Marrying Well

A Norton Professional Book

For Gabe & Jane 8/22/10
With deep affection,
Elena

Marrying Well

THE CLINICIAN'S GUIDE TO PREMARITAL EDUCATION

Elena Lesser Bruun and Anne F. Ziff

W. W. NORTON & COMPANY
NEW YORK • LONDON

For information about permission to reproduce selections from this book,
write to Permissions, W. W. Norton & Company, Inc.,
500 Fifth Avenue, New York, NY 10110

For information about special discounts for bulk purchases, please contact
W. W. Norton Special Sales at specialsales@wwnorton.com or 800-233-4830

Manufacturing by World Color Fairfield Graphics
Book design by Joe Lops
Production manager: Leeann Graham

Library of Congress Cataloging-in-Publication Data

Bruun, Elena Lesser.
Marrying well : the clinician's guide to
premarital counseling / Elena Lesser Bruun and Anne F. Ziff. — 1st ed.
p. cm. — (A Norton professional book)
Includes bibliographical references and index.
ISBN 978-0-393-70594-2 (hardcover)
1. Marriage counseling. 2. Couples–Counseling of.
3. Marriage. I. Ziff, Anne F. II. Title.
HQ10.B78 2010
616.89'1562—dc22
                                           2009047974

W. W. Norton & Company, Inc.
500 Fifth Avenue, New York, N.Y. 10110
www.wwnorton.com

W. W. Norton & Company Ltd.
Castle House, 75/76 Wells Street, London W1T 3QT

1 2 3 4 5 6 7 8 9 0

To my wonderful family and all of the couples who have let me into their lives.

—ELB

To Kostya and Alexandra, for your future happiness, and to my friends, patients, and multiple generations of my biological and extended family, who have helped me understand all that it means to truly marry well. *—AFZ*

Contents

Acknowledgments

I know from having planned birthdays, bar mitzvahs and weddings that inadvertently yet inevitably, someone is left out. If, as you read these acknowledgments, it is you, please let me know, so I can make it up to you somehow.

Of those I surely need to thank, those who come to mind first are my social scientist friends who gave me the benefit of their expertise. Judith Walkowitz read a rough draft of Chapter 2, giving me wise council, a reading list, and encouragement, as did Naomi Andrews, who also supplied historical material I would never have found on my own. Anita Bardin, former director of Shiluv, a family therapy agency in Jerusalem, read several chapters, providing an expert clinician's perspective. Wahira Abu Ras added immeasurably to my inchoate understanding of Muslim marriage in the U.S., and the role of imams. Suzanne Michael has been my supportive and stalwart friend and colleague, stepping in for countless hours toward the end of the project to help me think through certain theoretical and organizational issues, make editorial suggestions and refinements, and retrieve reference material. Without her, I would never have finished on time. To the extent that *Marrying Well* displays any depth of understanding of the history or sociology of marriage, credit belongs to all of these women.

Bill Northey, whom I knew as director of research for the American Association for Marriage and Family Therapy (AAMFT), was kind enough to read Chapter 3 and provide assurance that I had adequately covered most of the important developments in the field. His imprimatur gives me confidence that I am at least providing readers with a reasonably balanced perspective.

To the extent that my chapters contain thinking that is outside the box, some people in my life are more responsible than others for giving me courage and belief in myself: teachers, mentors, supervisors, colleagues, and therapists including Clarence Karier, Jerry Gladstein, Carol Fonda, Peter Dunn, Aaron Lipton, and Manual Brontman. When it comes to thinking outside the box, though, my son Noah takes the cake. He is the one who helped me see the potential for working a sense of social responsibility into the premarital counseling process and for convincing me that overpopulation was a problem with which childbearing couples must wrestle. When it comes to issues of social justice, I turn to my son David who keeps me informed, this time helping me to realize the connection between current same-sex marriage bans and recent miscegenation laws.

I must also thank Carl Rogers, whom I never had the good fortune to hear or meet in person (though I have read his books and heard him interview a client on audiotape), but whose simple core facilitative conditions—warmth, genuineness, unconditional positive regard, and perceived empathy—became the guiding principles of my life early on, not only as a therapist, but also as a person in all aspects. If I sometimes go astray, it is not Rogers's fault, but my own.

Kristen Holt-Browning, our wonderful editor at Norton Professional Books, was very brave in giving me, a first time author, this opportunity, and has been there every step of the way to be sure she didn't make a mistake! She allowed me to select a co-author, kept Anne and I on track with calm encouragement and advice time and again, and also deftly managed the disagreements that inevitably arise between co-authors. Casey

Ruble, copy editor par excellence, understood more of the content than we would have expected and was able not only to suggest more elegant turns of phrase, but ways to clarify and make some of our points more forcefully. I am grateful to Rachel Sussman, a marriage and family therapist colleague who recommended me to Norton (except late at night when I lost sleep worrying about how we would ever get this project done).

When I invited Anne Ziff to co-author, I was reasonably sure we were good-enough friends to be able to work together comfortably. The fact that we are still friends is proof that I was right. If Kristen has been the one to keep us on track, Anne is the one who has kept us more or less on time. Her sense of humor and consistent dedication have gotten us through many a rough spot, and I hope you gain as much from reading her chapters as I have.

What more can I say, except to thank my lucky stars that my husband, Nils, has been able to cope with my at times total self-absorption in this project. He has not only accepted it, but been there with me throughout, taking over jobs I used to do, helping me with computer glitches, reading and commenting on the manuscript, while seeming to get a kick out of the whole enterprise. I have promised to make it up to him, though I have to admit I am a little worried about the price he'll justifiably exact! There is no way I can really repay him, but I will try.

—*Elena Lesser Bruun*

I've learned about marrying well from my parents, my daughters and their husbands, friends, my caseload, and, of course, from my own personal experiences. Thank you all; thank you Charlie.

Furthermore, I am appreciative of the generous professional help and personal support on this project from friends and colleagues, including: Jacalyn Barnett, Esq.; Mariangela Carr, LMFT; Donna and "the gang" at Heco; Judith Kelman; Ashley Leiton; Gary Oberst, Esq; Heidi Opinski, Esq; Casey Ruble, copy editor; Harriet S. Selverstone; the Thursday Faculty Group and Family Therapy Conference, Division of Psychotherapy, Mount Sinai Hospital, and my Wednesday writing group. My special thanks to Elena Lesser Bruun, whose invitation to join her in this exciting project was the genesis for our collaboration, a friend whose warmth and intelligence throughout have been more than "good enough."

My thinking and methods as a clinician have been influenced by many pioneers and leaders in the fields of Marriage and Family Therapy, Object Relations Theory and Therapy, and Psychosynthesis. These include: Roberto Assagioli, David Bach, Ivan Boszormenyi-Nagy, Murray Bowen, Harry P. (Hap) Dunne, Tom Fogarty, Rosalind Gould, Melanie Klein, Monica McGoldrick, David E. Scharff, Jill Savege Scharff, and Judith Wallerstein. I am indebted forever to Marjorie Coogan Downing Wagner, teacher and friend.

Kristen Holt-Browning has been a creative and supportive editor, helping us to negotiate the rough spots, and responsive at all times. We thank you, Kristen!

—*Anne F. Ziff*

Marrying Well

Premarital Counseling: An Introduction

Anne F. Ziff

Love is not love
Which alters when it alteration finds,
Or bends with the remover to remove . . .
William Shakespeare, "Sonnet 116" (1609)

In the 15th century, Shakespeare, understood that acceptance was a prime value for lovers to be willing (and able) to offer each other. We psychotherapists, in the twenty-first century, suggest that before lovers can begin to offer acceptance to each other, they must know and accept themselves. Knowing and accepting the beloved is next. In the absence of this and other understandings that are commonly discussed in premarital education and counseling, marriages are so difficult to sustain that divorce is frequently considered a viable alternative. Neither divorce nor "alteration" (change or modification, according to the non-Shakespearean English of the *Random House Dictionary of the English Language*), we suggest, is required in a couple that has succeeded in *marrying well*.

This book is written primarily for clinicians—particularly those who work with, or are training to work with, couples. We use the term *clinicians* to refer to all professionals who work with the premarital population. The majority of the text focuses on our clinical experience. In accordance with the APA Psychology Task Force, the clinical work described throughout the book is primarily based on single case studies (sometimes composites) and other qualitative approaches, with an emphasis on process-to-outcome observation and exploration.

Both authors are marriage and family therapists specifically trained in the sometimes daunting, always exciting work with couples, couples and their children, and/or multiple members of a client's "family of origin." Couple therapy is reputedly difficult for mental health practitioners of any discipline because it requires the clinician to be constantly on his or her toes—both to avoid being triangulated or otherwise drawn into the couple's system, and to maintain focus while attempting to keep straight all the data that so often spill out into a session.

Our role as clinicians in premarital education and counseling is to guide couples to better understand themselves and to thereby make informed decisions about the marriage they are contemplating. In the case of Pat and Mike, which follows, we see challenges to the clinician these, to avoid being triangulated as a good parent or to avoid very quickly receiving a projection as the new, good therapist. Furthermore, we see a couple in need of discovering, examining, and implementing acceptance, boundaries, and loyalties (among other qualities).

Pat and Mike came to see me 3 months before their marriage. Theirs was to be a short engagement of 5 months, and the bride-to-be, Pat, had already talked once with a psychiatrist about some of her concerns.

A teacher in her mid-20s, Pat was an attractive, lively woman. She was the only child of parents who loved her very much but dis-

approved of this match. Her fiancé, Mike, 28, towered over her. He was a banker with a rather cynical sense of humor, and an obvious ambition to succeed in the cutthroat business world he had entered right after graduate school, 2 years ago. We met together in my office.

Two things became apparent from their first conversation: (1) Pat was seeking support for her choice to marry this man, and (2) Mike was seeking support for not continuing any sort of therapy—educational or otherwise!

Pat began by saying that she was worried about their marriage because her parents were so opposed to it. They felt that Mike's background was too different from Pat's and worried that the couple's expectations and goals might not be compatible. Despite anything Pat said, her parents remained adamantly opposed to her engagement and prospective marriage to Mike, although they agreed to support her choice publicly.

In contrast, Mike's father, also a banker, was fond of Pat. He applauded the couple's plan to marry after more than a year of going out together. Mike's mother, however, had an entirely different perspective. When Mike had phoned his folks to announce their engagement, his mom had asked to speak to Pat. Mike gave her the phone and did not stay on an extension to join the conversation. Happy, and expecting a joyful remark or two, Pat had a broad smile on her face as she said hello to her future mother-in-law.

"Remember this, Pat," she was told, "he'll hurt you. No good will come of this, believe me. You're not the woman for my son."

Pat described herself as being so shocked by this comment that she mumbled something like "oh, okay" and gave the phone back to Mike, nonplussed. It took her 3 weeks to bring herself to tell him what his mother had said to her.

And so, our first premarital counseling session had begun!

One of my early interventions that day was to ask each of them to tell me, and each another, what it was they hoped we could accomplish together and how much time they were willing to put into the work. Pat spoke first, saying that she wanted to understand her own reactions to her parents' unhappiness with the forthcoming marriage, and, if possible, how she could "best respond to Mike's Mom's prediction of a bad outcome for us."

I felt hopeful for them, hearing this, because Pat's attention was directed toward herself, her feelings, and her responses to others. She was not trying to change anyone else; she wanted to deal in the best possible ways with herself and others.

When Mike responded, he turned directly to Pat and pronounced, "You know how I feel about therapy, Pat. I'm only here because you say you want me to be here with you. I think that psychiatrist you saw was right; you're just a little overwrought because the wedding's coming up so quickly and that's all that's wrong with your parents, too. As for my mother—she just loves me, and yeah, she doesn't think you're good enough for me. That's so normal for mothers of sons! Just go with the flow like my sister does. My dad likes you enough, and my aunts do, too. Come on, Pat, lighten up for God's sake! Let's get this talking over fast, okay?!"

Acceptance? Mike wanted Pat to change: to stop being "overwrought," go with the flow, follow his sister's example, and lighten up. He was not accepting Pat as she was.

Self-knowledge? Mike knew his mother loved him. What more was there to say? Quite a lot, actually, from my therapeutic perspective!

Based on this first session, I wasn't sure which way this engaged couple was going to go. Would they be able to make and negotiate their own decisions regarding marriage, or would their parents' perceptions be too strong to defy?

Pat and Mike met together with me weekly, for 10 weeks. Although Mike never really wanted to think very much about himself in the context of any need to change, what he did become aware of was their need as a couple to put each other first, not their original families. During one session, Mike announced that he had started to hear his mother's "warning" to Pat as a last-ditch effort to keep him to herself, and he decided to talk with her about his loyalty to his bride-to-be. Once confronted, Mike's mother backed away from her dire predic-

tions and began to speak and act in ways that made it easier for both Mike and Pat to spend occasional time with her and his father.

Pat decided to ask her parents for their full support, or at the very least to continue keeping their misgivings to themselves. She had heard their thoughts and appreciated them, but had decided to go ahead with this marriage. She felt certain that she knew and loved Mike, and that they could indeed make a good life together. She loved her parents, and she wanted them to learn to admire Mike, too. Her parents agreed to remain publicly supportive, and in time, they actually grew to like their son-in-law, I was told subsequently.

The premarital educational counseling lasted 2 1/2 months, and the marriage has now lasted over 10 years. When we spoke early in 2009, in a follow-up session that they initiated, both Pat and Mike expressed agreement that the therapy had had a pivotal effect on their marriage. The essential element, from their perspective, was the loyalty issue. In turning from their original families to each other, and in making their new priorities clear (kindly and with love) to their own set of parents, they created a couple with the capacity to look within and make decisions as a unit.

"We'd have been a divorce statistic for sure," Mike pronounced, "if we'd seen you just that once, like with the psychiatrist, and then tried to make a go of it. Our parents would have torn us apart, and you know, they'd have thought they were doing what was best for us, too!" Pat nodded, adding, "I never think about divorce, even when things get tough, as, of course, they sometimes do." She gave Mike a sly smile. "Now murder, on the other hand—just joking!"

We have written this book to encourage clinicians who work with couples like Pat and Mike to use premarital educational counseling with more couples every year. We believe premarital counseling can do at least two very important things:

1. Help couples to marry well, and
2. Help to effect a reduction in the incidence of divorce.

Although the divorce "epidemic" in the United States seems to have moderated in the 1980s, we are aware that not all contemporary marriages last "happily ever after."

Lili A. Vasileff, President of the Association of Divorce Financial Planners, offered the following statistics: "The average marriage lasts 7.5 years. Forty-three percent of first marriages end in divorce, and nearly 60% of second marriages end in divorce" (Vasileff, 2008). She continued, " . . . eight to twelve million men think of divorce every single day."

Further, Vasileff and Palatnik (2008) stated that "in February 2007, [now retired] Chief Justice Judith Kaye of New York in her annual address on the judiciary, announced plans to create a new family law center in New York City that is intended to make divorce faster and cheaper for couples who want amicable settlements." Although we appreciate retired Justice Kaye's intentions, we believe that divorce is the wrong place for additional effort and focus for couples and their families. In most instances, by the time a couple is considering divorce, it is too late for effective marital education and remediation. We believe that premarital education can help *obviate* the need for divorce in enough families to warrant it in most, if not all, cases.

One of the couples I worked with illustrated this with an amusing remark near the end of therapy. They had initially worked with me a few months before their wedding, and then they took part in intermittent educational therapy as they contemplated pregnancy, and again for a few months after the birth of their first child. At the end of our work, the husband declared, a little shyly, "We've been debating telling you this, and it may sound odd, but you're our favorite wedding present!"

What they meant was that the lessons they learned in premarital counseling would last a lifetime, and, unlike gifts of fine crystal or china, insights could not be broken, damaged, or even permanently lost. They learned how to marry well, and then they learned together how to maintain their feelings and acts of love in their couple, even as it expanded into a family of three. This was a "gift" they valued above most others.

We think the majority of couples who have experienced effective premarital counseling would feel the same way! What's more, we suspect that marital outcomes would improve, both statistically and in terms of personal satisfaction, if more couples spent a small fraction of the time and money that goes into wedding planning and wedding events (not to mention divorce!) in educating themselves about marriage *before* the ceremony. The research in couple therapy (discussed at length in Chapter 3) appears to substantiate this.

Clearly we would like to help reduce the population that decides to seek divorce, but that is not our only aim. We believe that, to properly assist couples, the professional community needs to be better informed about contemporary marriage and its antecedents, as well as the clinical skills and strategies that are most likely to *help marrying couples meet the challenges that lie ahead.* We also believe that to be effective today, professionals need to have or acquire a broad, realistic, open-minded attitude toward twenty-first-century marriage and marriage trends. Without that, we all run the risk of being politely ignored by too many of the couples we so earnestly want to serve. We hope that the couples we work with can understand that although romance is a desirable aspect of a couple's relationship, acceptance, compassion, good humor, kindness, loyalty, respect, and understanding are all actually more desirable. They form the "A list" foundation of marrying well. Romance and great sex are "B list" components for marrying well.

We are writing this book because we are confident—based on thousands of hours of clinical contacts in nearly 50 years of combined experience as marriage and family therapists, in conjunction with an understanding of the research—that it is less expensive both emotionally and financially for couples to work *prior* to marriages, to talk and learn about themselves and each other, guided by knowledgeable professionals—both mental health and clergy. Premarital counseling can help couples marry well and will make the considered avenues for faster, cheaper divorces unnecessary.

We frequently work with people who have formed their couples (and, ultimately, marriages) in order to codify their closest relationship. And yet, too often, neediness, romance and fantasy, and sexuality turn out to be the glue that holds the couple together. These qualities cannot help the partners cope with the stressful realities of everyday life—whether it's a downturn in the economy that puts pressure on the family finances, the birth of a new family member or the disappointment and frustrations that come with infertility, or losses of health, parents, friends, dreams, and so on. When we work with couples before marriage, we can educate them about consciousness and about perceived realities; we can offer tools to fall back on "just in case" they are needed.

It is our hope that this book can serve as a valuable resource for clinicians from many disciplines who are working (or training to work) with premarital couples before, during, and after the decision to marry. *Marrying Well* will, for example, key readers in on how to listen acutely and prevent secrets from derailing a relationship. It will open your eyes and ears to the things that are apt to be set aside or completely ignored by couples in the early years of relationship and marriage but become more serious deficiencies later in life as other stressors compound.

DEVELOPING TRENDS

More and more, couples are choosing to engage in premarital education and counseling. Some of the issues they present are increasingly complex and less conventional than in decades past. Issues of intermarriages of all kinds are part of our new patterns. So are same-sex unions. Questions may vary, but an underlying reality prevails, and that, we believe, is the need for understanding, acceptance, trust, and loyalty between partners in a marriage. We believe that this pertains regardless of the religions and ethnicities of the partners.

Another trend is couples who marry "later in life"—in their mid-30s and beyond—and are interested in having children as soon as they possibly can. We are sufficiently optimistic to believe that couples who marry after premarital education or counseling will be well prepared for a lifetime together and prevented from living with remorse or regret. What's more, their children may be spared the pain of trundling between the two homes of divorced parents—dealing with rules in two families, constantly packing, having two bikes, two tooth-brushes, two pair of sneakers, two Elmo lunchboxes, and so on, when one of each would surely have otherwise been more than enough.

NEUTRALITY AND ETHICS

One of the reasons we wanted to write this book was to help professionals address the question of whether or when to be more forceful in their offices, or to back off. When there is a lot of conflict or no substantive interaction between members of a couple, we may privately wonder if we shouldn't take a position. What do we do? Sometimes we may become (or fear we will become) either excessively aggressive or excessively timid. In the field of premarital counseling, that often leaves the professional uncomfortably aware of herself or himself as not sufficiently neutral, not guiding a couple to come their own decisions about marrying. Conversely, professionals may close the file for a couple with whom they have finished premarital counseling wishing they had spoken up more explicitly, urging them *not* to marry.

We wrestle with these issues in the forthcoming chapters. In the end, fully informed and having adopted the most open-minded attitude possible, we believe that each professional has to be guided by his or her own professional ethics in these situations.

ORGANIZATION OF THE BOOK

Chapter 1 serves as the introduction to premarital counseling, in which we identify the value of this resource for clinicians and other readers. We describe our goals for the book, talk a bit about each author, and begin our journey into the exciting, relatively new field of premarital counseling.

Chapter 2 touches on the fascinating history of marriage, premarital arrangements, and premarital counseling. This chapter is an eye opener. It shows how incomplete and distorted many of our beliefs about marriage in the past have been! Chapter 2 is designed to help us rethink our image of the "good old days" and it guides us to approach contemporary marriage with a more open and realistic perspective.

In *Chapter 3* we review much of the extensive research that is being done or has been done on couple therapy and premarital counseling. These resources include prominent couple therapy research and assessment instruments, couples relationship enhancement techniques and literature, and much more.

Chapter 4 asks, "Who are your clients?" We begin with a discussion of the premarital counseling intake process, during which we ourselves begin to learn who our client is. Subsequently, we talk about many different characteristics of clients, including anxious clients, those seeking education, highly motivated clients, those embarking on second marriages, blended families, and so on. We mention couples' varying needs and expectations from marriage, as well as educational work together in and out of session. Chapter 4 demonstrates that knowledge is indeed power; in this instance, it's the power that guides premarital couples to marry well.

In *Chapter 5* we discuss many of the most common issues that arise in premarital education and counseling. These include: ethnicity, gender, income disparities, political or religious differences, sexual issues, communication, and more.

In *Chapters 6* and *7* we discuss what makes a satisfying marriage, in chapter 6 focusing on the individual factors, and in chapter 7, the couple predictors. In each chapter, we observe how the clinician can recognize, develop, and support these characteristics. For example, both people in the couple must be willing to consider their partner's needs or wants as equally important as their own. But when interests, needs, loyalties, or wants diverge, in order to survive, couples need mechanisms for addressing the differences and compromising creatively. This does not necessarily "come naturally," but it is a natural part of premarital education as we teach and practice it. We suggest that developing recognition, or awareness, is the first step towards change.

In *Chapter 8,* we offer a new frame for the premarital experience. We walk readers through the *eight premarital stages* that most couples experience, providing an understanding of both the needs and development of a couple on the way to marriage.

As premarital clinicians, we have the unique, specific opportunity to help couples develop enough knowledge about themselves, their partners, and the real-life institution of marriage to make good choices and decisions and to enter into prenuptial marriage contracts if needed. (Please see Chapter 8, stage 6, for a discussion on prenups.) Our premaritally counseled couples can create and negotiate marital relationships that will serve them well. As a result, they stand an excellent chance of surviving the inevitable difficulties as well as the joys that decades of life together will hold.

Chapter 9 presents a recap of our thoughts on the subject of Marrying Well, and the future of premarital counseling. There is also a provocative picture (the "not-so-modest proposal") of one direction the future of marriage as an institution might take, in this new century. In this final chapter, we also present our thoughts about the future of premarital counseling itself.

Both authors have been married and divorced and then formed new, lasting, primary relationships. We speak passionately about the need for education before marriage—and the need to *prevent* serious problems *before* marriages take place—because we have first-hand knowledge not only of theory and professional experience, but also of the pain of the divorce experience, extending to every member of the family. We have learned, on many levels, what it takes to have a satisfying marriage—to marry well.

We are trained in different ways, and our theoretical stances and ways of working may differ. Nonetheless, we respect each other's work and join in this collaboration with a willingness to recognize and accept our differences.

Elena Lesser Bruun obtained her master of arts in teaching from Harvard University and a doctorate in education (with a specialization in counseling) from the University of Rochester. She spent 25 years in medical education, first as an associate dean for curriculum at SUNY Brooklyn College of Medicine and then at New York University Medical School as associate dean for student affairs.

In addition, she holds a certificate of advanced study from the Ackerman Institute for the Family, and she taught family therapy at SUNY Brooklyn, where she was also associate director of the Family Therapy Institute in the department of psychiatry. As a clinical associate professor of psychiatry, she supervised residents and psychologists in the NYU Child Study Center. From 2003 to 2005 she served as president of the New York Association for Marriage and Family Therapy (NYAMFT), a division of the AAMFT, where she is both a clinical member and approved supervisor. She is a New York–licensed marriage and family therapist, and she currently has a private practice in Manhattan in individual, couple, and family therapy.

She is married to Nils Bruun, has "two wonderful sons, a lovely daughter-in-law, and two incredible young grandchildren, Sophie and Sam."

Anne F. Ziff holds two master's degrees, one in marriage and family therapy from the University of Bridgeport, and one in communication and education from Hunter College. She is an AAMFT clinical member and approved supervisor and an assistant clinical professor of psychiatry at Mt. Sinai Medical Center, where she teaches child psychiatry residents to integrate systemic and psychoanalytic thinking in treating children and their families. She has a postgraduate certificate in object relations theory and therapy from the Washington School of Psychiatry. She is certified as a group psychotherapist and as a psychosynthesist, and she holds MFT licenses in Connecticut, Massachusetts, and New York. Ziff is also an author, editor, and journalist. Prior to becoming a family therapist, she was an award-winning marketing professional at Pitney Bowes and in the healthcare industry.

From 1992 to 1994, Ziff represented AAMFT at the National Interdisciplinary Conference of Attorneys and Mental Health Practitioners (NIDF), served on a committee of the Academy for Matrimonial Attorneys (AMA), and was mental health co-chair of the NIDF in 1993 and 1994, leading groups, lecturing, writing articles, and teaching throughout the United States. Her theoretic approaches are eclectic and solution-focused in nature, reflecting theories including Bowenian family systems, Kleinian object relations, and Roberto Assagioli's psychosynthesis. Other theoretical influences and teachers with whom Ziff studied include Jill and David Scharff, Tom Fogarty, Judith Wallerstein, and Harry P. Dunne and David Ulrich, the last two of which were colleagues of Nagy as well as eclectic practitioners themselves. Ziff is in private practice with offices in New York City and Westport, Connecticut.

BENEFITS OF PREMARITAL COUNSELING

We've written *Marrying Well* to provide professionals with needed help to feel confident that they have used the best knowledge and tools, theory and research, and experience over time, so that, couple by couple, each therapist is able to guide the prospective partners to make the best possible premarital decisions. In some instances, that may mean not marrying at all, but more often, the couples we have educated will know that they *are* marrying *well*.

CHAPTER 2

Looking Backward: A Brief Foray into the History of Marriage and Marriage Counseling

Elena Lesser Bruun

"There is nothing new in the world except the history you do not know."

Harry Truman

Although there is no agreement among scholars as to how to define marriage, as far as we know, some form of marriage has always existed. For as far back as we know, human societies have always felt the need to bring some order to the conduct of couples' relationships. Though marriage is a very old institution, dating back at least to Old Testament times around 2000 B.C., professional marriage counseling is relatively new, beginning not very long before the year 2000. In those four thousand years without our professional help, people wrote legal codes and conducted their intimate relationships in ways largely unknown to us.

The story of marriage before we clinicians came on the scene is both fascinating and important, because it tells us that arrangements we think of as new, such as gay partnerships, are actually old; that many forms of marriage—not just the one we prize today—existed somewhere in the past; and that modifications we believe we cannot accept, such as group marriages, existed before, were accepted, and perhaps even worked well. In fact, much of what is feared as radically different today once did exist comfortably in the past. In considering the evidence history provides, it cannot help but open our minds and make us more tolerant, which as clinicians we must strive to be.

As clinicians, we need to know not only about the past, but also about what is actually new and contemporary, how the change connects to the emergence of premarital counseling, and the new societal need that premarital counseling serves. For some readers, this chapter will be a review; for others it will be an eye-opener.

MARRIAGE MYTHS DISPELLED

Myth: Marriages in the past were better than they are today.
Actuality: Whenever we worry about problems in contemporary life, such as what we believe to be the sorry state of marriage, we look back nostalgically to the past, where in hindsight it appears that almost everything was better. People cared about each other more, looked out for each other, and no one was left alone or behind. If pressed, we admit that we don't really know very much about how it actually was, and that our view of the past may be somewhat naïve, but we cling to it anyway, hoping to find answers there.

In fact, married life has never been easy, and the past may not be a particularly good guide to the attitudes and posture we need to adopt now. To decide what to retain, modify, or discard from marriage in the past, we first need to remove our rose-colored glasses and get a clearer view of how it actually was. Only then can we realistically approach our clients and address their needs.

Stephanie Coonz (2005, 2000), a well-known expert on the history of marriage, explained that we have idealized the American/ monogamous/ male breadwinner/female homemaker/ post-World War II marriage of the 1950s. Relationships were more stable, people married "their own kind" in religiously sanctioned ceremonies, no one divorced, and middle-class families were able to move with their children to the sparkling new, supposedly problem-free suburbs ringing our major cities. Though these relationships were relatively stable, they were not always satisfying. Betty Friedan called it "the problem that has no name" in her seminal book *The Feminine Mystique* (Friedan, 1963), which helped fuel the women's movement of the 1960s. The phrase spoke to the insidious blandness of existence and to the personal sacrifices that women—and men—had to make for that kind of marriage to succeed.

Far From Heaven (Haynes, 2002), a film made in the 1990s about marriage in the 1950s, shows how stultifying that life could be. The wife, played by Julianne Moore, and husband, played by Dennis Quaid, both try to ignore his suppressed homosexuality and their lives of quiet desperation; they stay together despite their complete incompatibility. She seeks solace in a relationship with their African-American gardener. *Revolutionary Road* (Mendes, 2008), shot in 2007, is in a very similar vein, with a horrifyingly tragic ending.

We therapists are no different than anyone else in wishing for the good old days, when marriages lasted, when husbands and wives were not just faithful, but utterly devoted to each other and their children through thick and thin. Our idealized image is something like the James Stewart and Donna

Reed marriage in *It's a Wonderful Life* (Capra, 1946). They are the perfect couple, with perfect children, coping with tremendous adversity but triumphing brilliantly in the end with the help of their small-town community and his personal, specially assigned angel.

It's a Wonderful Life, repeated on television every Christmas season, imprints on our minds a supposedly achievable model marriage. This film, and so many other films, canned television series, books and advertisements like it, skew our assessment of what is normal or abnormal in the couples we see, and it sets up expectations for what every couple should strive for. If we are not careful, preparing couples to live that life—or restoring our "sick" families to that "ideal" relationship state—becomes our twisted mission.

The most obvious problem with the model marriage portrayed in *It's a Wonderful Life* is its singularity. There is only one way to be married, one kind of couple, and one set of rules, and as long as we hold it as the standard to which we would have our clients aspire, the more we wind up forcing families to fit a mold that is too confining. And they fail. Less obvious, but at least as important, is the fact that those good old days of the 1950s were probably more cultural fantasy than reality, and certainly not the norm.

Though there certainly were many more typical small-town, Anglo-Saxon Protestant, male-headed, middle-class, nuclear, intact, lasting monogamous marriages in the 1950s, many were far from blissful, making Stewart and Reed an exception rather than the rule. And though divorce was initially lower during the Great Depression, when families had to hang together, not long after, the divorce rate increased and eventually exceeded the prior rate (Cherlin, 2009a p. A25). Moreover, if we look further back than the 1950s, we see how radically different the companionate model was from the actual scene on the ground.

Myth: Even if the 1950s produced imperfect marriages, there must be earlier examples of perfect marriages.

Actuality: In more distant times, we also idealized royal marriages as paragons of monogamous virtue, and it can be hard not to. I happened to be in Copenhagen a few years ago during the week the handsome young prince of Denmark was marrying a beautiful young commoner he met in Australia. The whole city was taken up with it, and everyone lined the streets to see the beautiful young couple as they rode through town to the church in their magnificent horse-drawn carriage. Could that marriage be anything but fairy-tale perfect?

Numerous historical examples belie this, but three familiar ones will suffice. First, there is Henry the VIII of England, who "married his 15-year-old son, Arthur, to 18-year-old Catherine of Aragon, daughter of the king of Spain. When Arthur died just 5 months later," Henry refused to send Catherine back to her father because "he would have lost his alliance with Spain and her dowry of 200,000 ducats." Instead, he married her to his second son, 12-year-old, Henry. "Although this violated Church rules on incest, the pope granted a dispensation." This young Henry became the infamous Henry VIII who broke with Rome to set up his own Church of England when the pope would not grant an annulment of his marriage to Catherine so that he could marry Catherine's maid of honor, Anne Boleyn, whom he had taken as his mistress. By the end of his life, Henry VIII, paragon of virtue, had either murdered or divorced five of his six wives (Coontz, 2005, p.133).

Looking even further back, Augustus of Rome's behavior would also be considered most egregious by today's standards. As Coonz (2005) described, he

> divorced his first wife who had just given birth to their daughter, Julia, in order to marry Livia, who was married to someone

else at the time and was pregnant with her husband's child . . .
When the marriage between Livia and Augustus produced no
children, Augustus appointed Livia's son Tiberius as *his* (italics
in the original) successor, then ordered Tiberius to divorce his
pregnant wife and marry . . . Julia. (p 83)

One can hardly follow the twisted incestuous marriage/
divorce sequence here!

A last example goes further back, to ancient times. In simple,
matter-of-fact reportage, the Book of Genesis tells us that Jacob,
the grandson of Abraham, married Leah, and then seven years
later her sister, Rachel. Polygamy was clearly accepted then and
was fairly common practice in the West until it was outlawed
by the Catholic Church in the 12th century. (Witte, 1997 p. 4;
Coonz, 2005 p.124).

Myth: Monogamy is the oldest form of marriage and has lasted
the longest.
Actuality: The truth is that monogamy is a relative newcomer.
Cultural anthropologists are fairly sure, for example, that communal marriage was the earliest form of marriage to appear
and that it was prevalent for many millennia in early hunter-
gatherer societies. Communal marriage meant that loyalty,
including sexual, was to the group, or community, not to
another individual.

Polygamy—polygyny and polyandry—has existed far longer
than monogamy. Monogamy only really became an ideal in the
16th century and only in northwestern Europe and the United
States (Coonz, 2005, p.6) Prior to that, most people entered
plural marriages or never married at all.

Early forms of monogamy were really quasi-polygamous or
transitional forms from polygamy to monogamy, such as co-mar-
riage in which two couples proclaimed oneness by having sexual

relations across couple lines, or men who were "monogamously" "married" but maintained concubines with legal standing in the couple's household as Abraham did with Hagar. Sibling marriage is another instance. It could involve one man marrying sisters such as Jacob with Leah and Rachel, or a woman marrying brothers; or it could even be a brother and sister (i.e., incestuous) marriage such as was referenced in an ancient Egyptian cautionary tale (Ahura, c 1100 BCE/1914). Bifurcated marriage is another transitional type in which an individual—usually the man—has more than one wife, but unlike in polygyny, the spouses are kept apart, each known only to the husband.

Myth: Early forms of marriage such as communal, polygamous, and arranged marriage are merely vestiges from the past, with no real staying power.
Actuality: Most forms of marriage, though they arose at different times, are all alive and well today. Most kinds have existed formally or informally, legally or illegally, sanctioned or prohibited, not just in one time or place, but *throughout* human history. Some types, such as polygamy, appeared early, whereas others, such as monogamy, came later; some were relatively rare even when they first appeared whereas others were the prevailing model for significant periods of time. The important point is that at any time in history one can find examples of every kind of marriage.

For example, in a 19th-century, upstate New York Oneida community, sexual exclusivity was explicitly forbidden and community members expected to have relation were with many members of the opposite sex (Muncy, 1974). In 20th-century Israel the kibbutzim retained a monogamous marriage form, but with communal childrearing and committing ones' deepest emotional attachment to the land. In the 1960s' and early 1970s' return-to-the-land movement in the United States, couples lived and slept communally and co-raised their children, breaking the previously self-contained nuclear family units of the 1950s, which coexisted alongside. Some communal families bought land or large houses together, or one couple might move in with another for a few months or years.

Though communal marriage is probably the earliest form of marriage, it still persists today. It has been relabeled "polyamory" and flies largely below the legal radar throughout the United States. We know there are numerous polyamorous families—or those involved in "polyfidelity," if only because there are polyamory websites (e.g. www.polyamorysociety.org) that cater to individuals in polyamorous relationships, as well as a website list of self-described "polyfriendly professionals" who want to assist them (see www.polychromatic.com). There are signs that polyamory may even become mainstream. We are not referring here to individuals who engage in recreational sex or swinging couples but relationships in which fidelity is maintained within a defined group of individuals that have become more frequently discussed in the media. For example, the *New York Times* recently published an article by Williams (2008) featuring a couple who agreed to be named. Although these people are not married, their ties and agreements closely resembled polygamous ones, down to girlfriend #1 having veto power over whomever else is allowed in. Similarly in *Newsweek,* Bennet (2009) described the practice of polyamorous relationships amongst a group of individuals living in Seattle. The *New York Magazine* just published a small cover photo of a "polyamorous paralegal (Polyamorous paralegal, 2009)."And finally, the *Guardian of London* recently reported that Siberian women are lobbying to legalize polygamy to respond to the low sex ratio of men to women and insure that women and children in such relationships receive legitimacy and the relevant state benefits (Katbamna, 2009).

Arranged, brokered, and bought marriages are still happening, even in the United States. One woman in her early

40s who was eager to marry, but had no prospects, converted to Judaism and went into the Orthodox community to find a husband. Her rabbi arranged three meetings, and she chose one man to marry. Another American woman of East Indian decent went to India and had a marriage arranged by her relatives there. Private matchmakers make a fortune serving the rich and famous; brides are bought by mail-order, sad to say; and green-card marriages of necessity abound in immigrant communities.

Myth: Polygamy was mainly an ancient, Eastern custom that never really existed in the West.
Actuality: Polygamy existed not just in the East, but also above in Western Europe until the 12th century (Coonz, 2005, p.124). It was the prevailing model for Mormons in 19th-century America, though it was ostensibly abandoned when it became clear that statehood could only be obtained for Utah by outlawing it. It still persists today, however, in the splinter Fundamentalist Church of Jesus Christ of Latter-Day Saints (FLDS) sect in Utah and Texas, as well as in a few other isolated communities elsewhere in the United States and Canada.

Under the Banner of Heaven, by Jon Krakauer (2004), richly details the ideas, complex interrelationships, and internecine warfare that have characterized Mormon family life in America. Apparently, there is at least one large polygamous community in Utah (though their leader, Warren Jeffs, was arrested in 2006 for encouraging marriage for underage girls). In 2008, an isolated polygamous Texas community was raided by law enforcement, but then reinstated after a widely publicized court battle.

Mormonism is spreading rapidly throughout the world, and though polygamy is no longer officially condoned or recognized, it is still in evidence in at least the splinter group. There

are several websites, for example, that advertise Christian polygamy, explaining how to get around legal prohibition of plural
marriage through a series of marriage and divorce contortions
(*christianpolygamy.com*).

Polygamy only begins to make sense to Westerners or
monogamists if placed in a plausible social context. There is,
for example, some evidence to suggest that polygyny increases
when men are in short supply after a war (Guttentag & Secord, 1983). "Sharing" a man might, in that case, be taken as
a sisterly act of generosity. Similarly, where older men prefer much younger women, as they often have for generations
in the United States and elsewhere, older women might well
opt for a polygamous situation rather than grow old alone.
It could also be argued that the demands of childrearing
are more easily borne by multiple mothers or wives sharing
responsibility.

Myth: The Judeo-Christian religions have always advocated
monogamous, lifelong marriage.
Actuality: Although Judaism may be credited with having "discovered" monotheism, it did not discover monogamy. The Old
Testament has many examples of polygamous relationships
and it is unclear whether monogamy ever existed in the early
periods covered by the bible.

In Islam, marriage is perceived as "half the religion" (Maqsood,
2000), however, the Christian church has actually changed its
mind more than once about marriage. In the New Testament,
Christ prophesied that in the resurrection, persons "neither
marry nor are given in marriage" (Matt. 22:30.p 10). And he
promised that in his time "there is no man who has left house
or wife or brothers or parents or children for the sake of the
kingdom of God who will not receive manifold more in this
time and in the age to come eternal life" (Luke 18:29:30). Par-

enthetically, about 600 years before Christ, Buddhism began with Buddha's own monastic choice. He reputedly left a comfortable life, his wife and newborn baby choosing to devote himself to what he considered a purer unencumbered unmaterialistic holy life of sacrifice (Armstrong, 2001).

In Christianity, this monastic ideal was undone by the fourth century, when there was a period in which "bishops, clergy, monks, and other servants of the church were ordered to be chaste, heterosexual, and monogamous" (Witte, 1997, p. 19). By the end of that century, however, the church reversed itself and "councils were ordering them (the "servants of the church") to be celibate and to avoid both marriage and concubinage on pain of losing their clerical offices" (Witte, p. 19).

From then until the thirteenth century, Christianity openly disparaged sex and love between men and women; nuns and priests were considered married to God, and lay marriage between men and women was barely tolerated—its only virtue being a way to avoid the sin of lust. Devotion to God was all and celibacy was considered the preferred state for everyone. Monasteries and convents abounded in western Europe, and a third to a half of the population either entered monastic life or remained outside, but never married (Coonz, 2005, p.127). Aristotle and others sought to legitimize marriage in the Church as a way to discourage pagan marriage and polygamy, but they still believed that marriage was a second-class state.

The sixteenth-century Protestant Reformers changed all that, primarily because some adherents felt that the clergy had become too powerful and hierarchical, but also because too many priests (and nuns) had difficulty keeping their vows of celibacy and were viewed as hypocrites. The Reformers closed the convents and monasteries and "rescued" the inhabitants; Luther himself married a former nun. From that point on, lay marriage gradually rose in estimation to the point that it is now nearly everyone's goal, leaving those who are not single by choice feeling lonely and marginalized.

Once the Church gave up the goal of celibacy for all—or most—it took monogamy under its sacramental wing and used it to its own advantage. If man-woman marriage was inevitable, the Church advocated that couples enter into it as soon as possible, which meant at puberty, to avoid the sin of premarital sex. Doctrine held that the couple, once married, belonged to God, and thus to each other and the Church for life. The sacramental bond, in other words, was indissoluble. Divorce was not permitted, except if a husband claimed his wife was not a virgin, or if it was discovered that she was betrothed or had been married before, or if it turned out that she was related to him, even distantly. That said, there were, in fact, many loopholes, and in those cases a marriage could be annulled.

Myth: Divorce is a new phenomenon. In the past, people stayed together.

Actuality: Divorce and even alimony are almost as old as the hills, as documented in the following decidedly unfair Mesopotamian prenuptial dated c. 2200 B.C.:

> If Bashtum to Rimum, her husband, shall say, 'You are not my husband,' they shall strangle her and cast her into the river. If Rimum to Bashtum, his wife, (a former slave) shall say, 'You are not my wife,' he shall pay ten shekels of money as her alimony. They swore by Shamash, Marduk, their king Shamshu-ilu-na, and Sippar.   (Halsall, n.d.)

Myth: Even if divorce is not a new phenomenon, it is much more common today.

Actuality: Yes, in the United States, the current divorce rate is high. But let us place this in context. The phenomenon is not nearly as alarming as it appears at first glance because of the following mitigating factors. First, for most of history, and for most people other than the elites, marriage was an informal, nonlegal arrangement that could be entered simply by setting up a joint household and terminated simply by walking out. No divorce necessary.

Second, although the average age of marriage, in most early times, was much younger than it is today, the life span was also significantly shorter. Prior to 1900, the average life span in the United States was roughly 40 or 45, half of what it is today, and there were very few golden anniversaries. The average length of a marriage might be 20 years, and a spouse might well die young of disease or in childbirth, all obviating the need for divorce.

Third, we need to take a closer look at what "staying together" meant prior to the greater accessibility of divorce. In some cases, like that of Franklin and Eleanor Roosevelt, it meant retaining a legal marriage, but living apart in a de facto divorce. In other instances it meant staying together, but one or both taking on another as a concubine, mistress, or lover such as Lady Chatterley did (Lawrence, 1928/2005). For most women in terrible marital straights, running away, going mad, or committing suicide were the only options. (Chesler, 1972/2005). Tolstoy's larger-than-fiction heroine, Anna Karenina, did all three. She left her husband for her heartless lover, Count Vronsky, went mad and committed suicide (Tolstoy, 1878/2004).

Finally, it is necessary to bear in mind that although the Catholic Church forbade divorce and still does, it has also allowed annulments on an increasing number of grounds starting, for example, with failure to be chaste, mistaken identity, extreme duress (i.e., compulsion to marry), marriage to a pagan, and a spouse leaving the faith. According to Witte:

the canon law of annulment is often described as the virtual
equivalent of the common law doctrine of no fault-based divorce
. . . any enterprising canon lawyer, it is said, can sift through the
multiple impediments to marriage recognized at canon law and
find one that applies sufficiently to allow an unhappy couple to
dissolve their union" (1997, pp. 34–35).

In Jewish law, at least for men, it has never been difficult to
obtain a divorce.

And though it is easier for all now than it was even 50 years
ago, it will probably never again be as it was for an Orthodox Jewish man, who could divorce his wife for as seemingly innocuous
an oversight as leaving "a hair in the soup." Judaism, however,
has also given women the right to ask for, and often be granted, a
"get" (divorce) in certain circumstances, such as if: her husband
is afflicted by various physical ailments or characteristics which
are deemed unendurable for the wife (e.g., "boils" or "poly-
pus"); her husband violates or neglects his marital obligations
(e.g., refuses to support); there is sexual incompatibility (e.g.,
she states that "he is repulsive to me") (Biale, 1995 p. 85–86).

Myth: People have always married for love.
Actuality: Not true at all! Historians do not agree on when
exactly love became the primary reason to marry. Most scholars do agree, however, that the love-based marriage became a
firmly ensconced ideal only in the past century or two, though at
least one highly regarded historian finds its roots go as far back
as the thirteenth century in northwestern Europe (Hartman,
2004) when young peasants, having to find employment off the
land, were thrown together in the houses of wealthy aristocracy,
largely unsupervised, and found mates for themselves by dint of
proximity (Hartman, 2004, p. 56). Prior to the twentieth century, people fell in love, of course, but love was not the driving
force behind marriage. And although sexual attraction always

drew men and women together, it wasn't until the 1920s that sexual compatibility or enjoyment became an important aspect of marriage. Around that time, love and marriage converged.

Until then, marriages were arranged for the sake of the family and couples stayed married for the same reason. Marriage in western Europe and throughout most of the world was designed for family and community stability, economic viability of the family, procreation or continuity, and advancement—not love. The Tina Turner song "What's Love Got to Do With It" (Lyle , Britten, & Hamilton, 1993) would have resonated with families then; it appears less applicable now, when love seems to have everything to do with it. Wonderful lines from the film *Moonstruck* (Jewison, 1987) also hark back to earlier times. Olympia Dukakis asks her daughter, played by Cher, if she is in love with her fiancé. When Cher answers "no," her mother immediately counters with "good!" Love only complicated matters; marriage was all about property, securing lines of inheritance, and increasing family power and viability. Owing to limited travel and local population homogeneity, the average citizen had few partner choices and more proscriptions regarding whom one could marry. Like married like.

In essence, marriage was to a family, not an individual, and the strongest connection, the primary relationship, might be between father and son or between siblings, not husband and wife. Perhaps surprisingly, these issues continue to complicate marriage today.

This point was brought home to us by a South Asian newlywed couple whose presenting problem was dissatisfaction on the part of the young wife, Aasha, age 25, with her husband, Ramesh, age 38. Aasha felt that Ramesh spent inordinate amounts of time catering to his parents and siblings. She complained vociferously about phone time he spent with his mother discussing, say, the minute details of the couple's home decorating plan and the insufficient attention Aasha felt he paid to her when they were out with friends or family. Ramesh was bewildered and unnerved by Aasha's seeming inability to go with the flow, sudden angry outbursts, and unwillingness to absorb perceived slights—all of which only led Ramesh to withdraw further.

The couple had met, though not formally introduced, at the strong suggestion of the two sets of parents, and they had a traditional Indian wedding. Ramesh's mother had every expectation that her daughter-in-law would join her household, at least in spirit, and defer to her wishes. Along with the normal cultural divide that had to be bridged by the therapist was the confusing fact that the contemporary thrust ("I want to be first in your life") was coming from the wife, who was born and raised in India, whereas the husband, of Indian descent, was born in the United States! Apparently, Aasha, from the old world, was looking for modernity, while the Ramesh, of the new, was looking for a more traditional relationship.

For those interested in further exploring this transitional period in the history of marriage, the novels of Jane Austin illustrate and help to mark the change from family-driven inheritance marriage to individual-partner love-based marriage, as well as the exquisite tensions that existed between the two, as do the works of so many other British and American writers including Henry James and Edith Wharton.

Myth: In the old days, married people were sexually faithful.
Actuality: Until quite recently, couples, especially women, were expected to have low expectations for fidelity. "Grin and bear it" was the mantra. In truth there has never been a time when sexual fidelity prevailed, regardless of the marriage form. The concept of fidelity itself has changed and been modified in different periods. And there have always been loopholes and escape hatches, even for priests and nuns, who are, in theory, married to God. Not long ago on a trip to Italy I visited one cler-

ic's former home that featured a hidden staircase used either to import female company or for the cleric to leave unnoticed for a rendez-vous. Perhaps sexual fidelity is an ideal that few can attain. Perhaps there are even arguments against it, such as the one made by the poet Percy Blythe Shelley, who claimed that:

> Love withers under constraint; its very essence is liberty. It is compatible neither with obedience, jealousy nor fear. It is there most pure, perfect, and unlimited when its votaries live in confidence, equality and unreserve. (From "Queen Mab" 1813).

On the other hand, if we are not made for fidelity, what do we do with feelings of jealousy and competition? Monogamy serves the human desire for primary exclusive attachment, sense of belonging, and security. But it doesn't always work. We are such contradictory creatures, desiring—perhaps even needing—both sameness and variety.

Myth: Marriage has always benefited women as much as men.
Actuality: No. Although marriage is better now for women than it ever was, at its worst one could say that the history of marriage is the story of the subjugation of women. If that is an extreme characterization, it is certainly true that marriage has not been as advantageous for women as for men. While even ancient Islamic law granted women the right to own and dispose of property independently of their husbands (Maqsood, 2000), it was not until quite recently in the West that women and children were themselves, in legal terms, no more than "chattel"—property belonging to their husbands. Under English and French "coverture" law as late as the 19th century, women had no legal standing, and little if any power over their own lives. Husbands represented wives in the world outside the home, and in exchange for protection, and her obedience, he

was to provide economic support and treat her fairly (Coonz, 2005, p.186; Blackstone, W., 1796/2005 pp. 72–79)

In Islam this kind of reciprocity was embedded in the rules of marriage. For example, in a Muslim marriage while the husband is considered

> the 'iman' and the head of the household, he has to *prove* himself worthy of that position. . . . .If the husband attempts to order her to do anything that clashes with Islam, it is her duty NOT (emphasis in the original) to obey him, but to point this out (tactfully and gently) and to change his orders (Maqsood, 2000 p.53).

However, in both the East and West, when a woman was not treated fairly, she tended to have little actual recourse. Virginia Woolf, writing in the 1920s, decried women's lot, pleading for just some financial independence and a "room of one's own" (Woolf,1929/1989). "The Yellow Wallpaper," a short story by Charlotte Perkins Gilman, published in 1892, details the descent into madness of a woman kept isolated from her children and away from her work "for her own good" by her condescending physician husband. In essence, women were financially dependent and treated as children who did not know what was best for them. They were often protected, but unbearably marginalized. The inception of the Women's Project at the Ackerman Institute for the Family in the 1980s was another indication that, despite the womens' liberation movement's efforts in the 1960's and 1970's, an egaltarian marriage ideal, modernized laws, and the right to vote, women had still not attained equal relationship status or power in marriage.

Myth: If we permit same-sex civil unions or gay marriage, marriage as we know it will cease to be.

Actuality: Just a few centuries ago Christianity held that the *only* valid marriage was between a Christian man and woman, blessed by the Church. But same-sex marriage is only the latest example of a movement to gain legal sanction for the right to greater partner choice. What is happening now as gays seek parity in marriage is no different from earlier struggles against prohibition of religious or racial intermarriage, thoughts of which horrified previous generations.

Moreover, there is more than one instance of same-sex civil union in the western European past. In late-medieval France and elsewhere it was called *affrerèment,* or "brotherment" (Tulchin, 2007). These contracts had much in common with legal marriage, and though they were designed to recognize biological brothers living together in an inherited home, the laws also applied to the union of unrelated same-sex partners. Because of their avowed affection for one another, the "brothers" pledged before a notary and witnesses to share "*un pain, un vin, et une bourse*" (one bread, one wine, and one purse) (Tulchin, 2007, p. 635).

Catholics were excommunicated for marrying out of the faith. Jews sat "shivah" (mourned as if dead) for children who married "goyim" (non-Jews), and some still do. Miscegenation laws were in place in many states, not just in the South, until less than 50 years ago, the last one struck down only in 1967. Fifty years from now, we hope gay marriage will seem no more outrageous or beyond the pale than Christian-"pagan" or black-white marriage did only decades ago.

We have the complete picture when we recall the early Christian notion that the only true marriage was to God, that marriage between a man and a woman was simply a necessary evil. As practitioners, we have an obligation to be at least one step ahead of the tolerance curve.

Myth: The survival of marriage itself is being threatened; it cannot sustain all of the changes that have been inflicted upon it.

Actuality: Contrary to the Beatle's claim that "All you need is love" (Lennon & McCarthy, 1967), many observers say that the pure love-based marriage bears the seeds of its own destruction. It certainly lacks the old power of religion—the fear of God—that held marriages together when divorce was considered a sin. Families of origin, particularly parents, have less sway as well. Economic necessity no longer provides as powerful a motivator bringing and keeping couples together, given women's ever-greater acceptance in the workforce. Further, overpopulation with its concomitant drain on vital planetary resources might sooner or later force countries to adopt policies, as China has, to limit the number of biological children per individual or couple, and encourage adoption or no children. Though couples without children may choose to marry, there is less pressure (some would say, no reason) to marry. Finally, a divorce is easier now than at many times in history.

On the other hand, although these trends might cause a student of marriage to be discouraged, the picture is actually less bleak than it seems. One growing positive trend is that couples have more partner choice. As we discuss in chapters to come, the choice is now not only broader in terms of religion, race, age, and gender, but, with globalization, in terms of socioeconomic class and cultural background as well. In some couples we are seeing several of these differences at once.

For example, in my New York City office this year, I saw a couple with widely divergent backgrounds: Daniel was a gentle giant, standing over six feet tall, originally a wild game preservationist, Muslim by upbringing but strictly agnostic now, with a large family farm and real estate holdings in Sierra Leone. He was also a painter, but earned his living here as an employment counselor. Annette was his 5'1" wisp of a Catholic Caucasian wife

from southern France, a professor of economics at a local university, 10 years his senior. She had three grown children from a
previous marriage, as well as a 6-year-old daughter, Nadine, who
was adopted from South Africa before she met Daniel but who,
coincidently (or perhaps not), looked exactly like him.

Back to back, in the next hour, I saw a 6-foot-tall Caucasian
woman from Oregon with two masters degrees—in music and
linguistics—and her 5'3", Peruvian significant other. He followed her to New York all the way from Oregon, where they met.
He wanted to marry her but she was still not sure. She came from
money; he had grown up dirt-poor and had left home at 12, eventually making his way to the United States. The challenges these
previously impossible global "mismatches" face and present to
clinicians are daunting, but often the underlying relationship
dynamics are the same, and learning from these couples as we
help them through their difficulties is endlessly rewarding, too.

Another positive trend is that decisions to marry are now
mostly made by mutual consent. Even when marriages are still
technically arranged, there is somewhat less dictation by outside parties and the couple is allowed to give more input. Certainly there is more equality and protection for women within
marriage, more belief that sexual fulfillment should be part of
marriage, and more leeway for couples' own creativity in fash-
ioning their relationship as they wish.

Birth control and the possibility of abortion (though still con-
troversial) are possible options for many who need or want to
avoid pregnancy, and there are fertility measures for couples who
desperately want to have children but require assistance. And
before we bemoan the fact that there is less external pressure to
be and stay married, we should remember that it is not clear that
pressuring couples to stay together always works or is always wise.

In researching marriage, we could find no consistent linear
progression from "primitive" to "modern" marriage. Lifelong
marriage and marital satisfaction between two people remain

the Western cultural ideal. However, only half of those who marry stay together; and of these that stay together only half report they are happy, i.e. satisfied. At the same time, other marriage trajectories and forms continue to exist. In the United States, we seem to be evolving into a variation on serial monogamy (Cherlin, 2009), and some individuals are rediscovering the earliest form, communal or group marriage.

We cannot even say that any model is inherently better than another. Each has advantages and disadvantages. There are healthy and unhealthy polygamous marriages, just as there are good and bad monogamous marriages. The popular HBO television series *Big Love* illustrates this point beautifully. On the compound, a dictatorial cult leader modeled after Warren Jeffs takes advantage of young girls and manipulates everyone to augment his power and position. Bill, one of his many sons, breaks away and lives nearby in a "normal" suburban community with three wives and their seven children in adjoining houses and shared yard, trying to keep their secret from their neighbors. . Bill, as head of this tripartite family, has his hands full but is an upstanding, honorable man, doing his best to satisfy the three wives.

In pondering the history of marriage from a twenty-first-century perspective, it is the variety of ways people have conceived of marriage that strikes us. We can draw on these models both to broaden our concept of what is appropriate for our clients and to help them make sense of their circumstances. We can also use our knowledge of the variety of marriage forms in history to help society consciously construct new and improved forms of marriage in the future.

HISTORY OF PREMARITAL OR COUPLING ARRANGEMENTS

Historically, introductions and courtship rituals have been long, short, and nonexistent; simple and elaborate; inclusive of involvement by other parties such as family, friends, match-makers, personal advertisements, intermediaries, and social-networking websites and not. I know one couple who literally "bumped into each other on a bus." Although we think of courtship as traditionally being initiated by the man, there was a time in the Victorian era when a young man would have been considered "cheeky" for asking to visit a young woman without an invitation (Humphry, (1897/1993a and b).

As would be expected, coupling has run the historical gamut. At one extreme, two families court each other, intentionally excluding the couple, who are betrothed by their parents with no knowledge of each other, meeting only at the altar. At the other extreme, couples meet on their own and go through elaborate or protracted dating steps, have sexual relations, and may even conceive children prior to marriage, with family being last to know. Between these extremes lie informally arranged meetings by relatives, friends, or professional matchmakers.

Although strictly arranged marriages have been in decline over the years, many couples have been expected to follow parents' wishes, and even today, some parents exert enormous influence. One of my couple clients, Linda and Don, were pulled apart over a few years by Linda's parents, who could not "allow" their Jewish daughter to marry a committed Catholic. They fought the young couple's relationship every step of the way, refusing to invite Don for holidays and pressuring Linda daily to leave him.

When couples have been free to select their spouses, the length of time they take to decide and perhaps fall in love varies considerably throughout history. Some couples are hooked after catching a glimpse of the other person, such as Rachel, whose eyes fell on Ian as she happened to look up after having a sip of water at a fountain. Instantly in love (we might say "captivated"), she adored this man forever. Others need substantial courtship time. It took Janet 6 months of dating to know she wanted to marry the man who would become her lifelong husband. She amused herself and others by relating that she initially thought so little of him that 3 months into the relationship she didn't even invite him to the New Year's Eve party she was hosting! A few months later, though, she suddenly saw in him a resemblance to her father and fell madly in love. Logic— and the research—say that time to develop a relationship predicts marital stability and satisfaction, but this is not always the case. Susan and Louis met on a dock at the beach, were married a week later by a justice of the peace, and were happy until the day Louis died 40 years later. Nicky and Tina dated for 2 years and lived together for a year before the marriage, only to separate a mere week after their large, extremely expensive destination wedding.

Courtship length also seems to be somewhat dependent on ethnic or social circumstances. The Irish, for example, are notorious for decades-long courtship. In times of war or population dislocation, when a couple could be forced to separate, courtship may be attenuated and marriages rushed. The same is true in cases of pregnancy, especially when out-of-wedlock births were taboo, and in cases where one member of a couple is ill. When people have begun seeing someone new after the death of their spouse, a lengthy "waiting period" before remarriage may be prescribed.

Approved courtship practices are also all over the map. When the age of marriage is late, cohabitation and premarital sexual relations are more common, but even in the eighteenth and nineteenth centuries there were certain forms of it in Europe and America—specifically the practice of "bundling," in which a young man and woman, often in their teens and under some level of parental supervision, were wrapped in separate blankets but allowed to sleep in the same bed and snuggle together for warmth in in winter and in order to get to know each other before marriage, while also preventing pregnancy. Sometimes a board was placed between them, ostensibly to prevent unbundling, sex play, and pregnancy, but it apparently did not always work (Hartman, 2004, p. 62)!

In each historical period, in every culture, and probably for every form of marriage, there seems to be a corresponding set of courtship rituals or rules. Knowledge of courtship and marriage practices in the past can help therapists be creative both in the suggestions they offer couples in the planning stages before marriage and in helping couples realize they have choices in what they can follow or discard from their family traditions, as well as in what they can create for themselves to suit their own specific needs. The point is that there are reasons for how customs evolved, and knowing those reasons can help couples decide what they want to preserve. The beauty of marriage today is that couples can essentially make some of their own rules. Of course, that is also the challenge. We return to this topic in Chapter 8.

HISTORY OF MARITAL AND PREMARITAL COUNSELING

Marriage counseling (including premarital counseling) as a distinct profession is a relative newcomer—it began around the 1920s. Some social scientists trace its roots back to primitive Shamans who they dubbed "the intellectual predecessors of contemporary counseling and therapy" (Gielen, Draguns & Fish, 2008 p. 18). Later, instruction and advice to marrying couples was dispensed by parents and other family elders, philosophers, clergy, physicians, social scientists, and even journalists. And just prior to the emergence of marriage counseling, the already established mental health disciplines of psychiatry, psychology, and social work brought their perspectives to the table. As a matter of fact, marriage and family therapy (MFT) has its roots in all of the aforementioned disciplines and in pastoral counseling as well. For a thorough history of these developments, see Gurman and Fraenkel (2002).

Historically, marriage advisors have tended to support the status quo, recommending conformity to the prevailing rules, mores and attitudes rather than helping couples modify existing customs, or invent new ones, to suit their own needs and circumstances. Advice givers have not been in the forefront advocating for change.

Because the scientific study of marriage is so new, it is understandable that advisors relied on custom and community standards. It is not very different from what happened in the medical field. Only a few years ago, physicians were still basing treatment more on standard practice than on real evidence of efficacy. Similarly, it is only recently that we have accumulated some solid evidence on what makes a relationship satisfying and likely to last.

Moreover, as long as marriages were held together by powerful external (religious, economic, familial, etc.) forces there was little perceived need for scientific evidence or professional help. However, as the external glue of relationships weakened, attention shifted to more internal emotional connections, and couples sought help with their relationships, the field of marriage and family therapy emerged.

Marriage and family therapists—and the traditional mental health practitioners who have advanced training in MFT beyond their original disciplines—depart from their root professions though, in two crucial respects. First, they tend to be systemic thinkers, resisting an ever-present temptation to focus on individual pathology, preferring the concept of "diseases of the relationship" rather than "diseases of the individual." Simply put, we say that there is nothing wrong with either member of a couple, but that there may be a problem in the way they relate or in the relationship. The job of the therapist is to help fix problems in the relationship, not in the individuals. Second, the new MFT field tends to focus on strengths, looking to build on what a couple already does well.

For example, one of our couple clients was a physician and an attorney—two highly talented professionals who never had sexual intercourse in their long courtship or in the first few months of marriage, although they had tried on a few occasions and it was established that they had no physiological problems. There were underlying relationship problems, however (he would psychologically withdraw or give in rather than engage or argue), and they had an overlay of sexual frustration that led to the wife's having had a premarital affair. In looking for strengths, it was discovered that they loved having dinner out, which they did together several times a week. They would then go home and cuddle in bed, feeling close if not sexually satisfied.

When this seemingly small strength was highlighted, the couple was surprised to learn that they were special in this regard and that not every couple experienced smooth sailing in restaurants. With this boost, they gathered the courage to tackle their sexual relationship and made their own plan for how to proceed. They would have sex every other night and keep trying even if it didn't go well at first. Neither would offer a critique afterward. The husband also agreed to complement his wife more, and she agreed to stay away from venues where she would be likely to run into the "other man."

Part of this strength-based approach is also that the therapist often assumes a "one-down" position in which the clients are seen as in charge of their relationship. This gives the couple a greater sense of their own power to change. An indication of this can be found in an anecdotal remark from a former director of the Ackerman Institute for the Family, "Think of yourselves as a benign aunt or uncle, caring about the couple and what happens, but with no personal stake in their decision-making process or in the therapy outcome. Then you will be properly positioned to help" (D. Bloch, personal communication, 1983).

Many premarital-advice books on the market have a primarily Christian orientation, preparing couples for a Christian wedding, and many are still steeped in the idealization of the 1950s-era marriage. We write this book in the hope that it will contribute to a more evidence-based pproach, as well as promote a broader, more realistic, global, accepting, and, yes, more appreciative and respectful attitude toward different forms of marriage and marriage arrangements. Rather than expecting couples to adapt to our ideal, we may have to adapt to theirs. The next chapters will offer more help.

CHAPTER 3

The Lay of the Land: Current Research and Practice

Elena Lesser Bruun

Ah, love, let us be true
To one another! For the world, which seems
To lie before us like a land of dreams,
So various, so beautiful, so new,
Hath really neither joy, nor love, nor light,
Nor certitude, nor peace, nor help from pain;
And we are here as on a darkling plain
Swept with confused alarms of struggle and flight,
Where ignorant armies clash by night.
                    Matthew Arnold, "Dover Beach," (1867)

Despite Matthew Arnold's romantic importuning on the eve of his marriage, the closeness and quality of a married couple's relationship remained relatively insignificant until well into in the twentieth century. What did matter was being able to establish paternity; having a social institution to support the care and rearing of children; carrying on the family name, especially as it involved the preservation and transfer of property; according to some, keeping women under control (controlling "women's lust"), and "marrying well," which used to mean moving up the social ladder. Early on, marriage was just a vehicle, a means to an economic or social end, not an end or of any real value in itself.

It is only since the mid-twentieth century that the relationship—how well a couple communicates or handles their differences, whether they stay in love or treat each other well—has been considered important. If the concept of fully egalitarian marriage is only about 50 years old, and if marital satisfaction is only a recent expectation, it should not surprise us that there was no perceived need for marriage counseling until now, no marriage counseling profession, no tested methods for teaching couples how to get along, and no research base to draw from in developing better methods of counseling. There was always advice, of course—originally from family and clergy, then from physicians and columnists—and there were proscriptions for how husbands and wives should behave, but there was no preventive help and no remediation for couples who couldn't seem to follow the "rules." Moreover, the rules were mainly designed to help couples keep the peace, not achieve satisfaction or happiness (see the Victorian Guide Books for men and women currently in print by "Madge of Truth" (Humphrey, 1897/1993a and b).

Over the past few decades, compelling sociological and psychological evidence has been accumulating to show that "marital distress, parental distress, and/or divorce is often harmful to children" (Amato Booth, 2007; Halford, Markman, & Stanley, 2008; Popenoe 2004; Wallerstein 2001; Wallerstein, Kelly & Blakeslee, 1996), resulting in academic underperformance, psychological and behavior problems, and conflict-ridden parent-child relationships. In addition, marital stress and divorce also seem to lead to job instability, reduced income, increased risk for drug and alcohol abuse, and crime (Lamb, 1997). Because these findings have been disseminated through the media and are nearly common knowledge, couples today are justifiably concerned about the quality and stability of their relationship and how their relationship could affect their children's well-being.

Most couples are aware of the high divorce rate in the United States, which may have peaked at around 50% from the early 1960s to the early 1980s, but still hovers somewhere between 40 to 50% (Popenoe & Whitehead, 2002, pp. 54–55). In part these rates may reflect the increasing ease of getting a divorce including no fault divorce legislation, expanded economic opportunities for women, and a cultural shift in which divorce has become more accepted. In some respect, divorce has become so commonplace that divorce services are glibly advertised on-line. For example, www.Document-Do-It-Yourself-Service.com, provides "marriage annulment on-line."

In response, about a third of couples seek relationship help prior to marriage, or seek out help when they run into difficulty. When they do, they are faced with a plethora of opportunities, and various levels of expertise and competence amongst the array of helpers, from educators, religious leaders, lay people, and mental health professionals. Furthermore, with changes in perspective about the institution of marriage and gender roles, as well as an ever-increasing complex body of research about the effectiveness of various approaches and strategies, couples are confused about whom to see, and practitioners are unsure about which type of intervention should be employed.

In this chapter, we explore the therapeutic models that are either most widely used, have influenced or been incorporated into preventive psychoeducational strategies, or simply seem most appropriate to use with premarital couples. Collectively, they demonstrate the range of possibilities. We also examine three assessment instruments and discuss several psychoeducational programs targeted to premarital couples (religious and secular). All of this is to ensure that practitioners of every stripe will be informed about exactly what is happening and available in the larger community and where else their clients could be or become involved. In addition, we discuss governmental involvement in marriage preparation and some programs that are currently available to assist premarital couples. The chapter ends with some general observations and suggested directions for future research.

TYPES OF RESEARCH: STUDIES, EVIDENCE, LIMITATIONS

Marriage research has come a long way from the early days when the first wave of marriage counselors emerged from the pastoral ranks with a strong bias toward keeping couples married no matter what. For these early marriage counselors—ministers, priests, and rabbis as well as the religious lay counselors who entered the field a little later—the usual measure of success was stability, or maintenance of the marriage, rather than improvement or the couple's estimation of marital satisfaction. Over time, as the importance of the marital relationship grew, and relationship quality, couple satisfaction, and patterns of interaction became the foci of couple counseling, new measures of "success" beyond "staying together" had to be developed. These new outcome measures had to determine not only what was accomplished through counseling, but also what interventions worked for whom, and for what types of problems. The earliest assessments of improvement or outcome amounted to anecdotal reports—counselors' impressions and the couples' own reports. Although these subjective measures were undoubtedly helpful to specific counselors or clinicians, they did not provide objective documentation of validity or reliability to influence overall practice.

Fast-forwarding to the present day, there are now at least two generally agreed-upon ways to determine the value of a given therapy, assessment tool, or program. The first is the American Psychological Association (APA) Division 12 Empirically Supported Treatment (EST) seal of approval (Jacubowski, Milne, Brunner & Miller, 2004, p.528). A "brand" of therapy, or treatment, meets EST standards for "efficacy" if it achieves the same positive results in two experimental independent randomized clinical trials comparing a group receiving treatment with no-treatment or wait-list controls. Additionally, therapists in the trials must follow a prepared treatment manual, and study results must be published in peer-reviewed journals. For many researchers, ESTs are the "gold standard," though many concede that efficacy is difficult to achieve in a field that is process-driven and hard to control outside of university lab conditions (Johnson, 2003). In fact, most EST studies have been conducted in academic settings, in departments of psychiatry or psychology, are over-controlled, involve only short-term follow-up, and have not been able to provide results for the typical range of presenting problems.

For example, the most highly distressed couples and those with multiple diagnoses are often screened out of efficacy studies, meaning that the results do not apply to many of the couples therapists actually see. Second, the level of competence and confidence in a model being tested are not generally used as criteria for therapists' inclusion. Snyder, Castellani, & Whisman (2006) have also summed up two other problems with large-scale randomized efficacy studies. They explained that although impressive improvement rates over no-treatment are typically found, previous research indicates that about a third of couples fail to achieve significant improvement, and an even greater percentage—between 30 and 60%—of couples show deterioration in gains, or relapse, at follow-up of 2 or more years.

As a result, although extremely helpful with regard to some specific issues, EST findings often have limited applicability. Regardless of the methodology of evaluation and assessment, it is of paramount importance to recognize that "virtually every recent review of couple therapy research has decried the lack of findings regarding the generalizability of treatment" and that a couple's "age, family life stage, gender, culture, and ethnicity (including interethnic couples), family structure (including composition of stepfamily and extended family systems), and nontraditional relationships (including cohabiting and same-gender couples)" are all factors that need to be teased out and studied (Snyder, Castellani, & Whisman, 2006, p. 337).

In response to these inherent difficulties of assessing clinical-practice outcomes using ESTs, a comprehensive and more flexible approach was developed by the APA, in the Family Psychology Task Force of Division 43. Their multifaceted approach provides a framework for different levels of efficacy: absolute, relative, change mechanisms, and contextual. Essentially, it recognizes a number of different methods in addition to ESTs, such as matched control groups, meta-analyses, and single case studies. Researchers and clinicians can choose the best means to investigate specific issues of interest: outcome studies, comparison strategy trials, moderator studies, effectiveness studies, process-to-outcome studies, and transportability (Sexton, Gilman, & Johnson-Erickson, 2005).

Such a multilevel approach is increasingly favored by those who believe MFT research must be applicable to the real clinical world, be cost-effective, and be possible for clinicians to conduct in their own practices and community clinics. The information that emerges from a variety of studies and settings can then go far in informing practice, helping clinicians to decide whether to include or discard different strategies or models.

In the following sections we draw from the research that has been done and identify the methods used. We identify which models have been found to work best and with which populations and problems or issues. Our goal is not to present only those interventions that have met the "gold standard" of peer-reviewed randomized empirical studies, but rather to present findings from other types of studies where useful, even anecdotal, information has been obtained. It is therefore important to understand that the inclusion of "untested" strategies or models does not mean that the strategy or model is invalid, but rather that it has not yet been thoroughly studied.

In this regard, we probably can draw some comfort from Gurman and Fraenkel's (2002) extensive millennial review in which they concluded that "every efficacy study (controlled, randomized clinical trial) of any method of couple therapy has found couple therapy investigated to date, has found treatment to outperform no treatment" (p. 242) and that "conjoint therapy was more effective than individual therapy for marital difficulties" (p. 241). Further, they stated that about 60 to 75% of distressed couples treated according to the most common methods showed medium to large "effect sizes" (i.e., improvement), as compared to 35% of distressed couples not receiving treatment in the same time period. "These effect sizes and improvement rates approximate or exceed what has typically been found in studies of individual (non-couple-focused) psychotherapies" (p. 243).

TYPES OF ASSISTANCE

As Gurman and Fraenkel (2002) suggested, a good way to conceptualize the types of marriage assistance now available is to use three categories borrowed from medicine—primary, secondary, and tertiary treatment. Primary treatment is preventive and most often purely psychoeducational. When these programs were first offered, they involved a standardized, one-size-fits all curriculum, were conducted only in group settings, and presumed a premarital couple was experiencing no or low distress. They were designed for couples functioning well early in their relationship and aimed to help them avoid possible problems in the future.

Secondary treatment programs also traditionally utilized standardized psychoeducational material and were taught in a group setting or in psychotherapy, but their goal was primarily "enrichment" for couples who were in established relationships, with low to only moderate distress, and who wanted to make a few selective improvements in their relationship.

Tertiary treatment was meant to alter the course of a relationship that was or could be in jeopardy of dissolution. It could contain a psychoeducational component, but it revolved primarily around individualized couple therapy, designed to "cure" couples in more severe or pervasive distress, often to "prevent" divorce.

It would be simpler if couples would sort themselves out among the three levels of care based on the severity of their problems, but it does not work out so neatly in practice. Therapists who rarely or never saw premarital couples 20 years ago now see them regularly. They see young premarital couples whose relationships are quite stable and healthy. These couples come for a few sessions to "prevent problems down the line" and might have done just as well or better in a bona fide prevention program. They are now seeing couples that have been together a long time and who would benefit from an enrichment program, as well as very distressed newly formed premarital couples who would benefit most from tertiary care.

To further complicate matters, the lines between the three levels of help and their respective modalities are becoming blurred. Therapists are employing psychoeducational approaches with low-distress couples, and some primary prevention programs are beginning to individualize their curricula according to couples' needs based on the results of the pre-program assessments they conduct.

This means that everyone involved in working with premarital couples should be able to identify and adapt to couples at any stage of formation or level of distress. It cannot be assumed that every couple registering for a premarital course will be distress-free, or that an engaged couple who contacts a private therapist is necessarily on the brink. It also means that leaders of premarital courses may need to refer a couple for therapy, and that a therapist will sometimes use a premarital assessment instrument and either do preventive work or refer a couple out to a premarital counseling course.

PREMARITAL AND MARITAL COUPLE THERAPY

Given that most therapists historically did not see premarital couples, there is very little in the couple therapy literature about premarital therapy per se. The few practitioners who did work with premarital couples understandably assumed that couples were couples, and consequently they relied on the theories, dynamics, and methods developed for married couples, using them without making modifications. Just in the past few years, a decade at most,

> Couples therapy for the unmarried has evolved as an acceptable, even desirable, way of navigating modern love for those in their 20's and 30's. Aware of the high price of divorce, comfortable with the idea of therapy in general and free from cultural pressures to rush down the aisle, modern couples are turning to professionals earlier in the game to help them work through their relationship problems (Wolff, 2005, p. G1).

Behavioral Couple Therapy

In the late 1960s, family therapy pioneer Don Jackson invented the speaker-listener technique, which taught couples to resolve conflicts by taking turns expressing one's views, followed by the listener's repetition or paraphrasing of what he or she had heard (Gurman & Fraenkel, 2002). Jackson emphasized behavioral specificity in making requests of one's partner and warned against mind-reading, and he advocated the use of "the floor" by the speaker and taking timeouts to prevent escalation, followed by calmer resumption of the conversation. These techniques became the hallmarks of behavioral couple therapy (BCT), were adopted by Imago therapy, and then provided the basis for a number of preventive psychoeducational programs like the Prevention and Relationship Enhancement Program (PREP), described later.

BCT combines the speaker-listener technique with negotiated "behavior exchange" (Jacobson & Margolin, 1979). It was the first therapy to be thoroughly researched by EST standards and is widely acknowledged as efficacious. Despite its scientifically approved status, Jacobson, Follett and Pagel (1987) found that a great many couples did not to hold on to their gains, which were moderate, and at a 4-year follow-up were divorcing at an alarming 38% rate. Their research, however, did show that BCT was most effective with younger couples who were less distressed, less gender-polarized, more emotionally engaged, and more committed to their relationship (Gurman & Fraenkel, 2002). In addition, couples able to form a solid alliance with the therapist around performance of assigned tasks seemed to do best with this approach.

Jacobson's disappointment in the longer-term outcomes of BCT eventually led to the evolution, with Christensen, of integrative behavioral couple therapy (IBCT); Jacobson & Christensen, 1996). IBCT added a cognitive component to BCT, assisting couples in accepting each other by converting their differences from negatives to be eradicated into positives to be appreciated and incorporated into their married lives. In essence the couples were helped to change "it's either my way or your way" thinking into "our way"—hopefully with a "value added" component in the bargain. With IBCT, therapists refined the speaker-listener technique and sought to convert the so-called harder emotions (e.g., hostility, bitterness) into softer emotions (e.g., hurt, sadness).

Christensen (2004) compared the two approaches in a large randomized efficacy study, which found both approaches having roughly the same impact, a 70% improvement or recovery rate in the 134 distressed couples who participated. At the same time, preliminary study suggested that IBCT was more effective than BCT in reducing blaming and promoting softer emotional expression in therapy (Cordova, Jacobson, Christinsen, 1998). Of note is that this is one of the few studies we reviewed that had a substantial number of ethnically diverse couples (22%). A few years later, Christensen and Atkins (2006) demonstrated the ability of both IBCT and BCT to promote positive change at 2-year follow-up.

"The Sound Marital House"

Based on the results of his sophisticated newlywed prediction studies (Gottman, Coan, Carrere and Swanson, 1998), and on studies of long-term marriages (Gottman & Notarius, 2002), John Gottman laid out his theory and therapy in *The marriage survival kit: A research-based marital therapy* (Gottman & Gottman, 1999) and also in *The seven principles for making marriage work: A practical guide from the country's foremost relationship expert* (Gottman & Silver, 1999). In what Gottman has called "the sound marital house," couples ascend from bottom floor to sixth floor and attic, with each floor representing a set of skills to support and sustain their relationship. The tasks on each floor are designed to counteract negative tendencies ("the four horsemen") that so accurately predict and inexorably lead to dissatisfaction and divorce.

Originally, Gottman intended his therapy for relatively new couples whose negative patterns were not too ingrained, to show them seven simple ways to behave well. In *The marriage survival kit* (Gottman & Gottman, 1999) he specifically stated that the population he studied may be less distressed than many of the couples seen in private practice, and that his therapy was not designed for couples in which there are serious problems such as major psychopathology, alcoholism, posttraumatic stress disorder, physical or sexual abuse, or an ongoing extramarital affair (Gottman & Gottman, 1999 p. 322). Gottman's therapy is offered both in individual couple-therapy format and in a weekend psychoeducational workshop format called "The Art and Science of Love"; John and Julie Schwartz Gottman even offer completely private couple therapy at their Orcas Island retreat off the coast of Seattle.

More recently, Gottman began applying his principles to more troubled relationships, conducting a large randomized quasi-control group study of a hundred couples (Ryan & Gottman, n.d.). Here he used an ethnically diverse representative sample, comparing moderately and severely distressed couples on Gottman therapy outcomes for friendship-building and conflict reduction. Both groups showed post-treatment improvement comparable to best outcomes for other couple therapies. Also, as would be expected, the moderately distressed couples made more gains and held on to them better than the severely distressed couples at a 1-year follow up. Severely distressed couples actually lost their gains (i.e., relapsed on the destructive-conflict dimension). Encouragingly, there were no significant differences in the results among the various ethnic groups. The quasi-control group was minimally "treated" with "bibliotherapy." They received and presumably read Gottman and Silver's book, and of interest, showed the most immediate post-treatment improvement! Control group husbands, however, did not hold on to their gains at follow-up.

This unpublished work aside, there do not seem to be published peer-reviewed EST outcome studies of or by Gottman, or other empirical or qualitative research to prove positive results from this therapy. A consummate researcher, Gottman has promised outcome studies, (Gottman & Gottman, 1999), so we can assume they will be forthcoming.

However simple Gottman's lessons may seem—he himself has said that it is only a matter of treating your life partner as you would a close friend or guest—they are deceptively so and can be devilishly hard for couples to implement. Traditionally, for example, men have been reared not to respect or defer to women. Gottman's position is that male dominance and emotional distancing ("turning away") are each capable of destroying a relationship, and that friendship-building can protect it.

Emotionally Focused Couple Therapy

Another major researcher, Susan Johnson, who calls her approach emotionally focused couple therapy (EFCT), is exclusively concerned with connectedness and attachment (Johnson, 2002; 2004). These concepts are very similar to Gottman's, suggesting that the two clinicians have kindred underlying views of what people are seeking from a primary relationship. In fact, both Gottman and Johnson owe much to attachment theory in terms of what they believe makes for healthy relationships, including the notion that mutual dependency in relationships is not something to be overcome, as some other theorists believe, but is actually a necessary foundation for healthy adult growth and development. Secure attachment—building and maintaining closeness—is where both Gottman and Johnson begin. However, they differ markedly in how to help couples get there.

Gottman is essentially a behaviorist in that his therapy first calls for behavior change, positing that changes in feeling toward the partner come as a result. Johnson, on the other hand, believes in the power of corrective emotional experience. Couples able to express and mutually soothe hurt feelings underlying negative blame-withdraw cycles will naturally change their behavior toward each other. When each one understands what the other is really feeling, and that there is no hostile intent, they experience empathy for each other and soften their approach. That empathy and softening is what heals. In comparing Gottman and Johnson, it's mainly a question of which comes first—the perennial insight versus behavior change debate.

Johnson and other EFCT therapists see couples over 8 to 20 sessions in private couple therapy. During these sessions, the EFCT therapist joins, collaborates, models, and "choreographs" the various steps couples need to take to correct their understanding of themselves and experience of each other. The aim is to catch, highlight, and disrupt a painful exchange that usually involves repetitive, harmful interaction cycles such as pursue-distance or blame-withdraw, and then replace it with positive interaction. The therapist proceeds to "unpack" the couple's emotions and the couple's labels for them. For example, anger might be translated "into different elements, such as exasperation, bitterness, helplessness and fear (Johnson, 2004, p.70)." The unpacking helps to reframe and to shift the couple's perceptions, thereby reducing their inclination to judge. The result is increased empathy and an enhancement of the couple's emotional bonds. In Johnson's work we see both Carl Rogers and John Bowlby, whom she never forgets to credit as her major influences.

EFCT has been thoroughly tested by EST standards demonstrating couple recovery rates, with EFCT posting gains greater than 70% over a wait-list control group. An amazing 90% reported substantial improvement. EFCT appears to maintain, and even improve its effects at up to two years follow-up (Johnson, Hunsley, Greenberg & Shindler, 1999). As is usually the case, not everyone benefits equally. It appears that somewhat older (average age 35), emotionally engaged couples who are able to "soften" their emotions seem to profit most from EFCT, and the model also works best with couples who have low to moderate distress levels (Johnson & Lebow, p. 9).

Insight-Oriented Marital Therapy

Insight-oriented marital therapy (IOMT) works by means of therapist interpretation of each partner's behavior. Insight-oriented therapists help partners come to understand their own internal conflicts, contradictions, inconsistencies, and needs, and also to uncover inherited dysfunctional beliefs and dysfunctional ways of behaving from the past. It seems to be a combination of individual and couple therapy conducted in conjoint sessions. Unlike Bowen's psychoanalytically based therapy, or Imago therapy (both discussed later in this section), this model does not press partners to research their past by interacting with and engaging in live discussion with family-of-origin members or others. According to Gurman and Fraenkel (2002), IOMT is "decidedly psychoanalytic, and overlaps with models based on attachment theory. Like EFCT, IOMT seems to work best with low- to moderately distressed, younger, emotionally engaged couples; IOMT is another EST treatment" (Jacubowski, Milne, Brunner and Miller, 2004).

Imago Relationship Therapy

In contrast to Gottman, EFCT, and IOMT is the work of Harville Hendrix, who developed Imago relationship therapy (IRT) (Hendrix & Hunt, 2008). Hendrix, whose thinking is also rooted in psychoanalysis, is less interested in the systemic or interactional problems of the couple; he focuses on how couples can help each other recover from wounds unwittingly inflicted by parents or other caregivers in childhood. The most basic assumption of IRT is that we unconsciously use our earliest experiences of imperfect parents to form an image of them (our Imago), which we internalize, carry into adulthood, and apply in selecting our romantic partners. According to Hendrix, we choose someone for better *and* for worse, in the sense that our partner embodies both positive and negative characteristics of our parents. Unconsciously, we believe that we will have a second chance to have our needs met, this time by our partner. We will remake the partner into a perfect parent who will help us heal from the frustrations, disappointments, and wounds we sustained growing up. If, or when, the partner fails to deliver the needed solace and repair, marital distress follows. And, in part, like other psychoanalytically oriented therapies such as attachment and object-relations therapies, IRT attends to the projection processes between partners that stem from family-of-origin and other significant relationships (Scharff & Scharff, 1991).

There is a crucial difference, however, between Hendrix's quite radical therapy and more traditional psychoanalytic couple therapy like IOMT. Traditional psychoanalytic therapy helps the individual heal by accepting the "fact" that an adult partner can never be and should not be expected to compensate for what the other was denied by parents. Hendrix questioned this supposed dose of reality. Too often, he observed, couples try to hide their true needs from each other, but are never really successful. As a result, these needs burst out obliquely, in resentment, anger, sniping, and withdrawal. It is precisely couples' quashing their needs and their failure to seek assistance in healing from their partners that gets them into trouble. Hendrix claimed that partners can and should help each other heal from past hurts, abuse, and trauma.

Whereas there is substantial empirical validation for Gottman's predictive studies and for EFCT and IOMT outcomes, IRT is thus far essentially untested by EST standards (Jakubowski, Milne, Brunner & Miller, 2004). On the other hand, "in-house" qualitative studies cited by Hendrix & Hunt (1999, pp.191–192), accounts of life changes couples in his care are able to make, and anecdotal reports of couples' experience in IRT can be very persuasive. Although it may not be necessary to ask partners to help each other overcome early family-of-origin difficulties—EFCT, for example, succeeds without doing so—some couples, not only the most troubled, want and need to go there.

Bowen Family Systems Theory

Murray Bowen shared a profound belief with Hendrix that unexamined past relationships determine one's relationship fortunes in the future. Practically since he conceived Bowen family systems theory (1978/1994), he and his disciples have maintained his status as a leading pioneer of family and couple therapy. For Bowen, all pathology is caused by unresolved entanglements from the past. The couple is always the main target of treatment, and the goals of therapy are the establishment of individual autonomy and differentiation (sense of separate identity) from family of origin. On the roof of Bowen's marital house, there are always two flags flying. Partners look backward and literally, purposefully go back to their immediate or extended family of origin, or to generations further back, to discover and disentangle themselves from longstanding family problems that now restrict their individual growth and development.

Unlike Hendrix, who, as described earlier, expected couples to help each other heal from past wounds, Bowen believed that the true path to psychological health was gaining insight into how one has been entrapped in the past and, when possible, resolving problems directly with parents or whoever caused them. Freed from the past, an individual will be mature enough to be part of a couple. Importantly, Bowen's followers have also encouraged couples to explore larger cultural forces such as gender, class, and race, which so heavily affect couple and family relationships (Carter & McGoldrick, 2005).

Although Bowen is a highly regarded pioneer in the field, there are no efficacy studies supporting his therapy. A wealth of single case studies suggests that it works, especially for couples who can see the wisdom of preparing for marriage by returning to work extensively on family-of-origin issues.

Solution-Focused Brief Therapy

Solution-focused brief therapy (SFBT), developed by Steve de Shazer and Insoo Kim Berg (de Shazer, Dolan, Korman, Trepper, McCollum, & Berg, 2007), is a refreshingly upbeat approach that is health-, goal-, and future-oriented. Because its emphasis is on identifying couples' existing relationship strengths and harnessing them to help reach future goals, it is appealing to MFT's training which tends to be strength-based and for all. Proponents believe that people can and want to change using their own resources and talents, and that they already have the strengths and resources within them to solve their problems. This therapy is a direct attack on the pathology-focused medical model. SFBT is also a reaction to the early years of family therapy, when therapists were on a steep learning curve, often felt overwhelmed by the problems couples brought, and bought into the idea that families and couples were determined *not* to change—that despite coming for help, couples preferred homeostasis (staying the same) and would generally use the power of the family system to resist change.

There are three elements in SFBT that are of particular importance in implementing the model. First, a couple's "resource map" is used to assesses each partner's individual strengths (such as self-esteem, self-awareness, coping skills, and self-soothing strategies), then each partner's perception of their strengths as a couple, and finally resources in their family of origin and the community (including at their workplace). The therapist works collaboratively, assisting the couple in creating a shared vision of their future from their individual maps. "Solution–oriented questions" are asked by the therapist to facilitate the process, such as "What is right and working in your relationship?" or "What is the most helpful thing your partner does when you experience problems in your relationship?" Routinely, "feedback" is provided at the end of each session to consolidate what has been accomplished and homework is given.

Critics of SFBT are concerned that it is "overly simplistic, it has the potential for minimizing the client's problems, and the possibility that some clients may not possess the skills and resources to solve their problems" (Clark-Stager, as cited in Murray and Murray, 2004, p. 356). Adherents respond that SFBT was not designed for couples engaged in violent behavior or who have other severe problems (Murray & Murray, 2004). Furthermore, there are a number of studies, less rigorous than ESTs, that lend support to SFBT (Trepper, Dolan, McCullum & Nelson, 2006), and one randomized controlled study conducted in Sweden showing positive results for SFBT (Murray & Murray, 2004). (It should be noted, however, that the population in the Swedish study was a nonpsychotherapy group of temporarily disabled people returning to work.)

As none of the therapies discussed in this section have yet been disproved, clinicians should feel free to use them as long as they keep in mind that none have yet been proven to work with all populations, on all kinds of problems, or with lasting results. Each therapeutic model presented contributes an important and valuable perspective.

It is interesting to note that each theory concentrates on a particular period of time. Bowenians take couples back several generations to work through their past problems directly with the people involved whenever possible. Imago therapists go back one generation, and say that partners heal each other. Insight-oriented marital therapists have couples go back one generation but keep their own counsel. Emotionally focused couple therapy takes couples back, but only to past hurts sustained in the current couple relationship, where healing also takes place. The "sound marital house" addresses issues in the current couple relationship and considers the couple's dreams for the future; solution-focused therapists mainly look ahead.

Despite these and other different theoretical emphases, there are more commonalities among theories than staunch proponents of given schools have been willing to admit. Bill Northey, former research director for the American Association for Marriage and Family Therapy (AAMFT), reported that of the 128 core therapist competencies identified by an AAMFT task force in 2005, "not one . . . is specific to any single MFT model" (2009, p. 79) Several competencies expect practitioners to be knowledgeable about the important theoretical models and evidenced-based practice in the field, but Northey concluded that "this suggests that the vast majority of competencies that MFTs possess cut across therapeutic models" (p. 80).

As the outcomes research across these and other theoretical approaches yields similar results, Sprenkle and Blow proposed that certain basic common factors may be responsible (Sprenkle, 2009; Sprenkle & Blow, 2004). It is interesting that these findings are consistent with the oft quoted long standing clinicians' hunch which is that experienced therapists actually function more like other experienced therapists of different theoretical persuasions than like inexperienced therapists within their same school. Such universal or common factors appear to be qualities lodged in the particular people involved—the therapist and the particular couple. Client characteristics such as communication style, socioeconomic status life experience, belief in the therapy process, motivation, and emotional intelligence (including the ability to regulate affect in interpersonal interactions) are a few things that influence how clients behave.

As Carl Rogers knew, therapist genuineness, warmth, unconditional positive regard, and empathy (picked up and perceived by clients) deeply matter, but are difficult to measure and establish as prerequisites for selection of therapists for efficacy studies. Efficacy studies only require a certain number of years of experience, and they inhibit therapists' instincts and judgment calls by asking them to standardize their responses according to predetermined treatment manuals. Meanwhile, there is evidence from as far back as the 1970s that a confrontational style early in therapy without support or structure is associated with a negative outcome for some couples, an important finding that has been corroborated in more recent studies (Gurman & Fraenkel, 2002).

ASSESSMENT INSTRUMENTS

An assessment can be informal, as when the therapist observes a couple interacting in the course of a session and forms a preliminary clinical impression, or it can be a full-fledged videotaped session reviewed by independent observers using a reliable formalized coding system for every utterance. It can be a diagrammatic instrument such as a genogram or a diagnostic questionnaire to tap the couple's beliefs, attitudes, expectations, or assessment of change.

The kind of assessment a clinician undertakes should (and usually does) flow from his or her theoretical orientation and way of working with couples, and it takes into consideration the couple's own style, preference, and point in the therapy process. An EFCT therapist, for instance, would use a measure of the security of the couple bond and be less interested in whether the couple could adhere to a speaker-listener protocol. One couple might request an objective test of their suitability for marriage; another couple might find such a test hokey or disruptive of the counseling process. There is no point in administering a questionnaire about something the therapist can ask about directly, such as a couple's feelings about having children. The assessment should rather contribute to a broader understanding of the couple and their issues. We encourage clinicians to familiarize themselves with these instruments and use them not only to help each couple they see, but also to inform their practices and improve their own performance (i.e., for research purposes).

Genograms

Conceived by Bowen in accord with his theory emphasizing the importance of family-of-origin issues, genograms allow the therapist and couple to visualize and conceptualize the couple's intergenerational family composition, structure, and many of its features (Kerr & Bowen, 1988). It looks like a family tree, and by its very concreteness it encourages couples to try to understand themselves in relation to family of origin. For Bowen, as we discussed earlier, context and the issues and themes brought to the marriage matter most—more than, say, how well a couple communicates or whether their goals for their future mesh.

The possibilities of the genogram for both assessment and therapy have been fully explored and elaborated on by McGoldrick (McGoldrick & Gerson, 1985; McGoldrick, Gerson, & Petry, 2008). For our purposes in premarital counseling, genograms can be used by both therapists and couples to foster and better understand the new couple entity that is being created through marriage. We advocate using it with premarital couples to highlight family-of-origin strengths, patterns, and potential problems. We also use genograms to help couples become familiar with each other's family histories and see how and where they each "fit" in the other's intergenerational family. It is often amazing how much symmetry is uncovered in the two families, how much information unearthed, and how much mutual understanding a couple can derive. We advocate that almost all clinicians learn how to use genograms, especially when it seems most appropriate for a premarital couple to take a historical look backward.

FOCCUS, PREPARE, and RELATE

Three of the most widely recognized premarital assessment questionnaires (PAQS) are: Facilitating Open Couple Communication Understanding and Study (FOCCUS); Premarital Preparation and Relationship Enhancement (PREPARE); and Relationship Evaluation (RELATE). According to an analysis by Larson, Newell, Topham, and Nichols (2002), each of these questionnaires has the benefit of being: (1) designed (or modified to suit) premarital couples, (2) comprehensive in its coverage of premarital predictors, (3) relatively inexpensive and easy to administer and interpret, and (4) psychometrically reliable and valid (p 234). Unlike a genogram, which requires dialogue between therapist and couple as it is being composed and interpreted, each of these questionnaires are paper-and-pencil or computer-generated inventories completed by the couples independently. Most PAQs do require or offer some professional or trained lay interpretation, and they are used either as part of an overall assessment process in couple therapy or in premarital courses or programs that also teach communication skills, conflict reduction, problem-solving and so on.

FOCCUS

Developed by Markey, Micheletto, and Becker (1985), FOC-
CUS is used primarily in premarital Catholic and Protestant
programs and "was designed to reflect the values and ideals
of marriage as sacred, including issues of permanency, fidelity, openness to children, forgiveness, shared faith in God, and
unconditional love" (Williams & Jurich, 1995, p. 145). The
questionnaire also taps such topics as sexuality and management of finances, as well as an optional set of items for interfaith, cohabiting, and remarrying couples. The basic FOCCUS
questionnaire has 156 items and takes about an hour or slightly
more for couples to complete. It also has an optional set of
items for interfaith couples, cohabiting couples and remarrying couples.

Items are grouped into four categories: personality, life-
style/friends, communication and problem-solving skills, and
religion/ values/ readiness for marriage. A summary category
identifies potential problem areas. The test can be adminis-
tered to one couple or to small or large groups, but it must
be interpreted with the help of a professional. Finally, there is
a short, 14-item form called "FOCCUS for the Future," which
the couple can purchase to help them plan how they want to
address the problems they uncovered.

In Williams and Jurich's (1995) study of the effectiveness of
FOCCUS, 200 engaged couples were contacted 5 years after
they had completed a FOCCUS questionnaire to see how well
their scores predicted their future marital "success" (i.e., satisfaction). FOCCUS did successfully predict future marital
satisfaction of most couples (with about 60 to 70% accuracy),
supporting its predictive validity. The results also showed that
FOCCUS and PREPARE were roughly comparable in this
respect. However, although the study was large, with a significant 5-year follow-up, it is important to note that the sample

was entirely Midwestern Caucasian Roman Catholic, and there was no randomization or control group, thus limiting the study result's ability to generalize to other groups.

To meet the needs of the increasingly diverse couples who seek assistance, FOCCUS now comes in four editions: a general edition that has no Christian language or references; a Christian nondenominational edition; a Catholic edition; and an edition for those with limited reading ability or who have English as a second language. In addition, FOCCUS is available in Spanish, Vietnamese, Italian, Polish, Braille, and on audiotape for nonreaders. Providers interested in using FOCCUS can participate in a daylong training session or watch a video. But both are optional.

PREPARE

PREPARE (Olson, 1996) consists of 195 items and also takes an hour or more to complete. There is a companion version called "ENRICH," an instrument later developed as secondary treatment for married couples. In addition to the original PREPARE and ENRICH, there are several newer modifications to make the instrument appropriate for different premarital populations. There is PREPARE-MATE for couples marrying over age 50, PREPARE-CC for cohabiting couples, and PREPARE-MC for couples who come into a marriage with children. All versions are available in English, Chinese, German, Japanese, Korean, Spanish, and Swedish. All of the PREPARE questionnaires measure couple cohesion (closeness) and adaptability (flexibility), and based on the test results, couples are placed in one of four categories: vitalized, harmonious, traditional, or conflicted. Vitalized couples are the most satisfied and conflicted couples, the least. Inventories completed prior to marriage were able to predict with 80 to

85% accuracy which couples would be either unhappily married or separated or divorced 2 to 3 years later (Olson & Olson, 2002 p. 210). Because of its emphasis on closeness/cohesion, PREPARE may be of particular interest to clinicians drawn to EFCT. Among the PAQs, PREPARE stands out in requiring counselors and others administering the assessment to take a daylong instructor's workshop or watch a video and pass an instructor's examination.

RELATE

RELATE (Busby, Holman, & Taiguchi, 2001; Holman, 1997) is a 271-item instrument with nondenominational English and Spanish versions. Like FOCCUS and PREPARE, RELATE is intended primarily for assessing premarital relationships. It can be used with premarital couples at all stages from casual dating to cohabiting or engaged with a set wedding date. Four major relationship areas are covered: individual personality characteristics, similarity of values, relationships with family of origin, and relationship experiences (i.e., communication and conflict-resolution styles based on Gottman's research). A subsection on problem areas in the relationship is included. Larson, Newell, Topham and Nichols considered RELATE "the easiest to interpret and the easiest to use in large groups and teaching settings" (2002, p. 237). RELATE is also the least expensive assessment if using computer scoring and can be done on the web at (http://www.relate-institute.org). It is the only PAQ that can be completed and interpreted without professional administration or feedback, though couples accessing the instrument on the web can request a professional contact. To qualify as a professional contact, therapists, clergy, and educators submit proof of certification and licensure. Clinicians interested in using RELATE should know that no in-person training is required or offered, but a manual is available for those who wish to study on their own.

Although PAQs are widely used and supported in a host of psychometric studies, until recently there were no published experimental ones that used randomized controlled (EST) conditions (Halford, 2004). To remedy this gap, Larson, Vatter, Galbraith, Holman & Stanman (2007) recruited 39 unmarried couples to complete RELATE, by themselves, with a therapist, or at the study conclusion after serving in the control group. The results showed significant growth or increased relationship satisfaction in the two treatment groups, whereas the control group remained static. It also revealed that a therapist's presence kept anxiety lowered. This is clearly an important beginning toward establishing the efficacy of PAQs. However, the study was flawed in some key respects. The 2-month outcome effect was decidedly short-term, and the sample size was small and homogeneous (nearly all were young, Mormon college students). Further, the researchers were associated with the development of RELATE and thus may have inadvertently contributed some bias to the process.

PREMARITAL PRIMARY PREVENTION PROGRAMS

Premarital primary prevention programs offer psychoeducational, usually skills-based, largely standard curricula. A given program may or may not utilize one of the PAQs just described to assess how couples are fairing pre- or post-participation. Programs are usually led by mental health professionals, clergy, or trained lay leaders, but recently Internet and self-help-book options have also become available. The reader is encouraged to scroll through such sites as www.premaritalonline.com, www.stayhitched.com, and www.whenharrymetsally.com to see how common these programs have become. Apparently, there are over 40 such programs available (Lebow as quoted by Boodman, 2006) which, we should add, vary widely in quality.

Programs with a Religious Focus

In contrast to earlier times, many clergy who lead religiously sponsored premarital programs today have a considerable amount of post-baccalaureate training in counseling or in marriage and family therapy. Those most qualified have a pastoral care masters degree in divinity and they may also be state licensed to practice privately either through their own degree or with an additional masters or doctorate in counseling, social work, or marriage and family therapy. This is a sea change from the 1930s, when Catholic Priests, through the local archdiocese, first began offering private marriage preparation.

The Catholic Church began to offer actual courses for couples wanting to marry in the Church in the 1950s (Hunt, Hof & DeMaria, 1998). Today, clergy and specifically trained lay people, along with professional clinicians, sometimes collaborating, offer these programs in a variety of settings and formats. But although there is considerable overlap between religious and secular programs, and religious programs may utilize recent significant research findings about what makes marriages work, it is still true that programs run or sponsored by the religious groups expect and prepare couples to follow the specific tenets and rituals of the particular religion and offer "universal truths" about marriage. As of 2006, an estimated 30% of marrying couples were involved in some form of premarital counseling program (Halford, O'Donnell, Lizzio, & Wilson, 2006; Stanley, Amato, Johnson, & Markman, 2006). Premarital prevention programs are now big business, all the more so because they are relatively easy to standardize and amenable to being researched.

Catholic couples preparing for marriage are now required to

take Pre-Cana classes, either in small couples groups or privately with a priest or other parishioner trained for the role. The classes generally meet in 2-day intensives, or in a 4- or 6-week series. The topics discussed in these sessions include: the purpose of marriage, habits of connection, communication and conflict resolution, finance (priorities and working as a team), sexuality as a gift, and couple spirituality. Before the start of class, as well as when the course is completed, the couple meets with the priest. Additionally, the couple takes the FOCCUS PAQ test and has assistance from the course leader in interpreting the results. Finally, the couple is strongly encouraged to take a separate fertility-care class wherein the intricacies of the rhythm method for timing intercourse and pregnancy are covered. As one would expect, the classes have a strong religious underpinning and are valued as such by many couples, though feedback from some suggests that it can be a strain to keep up "the pretense," as one engaged couple put it, when they were already having sex, using artificial birth control, and living together.

There is limited research on the long-term success of Pre-Cana programs. The only study we found was undertaken in 1999 by the Center for Applied Research for the Apostolate. In this study 9 out of 10 couples who attended a Catholic "engaged encounter" weekend said they learned important skills for their marriage; in a first-anniversary follow-up, more than three-quarters reported that they felt prepared for the challenges they faced (Whelan, 2007). Although these data are encouraging, from a research perspective the findings are preliminary at best. The sample size is very small, there was no control group, and clearly there is built-in bias here. Those who take the course, and then evaluate it, know in advance that they must be approved of and found prepared for marriage by the priest in charge. They therefore would be reluctant to give what they perceive as true but "wrong" answers, or to criticize any aspect of the program.

Most of the Protestant churches have gradually followed the Catholic example, and as of the millennium, churches in at least 100 cities in the United States were making marriage-preparation classes a prerequisite for a church wedding. Although the Protestant denominations do not view marriage as a sacrament or indissoluble in the eyes of God as Catholics do, they still view marriage as essentially a life commitment and the ease of getting a divorce with alarm. The covenant marriage movement was an effort by the Protestant political right wing to shore up marriage in the southern states, where the divorce rate has been especially high. And although it did not succeed, it was not for lack of trying.

A very popular nondenominational Christian-based enrichment program is offered by Alpha USA. Its primary mission is to bring Christians into or back into church affiliation by offering evenings "at home," run by volunteer church members, starting with a meal and covering a number of topics and exercises in a relaxed group setting. Alpha USA also offers a similar series for engaged couples. As in other similar programs, couples share with each other, but need not open up to the group at large. Some of the areas touched on in the five-session series are: the importance of commitment, how to recognize and appreciate differences, the art of communication, resolving conflict, spending time together, nurturing friendship, making each other feel loved, developing a good sexual relationship, and the importance of talking together about goals, values, and dreams. This all sounds rather like Gottman, does it not?

Engaged Encounter, an outgrowth of Marriage Encounter, is a prevention program for couples who are engaged, seriously contemplating becoming engaged, or in some instances newly married. Founded in 1974, originally under Catholic auspices, it is now quite ecumenical, offering programs all over the United States and internationally in many churches including

Catholic, Episcopal, United Methodist, Lutheran, and Assemblies of God. A Web site about this program mentions the still-high divorce rate in the United States and the need for good communication skills to ensure a strong union from the start (http://www.engagedencounter.org/).

Formal marriage-preparation courses were neither mandatory nor offered in Jewish synagogues until recently, but individual rabbis usually met informally with a couple one or more times before the ceremony.

In recognition of the fact that the divorce rate in the Reform branch of the Jewish community is now as high as in the population at large, the Beyond the Chuppah Project was launched in 2001. It is a strongly encouraged daylong workshop (or in some places, a series of 2-hour classes) in a small group setting with other Jewish engaged couples. The project is approved by Reform rabbis and facilitated by Jewish Child and Family Services (JCFS) agency social workers. Couples learn about marriage "within a Jewish framework"; in addition to covering what it means to be a Jewish couple, they discuss issues that all couples confront in marriage, including expectations, personality issues, communication, conflict resolution, finances, leisure, sexuality, children and parenting, egalitarian roles, religion, and extended family. In many places the research of Gottman and Johnson has been incorporated and the PREPARE inventory is employed as well.

In 2007, the Chuppah Project was expanded to include another marriage-preparation program. The newer program provides premarital counseling similar to the Chuppah Project, but it is conducted in a private setting. Individual couples can attend up to eight sessions with a JCFS social worker. Prior to counseling, couples also complete PREPARE on-line and the results are discussed in the sessions.

Because of the high rate of intermarriage among Christians and Jews, over half of the more liberal rabbis who identify as Reform, Reconstructionist, or Progressive will marry an interfaith couple. In 2008, the Reform movement introduced another variant of the Chuppah Project called "Alpha Bet" to meet the needs of interfaith couples who plan to keep a Jewish home and raise their children Jewish. These programs welcome gay and lesbian couples. Note, however, that Conservative and Orthodox rabbis will not marry an interfaith couple under any circumstances, except conversion to Judaism by the non-Jewish partner.

To our knowledge, there are no premarital preparation classes offered by the mosques in the United States or elsewhere in this country's Muslim community. Historically, there are probably three reasons for the absence. First, it may be because Muslim marriage in predominantly Muslim countries was traditionally arranged by the parents or other designated religious guardians, leaving couples "free" of having to decide if they were making a right partner choice. Second, cultural and religious definitions of gender roles and responsibilities were quite fixed. Therefore, learning about marriage from one's parents was in most cases sufficient, and if there was marital conflict, the husband, an elder, or an imam generally settled it. Third, as in earlier forms of Western marriage, the family connections created by marriage and the stability of the marital dyad were more important than marital satisfaction of the couple. The bottom line seems to be that when divorce is forbidden and the divorce rate kept low, there is less perceived need for premarital preparation to hold marriages together.

Although marriage preparation courses for Muslim couples are lacking, there are at least two modern, highly informative self-help preparation books in English, one by a Muslim marriage and family therapist (Ezzeldine, 2003) and the other by a British Muslim scholar (Maqsood, 2000). We recommend them highly to clinicians who may not yet be familiar with modern Muslim marriage and who may want to recommend these guides to their Muslim couple clients.

Secular Programs

The Prevention and Relationship Enhancement Program (PREP) (Markman, Stanley, Blumberg, Jenkins, & Whiteley 2004), is probably the best-known prepackaged psychoeducational prevention program designed for premarital couples. Started in Colorado at the University of Denver as an outgrowth of Imago therapy, it utilizes the speaker-listener technique to deescalate conflict and incorporates some of Gottman's approach to provide a well-integrated and comprehensive curriculum. Group leaders distinguish between "static" factors, such as parental divorce or age at marriage, and "dynamic" factors—both of which contribute to marital satisfaction or unhappiness—but build the course topics around the dynamic factors, learning things such as talking without fighting, identifying "hidden issues" in gridlocked discussion, and setting aside time for fun, friendship, and sexual intimacy.

PREP recommends four to five session modules for therapists and clients to use in various in-person group formats. All PREP groups are led by licensed mental health professionals or trained clergy. Couple Commitment and Relationship Enhancement (Couple CARE) is a self-help, in-home version of PREP available on the web and in smaller stand-alone modules that can be introduced in part or as needed into a more open-ended couple therapy plan. Although PREP has "multiple foci of intervention, most time is devoted to prevention of destructive conflict" (Halford, 2004, p. 560). PREP is considered an efficacious program by empirically supported treatment standards, and its effects have been shown to last up to 5 years in long-term follow-up studies (Jakubowski, Milne, Brunner, & Miller, 2004).

Relationship Enhancement (RE) (Guerney, 1977) is another empirically validated set of programs. Originally designed for married couples as enrichment (secondary prevention), it was expanded early on to serve premarital couples, other family subgroup combinations (such as fathers and sons, mothers and daughters, and parents), as well as some underserved nonfamily groups such as prisoners and the mentally ill. The couple workshops are limited to 4 to 10 couples and are run on 2-day weekends throughout the year. The Couples Relationship Enhancement Weekend is an intensive version more appropriate for couples in moderate distress. The RE website (www.nire. org) describes the weekend as offering "unique and innovative skills-training . . . empowering couples to resolve current and future problems on their own while also deepening their sense of connection"(National Institute of Relationship Enhancement, n.d.)

In both levels of prevention and both formats, RE aims to help couples:

> establish a constructive, cooperative atmosphere for resolving difficult relationship issues, foster increased openness and trust, reduce defensiveness, anger, and withdrawal, express deepest feelings, concerns, and desires openly, honestly, and safely, deepen caring and compassion, increase love and affection, create solutions to conflicts at their deepest levels, successfully implement agreed-to solutions and behavioral changes. (National Institute of Relationship Enhancement, n.d.)

In some respects, RE is similar to PREP, but it is more clearly grounded in the experiential therapy tradition. In fact, the RE website specifically mentions indebtedness to Carl Rogers and refers to the EFCT work of Susan Johnson. Accordingly, the emphasis of RE is less on skill-building, is less behavioral, and is more focused on the development of partner empathy. Both in-residence and self-study training are offered to professionals and lay persons interested in RE coaching. There are also phone consultations available for couples that cannot travel to participate on site. RE also meets the standards of an efficacious (EST) program (Jakubowski, Milne, Brunner, & Miller, 2004).

Couples Coping Enhancement Training (CCET) (Bodenmann, 1997) is an approach developed in Germany that shows great promise. Its premise is that in addition to learning communication and problem-solving skills, couples also need to prepare for, and learn how to cope with, external stresses that can otherwise negatively affect marital quality and satisfaction and even lead to divorce (Bodenmann, 2005; Gottman & Levenson, 1992). Like the other programs described in this section, it is designed for premarital couples and for long-term couples experiencing early warning signs, and it is marketed as distress prevention. Couples in crisis—close to divorce, violent, and so on—are screened out and referred for therapy. The program is standardized and there is a treatment manual trainers must follow. CCET is an 18-hour program offered in weekend formats and in six 3-hour blocks; groups are recommended to be limited in size from four to eight couples. Four of the six modules differ significantly from other programs, teaching individual self-assessment of stress levels and coping skills, as well as stress management and dyadic coping. CCET is educationally sophisticated, employing a variety of educational methods such as video and live demonstration, supervision and feedback on couples' role-playing, and both the trainer and the couple's own evaluation of progress. In 2004, the CCET was found to be just "possibly efficacious," but only because the "control group" in one of two randomized controlled experimental studies actually received treatment via a short version of CCET (Jakubowski, Milne, Brunner, & Miller, 2004).

As may be clear now, the programs described in this chapter and a host of other premarital course offerings for couples are available and often aggressively marketed. They attract couples to counseling in a socially acceptable way. They help some couples realize that their differences are too great and pull back before making the marriage commitment. In addition to prevention of marital distress, these courses provide a valuable service to their communities, as they enable professional clinicians running them to screen for couples whose troubles are more complex or severe than brief group counseling can reasonably be expected to address. But they should not be viewed as a panacea. According to Jay Lebow, "It's easy to oversell these programs. They have a nice effect, but it's not life-changing. They are not going to fix an incredibly bad choice or a relationship that's deeply troubled" (Lebow as quoted by Boodman, 2006). Also of concern is that there are no universal standards for workshop leaders, and when courses are run by a briefly or superficially trained lay leader, problems may come to light that are more serious than a couple or the leader can effectively handle.

Overall, there has been relatively little research specifically on first-marriage educational program outcome. Much of the data that would pertain to first marriages has been embedded in studies of all marriages, first and previously married couples combined, or lumped in with a larger data set of married couples. Nonetheless, the separate data from an oft-quoted meta-analytic study suggests that, like couple therapy outcomes, in nearly every case premarital education programs appear to be very effective as compared to no education for the acquisition of "interpersonal skills (e.g. communication, problem-solving, empathy for partner, self-disclosure) and overall relationship satisfaction" (Carroll & Doherty, 2003, p.

111). A large ex-post facto survey lends further weight to these findings, which held true across race, income level, and education (Stanley, Amato, Johnson, & Markman, 2006). And all studies of premarital education generally support the value of couples' learning and practicing communication skills, problem-solving, and conflict management over programs that focus solely on enrichment and identifying problem areas but do not teach skills (Stanley, Blumberg, & Markman, 1999). Unfortunately, couples tend not to prioritize the opportunity to learn and rehearse new skills in choosing a premarital education course, perhaps because they are shy at the prospect of performing.

Recently, some quasi-experimental studies have found that the benefits of skills-based relationship courses for premarital couples are greater when it comes to the stability of relationships, even among high-risk couples, than with regard to couples' satisfaction with their relationship 2 to 5 years after participation (Halford, 2004; Halford, Markman, & Stanley, 2008). These findings are obviously encouraging for combating divorce, but less so if the object is to increase marital satisfaction. Another meta-analytic study of couples in relationship enrichment (though conducted overwhelmingly on married couples) yielded similar results (Hawkins, Blanchard, Baldwin & Fawcett, 2008).

In addition, like with the religiously based classes, the high marks these courses generally get from couple graduates may be due in some measure to selection bias. Couples attracted to these programs in these studies are rarely representative of all sizable subgroups in their community and tend to be white, middle class, educated, and affluent. It is quite possible that couples drawn to these workshops already know their relationships are good and are simply looking for affirmation; or they know that marriage can be difficult, are more committed, and are more inclined to work hard at it. Ultimately, for more definitive research about the efficacy of these programs, we may have to rely on the religiously based programs, as these programs are often required. But even here there is a selection bias in that those couples who choose religious weddings may be different from those who do not, possibly being more dutiful and less likely to divorce even if miserable.

Evaluating the research on premarital education programs, Halford, Markman, and Stanley concluded that researchers still do not know much about long-term effects past a year or two, or to what extent these programs reduce rates of divorce—but we do know that "couples that show sustained enhancement of relationship satisfaction from skills-based Couple Relationship Education seem to be couples in early-stage relationships who are at high risk for developing future relationship problems" (2008, p. 500). Gottman added to the concern about the lack of long-term follow-up by pointing out that few divorces occur in the first year that half of all divorces happen in the first seven (Gottman & Silver, 1999 p.4).

SELF-HELP BOOKS FOR PREMARITAL COUPLES

In addition to the two marriage-preparation books for Muslim couples mentioned earlier, there are almost too many other books on the market—religious and secular—to help couples prepare for marriage, as well as a host of websites that cater to the concerns of premarital couples. We also encourage providers to visit local bookstores and surf the Internet—with a critical eye—to identify books that they may want to recommend to their clients as well as books they would not recommend. Ideally, therapists would keep a list of currently available self-help books to recommend and offer to discuss them in sessions if the couples want to. Those that have some scientifically derived information and advice, such as Gottman and Silver's (1999)

The seven principles for making marriage work, and Susan Johnson's *Hold me tight* (2008) are what to look for.

COMMUNITY AND GOVERNMENT INVOLVEMENT

Since the mid-1990s, unbeknownst to many in the professional community, there has been a grassroots movement to combat divorce in the United States, and since the late '90s, marriage relationship education "has grown beyond programs offered by private professional and lay practitioners to become a tool of public policy" (Hawkins, Blanchard, Baldwin & Fawcett, 2008, p. 723). These efforts have often been sparked by professionals such as Diane Sollee, a family therapist who once was conference planner for the AAMFT. She went on to found the Coalition for Marriage, Family and Couples Education, organize the "Smart Marriages" conferences, and "galvanize public policy, professional, and community interest in skills-based education for marriage" in a variety of community settings including churches, schools, and businesses (Doherty & Anderson, 2004, p. 426).

In other instances, the impetus has come from lay organizers, such as Michael McManus, a journalist who promoted the concept of a "community marriage policy," by which clergy would refuse to marry a couple who had not taken a premarital counseling course (McManus, 1995). This community activism is what induced the Churches to set required courses as a standard, which, as we mentioned earlier, has been implemented in a host of cities and churches across the country. In most cases, the planning, implementation, and program evaluation is a collaborative process between community leaders (business, religious, educational, governmental) and mental health professionals. Doherty and Anderson (2004) described five programs they believe can serve as examples for other states or

communities to follow: Marriage Savers (a national organiza-
tion), Healthy Marriages (in Grand Rapids, Michigan), Families
Northwest (in Washington and Oregon), Oklahoma Marriage
Initiative, and First Things First (in Chattanooga, Tennessee).

As these community-wide programs are relatively new, complex, intentionally not standardized, and unwieldy to manage, it is not possible to say yet how effective they will really
be. Some have questioned their goals and near-religious zeal in
efforts to lower the divorce rate by keeping marriages together
that would be better off dissolved, in their absolute rejection
of cohabitation, denigration of single parenting, and rejection
of gay marriage. To some extent this has become a political
battle between conservative and liberal forces in the country,
each with an agenda larger than marriage alone. The Institute
for American Values think tank and the National Organization
for Marriage, which explicitly oppose gay marriage, are good
examples of involvement on the conservative end.

Under pressure from these and other "pro-marriage" groups
such as the National Council on Family Relations, the U.S. government under the second G. W. Bush term began to take an
active role through grants to "faith-based" and secular organi-
zations committed to "encourage marriage and promote the
well-being of children" (Department of Health and Human
Services, n.d. p.1). In 2006, for example, the Department of
Health and Human Services Administration for Children and
Families distributed 150 million dollars to fund programs in
five areas related to its mission, one of which is "services and
support" for low-income married or engaged couples with children. Unfortunately, cohabiting and engaged couples who do
not (yet) have children are excluded. Funds also have been
used for demonstration programs to further diversify the
group of couples who have been served to date. There is more
information on the Healthy Marriage Initiative website (www.
acf.hhs.gov/healthymarriage).

In addition to federal legislation and funding to support marriage, at least five states—Texas, Oklahoma, Florida, Minnesota, and Wisconsin—have passed legislation offering a small financial discount as an incentive to couples applying for a marriage license if they have taken a premarital education course. Some experts believe that premarital counseling courses should be required by law (Licata, 2002), and Gottman, the prediction guru, believes that in the near future it might well come to pass (2008, p. 120).

LOOKING AHEAD

As we move forward, researchers and clinicians need to think of premarital couples as a more distinct subcategory. As Gurman and Fraenkel (2002) noted, we need more studies on the effectiveness of couple therapy—and, we would add, on preventive programs as well—specifically with *premarital* couples.

If we take seriously the importance of therapist characteristics for therapeutic outcome, researchers, even in efficacy studies, will have to ramp up the criteria for therapist recruitment and stipulate that only those who can provide a predetermined level of facilitative conditions need apply. This will be difficult to implement and adhere to, but years of experience and willingness to stick to a particular protocol are not enough to test the efficacy of an approach or program. If therapists in these studies were all offering high levels of Rogerian conditions, the results would probably be even more positive than they already are.

As the notion of prevention of marital difficulty catches on more and more, marrying couples will increasingly turn to psychoeducational approaches for help with low and moderate distress. Practicing therapists will need to retool to be comfortable working in psychoeducational, preventive mode as well as to provide private couple therapy. Mental health degree programs and post-degree training programs will increasingly be called upon to teach these approaches.

Help will need to be made available in newer immigrant communities or in communities that tend to be more ingrown or cloistered. Training of clerical imams and mental health agency workers to provide meaningful premarital counseling to the Muslim community in the United States would be a good place to begin.

There is an urgent need for more promotion of prevention programs so that more couples will seek marriage preparation. Part of the advertising/marketing challenge will be to convince more couples to take advantage of the opportunities that exist and to focus at least as much time and effort on preparing for marriage as they do on planning the wedding. There is some evidence that couples will seek these courses out if they are convenient, low cost and when recommended by respected members of the community such as clergy, doctors, or elders (Gurman & Fraenkel, 2002; Sullivan, Pasch, Cornelius & Cirigliano, 2004). Also, an experienced, trustworthy professional course leader and insight-oriented educational content may be most important to engaged couples considering taking a course (Sullivan & Anderson, 2002).

Although the couples in the Sullivan and Anderson study placed less value on being able to practice skills, it is possible that this was due to a bit of fear and that an experienced course leader would be able to allay any trepidation. A post-test on the couples might have found skills-building much higher on the list. Apparently, post-course ratings suggest that although clergy and trained lay leaders may be just as effective as mental health professionals, utilizing clinicians as professional leaders may be important in being able to recruit more couples. Allowing couples to work on problems they select themselves might also help.

Although most clinicians would applaud efforts to increase

participation in premarital education, counseling, or therapy many would undoubtedly stop short of calling for it to be a prerequisite for obtaining a license. This is an important question we discuss further in the summary chapter, along with the question of whether there should be an across-the-board, same-size-fits-all course requirement or universal application of a screening instrument to identify couples most at risk. Although it is certainly appropriate for preventive programs to screen out and refer couples already engaged in violent behavior or who have other serious problems, programs should still address these issues as potential marital problems in all cases and discuss what to do should these kinds of problems ever arise. Many clinicians lack confidence and understanding of these problems and fail to broach these topics; more time training therapists in these areas is sorely needed.

At the very least, there should be a concerted effort on the part of all professionals who intersect with premarital couples to push premarital preparation; wedding planners, catering hall operators, gynecologists, clergy, bridal shop owners and employees, and even real-estate brokers showing apartments or houses to premartial couples could be recommending premarital education.

CHAPTER 4

Who Is Your Client?

Anne F. Ziff

What do you get when you fall in love?
You only get lies and pain and sorrow
So, for at least until tomorrow
I'll never fall in love again
    Dionne Warwick, "I'll Never Fall in Love Again"

Dionne Warwick, the Carpenters, and other entertainers refer to the pain so many people have experienced after they fall in love. Indeed, there often *is* pain if you've made love-object mistakes. This is as true of people choosing partners who are incompatible for a dance, a party, a college weekend, a wedding, or life! Having chosen foolishly or erroneously, one or both members of a couple may very well feel as if "you get only lies and pain and sorrow" as the result of falling in love.

Clients who come to us for premarital counseling and education have probably had at least one taste of that pain—either while dating or in an earlier marriage—and, even so, have now been able to find a potential life partner with whom it seems safe enough and more satisfying to go forward.

Clients who seek premarital counseling come from a variety of backgrounds, face a wide range of issues, and often have differing ideas about what makes a good marriage. Knowing who your clients are is a crucial part of helping them. We begin this chapter with a discussion of that exploration through the premarital intake process, then describe some of the main characteristics of clients who seek premarital education and counseling, and close with a section on referral sources and other ways clients find us.

INTAKE

During intake (a double session), we ask a number of questions, most often in conjunction with drawing the premarital couple's genogram, designed to focus the attention of the couple and the therapist on the couple's needs. These questions, which we ask aloud, first of one partner and then the other, are designed also to guide us in creating a therapy "contract." And they help each partner in the couple describe his or her model for good and poor relationships.

It's important to note that on occasion, during the course of intake discussions, we recognize that the couple is not a good candidate for premarital counseling. Difficult as this may be, we need to address the problem and suggest another option or two, rather than create a contract for such couples. The questions we find useful in the majority of intake sessions, follow.

- "Are your parents both living?"
- "Do they live together?"
- "How would you describe their marital relationship?"
- "What would you guess are the reasons their marriage has lasted?" (if the parents are still married)
- "What do you think are the reasons their marriage did not work?" (if the parents are no longer married)

- "How do/did you feel about their divorce? How old were you when it took place? Which parent did you live with? How often did you see the noncustodial parent?"
- "If either parent (or both) has formed a new couple, how do you see it as different from their couple in your family of origin? What are the admirable changes you observe? What mistakes do you think you are seeing?"

Responses to these questions help us develop an insight into each partner's experience with, and expectations about, relationships and marriage. In addition, the questions catalyze discussion and allow both partners to hear each other's story with fresh ears while an objective observer listens in. We typically follow the initial round of questions for either partner with this pair of questions to the other:

- "Is any of this new news for you?"
- "Are there any comments or additions you would like to make at this point about your partner's family story as you understand it?"

The answers to our questions are useful as we focus our therapy "contract." They serve as an initial guide, with a genogram in front of us, so a clinician can begin to know the two people who have come to us for premarital counseling. Further, we (and the couple) begin to understand a bit more about their expectations of themselves, of their partner, and of this institution called marriage.

ANXIOUS CLIENTS

One characteristic of clients who come to talk to us is anxiety. Clients frequently describe themselves as anxious or uncertain. They crave reassurance that they are making a good choice;

they long to know in advance that they are, in fact, marrying well. Libby was an anxious client.

I first met Libby, a 28-year-old woman, in a 6-week seminar I conducted for "Women Who Love Too Much." At the end of the seminar, she left me a note, asking if it would be all right for us to talk further in individual sessions. A child of divorce, her anxiety at this point in time was focused on fears of being a failure in marriage herself.

Libby denied anger at her parents, although she admitted she didn't like either of them very much and wanted to live far away from them if possible. She described her mother, a pediatrician, as a woman who "worked too many hours and didn't seem to care very much about her second husband and stepkids, either." She added, "She's more the cheerleader type than someone who's comfortable with soft fuzzy feelings." Her father, an orthopedic surgeon, was "handsome, arrogant, and a womanizer," she reported. "He'll never remarry! And that's a lucky thing," she added.

Libby's own love life was sufficiently overwhelming that, at first, she bought a dog for companionship, returned to graduate school, and decided not to dwell on being single. In fact, she dated so much that she hardly had time to feel single! But one relationship failed after another. Guys drank too much, or left their jobs, or otherwise disappointed her. She'd begun to worry that no one would ever meet her standards, or love her, and she'd always be alone.

Libby and I had worked together for roughly a year at this point, discussing how her anxieties were affecting her. She felt numb now in all aspects of her life, but especially in relationships. Once she could recognize her own survival technique—namely, not feeling anything—she was able to begin to make some more changes, which, in turn, reduced some of her anxieties. Among the feelings she allowed to surface were anger and sadness. In time, Libby faced both (and kept a journal about the process, "so I can always remember this"). She became better able to maintain healthy relationships, particularly friendships. She became very aware of the choices she was making as she developed a new, expanding lifestyle, both in graduate school and out, and of how anxiety was apt to complicate things if she "just went back on auto-pilot.."

Two years after our "last" session, Libby came back to therapy. She had had three dates with Paul, a man her father had introduced her to. Paul was the middle child in a family of three boys. He was bright but, more important to Libby, he was "really nice"—kind, and with a good sense of humor. He cared about his family and expected to marry and have kids of his own some day. Libby didn't want her fears to get in her way with him.

She'd enjoyed their first date but found herself feeling surprisingly suffocated by the end of it, a feeling much like the anxiety she had felt in adolescence in her family home. That puzzled her. Despite her wariness and fear, she'd accepted a second date when Paul called, and this time effortlessly enjoyed herself all evening.

That night, though, she had the first of several dreams about being trapped in an elevator that was falling from the 37th floor. Each time, she woke up in terror. Falling in love was not the metaphor she linked this freefall nightmare to until after their third date, and that's when she called me. She felt she needed to think this through, and wanted to do that in therapy.

Libby had begun to sense that this relationship was special, and she wanted to understand herself better and "not mess this one up." She began to explore more fully the origin of her anxieties in this phase of our work together, and to manage them consciously. She knew the anxiety had begun around her 10th birthday, when her parents had been divorced about a year and her mother remarried, and she associated these anxieties to her fear of making a mistake with her own marriage someday.

Hoping to reduce feeling "revved up and nervous" about her current situation, Libby stopped drinking coffee and soda and switched to herbal teas, especially remembering to have Sleepy Time tea at bedtime. In addition to weekly therapy, she began a yoga practice in a group at her health club, and, at my suggestion, wrote in her journal each morning for 10 minutes and race-walked for 20 minutes at least three times a week. All of this, plus increasingly good experiences with Paul, seemed gradually to be making a difference. Although Libby wasn't rid of her anxiety, she was in control of it. She had learned that having anxiety was different from being anxious (Assagioli, 1965, 1974), and she was becoming in charge of her own emotions, no longer frightened by them. Her sense of self was developing, and with it, her self-esteem.

Paul joined her for a session in my office, 6 months into this phase of our work together. They'd had dinner with her father and his current girlfriend in celebration of her father's birthday, and Paul wanted to talk to me about Libby's dad.

"I can really understand why Libby's afraid to trust men after seeing him in action," he said. "What a bozo!"

I asked him to explain.

"Well, his girlfriend's questioning him about their commitment to one another after 2 years of dating, and he mocks her. He's mean and sarcastic to her face, and we know he's cheating behind her back with a much younger woman—some au pair who works on his street! He's a catastrophe. Thinks only about himself."

Libby kept nodding as he spoke. When I asked her what she was feeling, she quickly responded, "Validated!"

At her next session, a few weeks later, in September, Libby reported that she and Paul had started talking about marriage and making a life together. Paul had his priorities "where they belong" she told me, and now, having clarified the seriousness of their relationship, her anxieties were no longer in her way. They were planning to become engaged by Christmas and marry before the summer. Our premarital therapy continued intermittently until the week before their wedding, with what I think of as "a two-pronged attack." On the one hand, when Paul was in session, our concentration was on premarital issues, emphasizing marital models in their two families, their own ideal marriage, and tracking and discussing their progress through the 8 premarital stages. This was the first prong. The second was Lib-

by's emphasis on learning what she felt was "enough" about her own anxiety, and then developing ways to manage this often wayward emotion. For Libby, the techniques of identification and disidentification (Assagioli, 1965, 1974) were key. Her mantra became: "I have anxiety, but I am not my anxiety; I am a center of pure self-knowledge and of universal knowledge." (A mantra is intensely personal, created by the individual using it, and, in Libby's case, highly effective as an antidote to the nearly lifelong anxiety that she had been working diligently to overcome.)

An interesting side note is that, several years and a couple of children later, Libby got in touch with me because she was thinking of making another career change, this time from her successful career in business, into Marriage and Family Therapy. She wanted to work in the field that she felt had made such a difference in her own life.

STEP AHEAD OF THE DIVORCE CURVE

Although some of our clients come to see us because they, or someone who knows and cares about them, recognize a specific "issue," such as anxiety, many others come in for premarital counseling and education because they want to be "a step ahead of the divorce curve." They hope we can teach them enough about marriage that they will be able to circumvent ominous surprises and replications of toxic family-of-origin patterns as they walk through life. These clients quickly learn to recognize that life doesn't arrive beautifully designed and neatly packaged, and that although having knowledge (conscious knowledge, that is) is an advantage, it can't completely prevent disappointment, frustration, or trauma. Humans err; we make mistakes. The skill we advocate in couple counseling and premarital education is to recognize each mistake as quickly as possible and correct it. And, of course, we hope to help clients use awareness to prevent a repetition of the same mistake whenever possible. Clients seek premarital counseling and education for many of these reasons, as Marilyn and Al illustrate in the next case.

Marilyn and Al were eager for their marriage to be a successful one. They'd been together since college, and had lived together for nearly 2 years when they decided to take the next big step and marry. They had just one problem: their families.

Al's family was only a problem in that it was so different from Marilyn's. He was the third of four children, and the only son. Although both of his parents now worked, his mother had stayed at home until his youngest sister was in high school. A close-knit family, they had faced their share of typical life challenges, but the family bonds had always remained strong.

Marilyn came from an entirely female household. She had three older sisters and two younger. Closeness patterns between the girls varied from time to time, as did distance. Triangles formed and were broken haphazardly within the sibling subset. Marilyn's parents had separated when she was 12; years later, they divorced. Her mother's patience was almost always in short supply, and she had little to give any of her daughters except demands or competition. She could be mean and even verbally abusive with whichever daughters were not, at any given time, "on her good side." Marilyn attributed her feelings of helplessness and panic attacks during college to these unstable family alliances, so different from Al's home life. She had only one ongoing, close, sibling relationship, with her eldest sister, who acted as a quasi-mother to her. It was, in fact, this sister who encouraged Marilyn to first seek therapy as a freshman in college.

In her second year at school, Marilyn met Al. It was difficult for Al to understand the love/hate relationship Marilyn had with her family of origin. Over the course of their dating, Marilyn was gradually able to allow herself to believe she was accepted by Al and his family, and her comfort with them grew slowly; they were so different from her own family.

*One huge question remained however, and it worried Marilyn a
great deal. (Al did not seem equally concerned about this.) She fret-
ted incessantly: How could she guarantee that she would not revert
to old family patterns and grow into a shrewish woman like her own
mother? Al felt certain there was nothing to worry about, but there
was no way to mistake the earnestness of Marilyn's concern. "Teach
me to stay me, never to become her!" was her plea.*

*This couple did their premarital work for over a year, beginning
prior to their engagement and continuing until 5 days before their
wedding. They faced their differing expectations head on, especially
the varying communication models they had grown up with. They
had some experience talking about good things like being happy
together. They built on that, and learned to talk openly about anger
and misunderstandings without feeling threatened. In the end,
Marilyn was able to disidentify from her mother and original family, recognizing that she "has a mother, but is different from her
mother" (Assagioli, 1965, 1974). Marilyn learned a whole new
style of self-expression, and even chose to get a masters degree in
Communication because she was so fascinated by her experiences of
effectively communicating, and the changes she was able to make
in her life.*

*Ultimately, one of the new steps Marilyn was willing to take
involved breaking with some of the expectations her mother and siblings had, on the subject of her bridal shower. She found the nerve
to tell one envious, cranky sibling not to come to her bridal shower.
This sister had not sent an r.s.v.p. but was telling family members
she wanted to go to the movies that day, and since she wasn't "in" the
wedding, she didn't have to go to the shower . . . unless she decided
to at the last minute and crashed. Initially panicked and feeling out
of control, Marilyn found the strength first, to tell her mother that
her sister was being disinvited, and second, that she was expected
to either support this decision or to not attend as well! The divisive
games Marilyn had grown up with were no longer "normal" and
acceptable to her, and she was able to be both loving and firm about*

this. She had sought education in her premarital therapy, and she learned a great deal about herself, communication styles, and healthy families, in the process.

CLIENTS WHO ARE SELF-AWARE

Our most successful premarital counseling clients tend to be those who approach marriage with self-knowledge and awareness, acceptance, sensitivity, good humor, a willingness to be flexible and to compromise, and an ability to listen thoughtfully. With such an abundance of fine qualities, what could these people need premarital counseling for? Even with clients who are lucky enough to be able to love deeply and be deeply loved, there can be issues. In the following case, of Harold and Maggie, both age and geography were potential "deal breakers."

Harold, a 55-year-old client (for two years), was a long-divorced, noncustodial father of two, when he took a sabbatical year in China, teaching English as a second language to advanced students in Beijing. One of his students was Maggie, an articulate Chinese woman whom he found beautiful as well as bright. Maggie was 25, never married, and the eldest of her four siblings. This pair developed a warm friendship during the school year, often having vibrant discussions over tea or in the company of Maggie's family. They laughed "at the world's foibles," enjoyed art and literature, felt strongly about "the need to stop terrorism through education," and they each valued family, religion (he was Jewish; she Buddhist) and friendship. When the year was over and Harold came back to therapy, it was to discuss his inclination to bring Maggie to the United States so they could live together and explore the romantic dimension to this relationship.

Their age difference was striking in American terms. In Asia, it was much less unusual, Maggie and her family assured him. She

was fine with the prospect of their living together; so were her par-
ents. We did some premarital counseling while Maggie's visas, et
cetera were organized, and, once she was in the States, they began
their work as a couple. Here we had two very introspective, aware
partners, sensitive, accepting, flexible, and quite ready and willing
to compromise. The problems they faced were largely external ones:
How Harold's family felt about his choice of wife, the age-complicated
cohort groupings, Maggie's need and ability to become financially
independent here in the United States (and her citizenship), the tim-
ing and cost of visits to Maggie's family in Beijing, et cetera. And yet,
they did marry, and had been living happily together for over 5 years,
successfully working through the thorny issues, no longer in therapy,
when I heard from them last. While Harold and Maggie's story is
one of disparate opposites, what makes it useful is to see beyond age
and geography, into the character of these two already formed human
beings, who "found" each other and chose to overcome obstacles in
order to successfully create a life together.

PREVIOUSLY MARRIED CLIENTS

Previously married premarital clients, often faced with blending families, are an interesting category that actually deserves
its own separate book. This group encounters problems and
carries baggage that previously unmarried premarital couples
generally do not have to deal with.

This unique subset almost always presents as couples in which
one or both partners have had a previous marriage that ended
in an annulment, dissolution, divorce, or death of the spouse.
In most of the cases we have seen, divorce is the method by
which the marriage ended, and there may be significant emotional wounding that is still unresolved prior to the new relationship. These "second time around" partners are, however,
highly motivated to have a successful marriage this time, and
they may be able to understand what it was like to be married

to them. In initial interviews and at other times during work with these clients, we specifically ask a question developed by Dunne (1991): "What is it like (or likely to be like) to be married to me?"

CLIENTS WHO ARE BLENDING FAMILIES

Many problems can arise for partners bringing children from a previous marriage into the new marriage, and therapists or other trained counselors can help these clients to anticipate them. That said, however, it is never possible for anyone to anticipate all of the problems and anxieties a child will experience when his or her life is being scrambled.

The "blending" family in the following vignette came to see me in advance of their engagement, hoping to ease the groom-to-be into his new step-parenting role.

Jonathan, never married, was in his early 40s. He had waited "a long time" to find the truly right woman, and he was confident that Audrey was it. He frequently remarked, "One of the things I love most about Audrey is the kind of mother she is. I trust and admire her kindness and patience and love for her children. It's not easy, I think, but she does it so naturally."

Jonathan very much wanted to blend into Audrey's three children's lives. He was looking forward to being stepfather to her children, as well as to creating an entirely new life for himself with their mother. How he could accomplish this rather Herculean task was initially the primary subject of our work.

As their wedding approached, anxieties increased. Jonathan and Audrey both considered themselves Unitarians and had easily agreed on the selection of a minister who would perform their wedding ceremony. They were planning what they described as a "tasteful, small ceremony" at a hotel not far from their home. At one session, Jonathan brought up his hope that Audrey's children would participate in their wedding ceremony. Pleased, she agreed that it would be really nice. They left the session excited, with plans to invite the children to walk down the aisle as flower girls and ring bearer.

Audrey's 6-year-old son was thrilled to be asked to be their ring bearer and gave an immediate and enthusiastic "yes," as did Audrey's 5-year-old daughter, who was delighted with the idea of wearing a new dress and tossing rose petals as she walked down the aisle. The 8-year-old daughter, however, had balked and cried at the prospect, and she had been withdrawn and rather grumpy since their conversation.

Both Audrey and Jonathan were upset as well. They had not imagined being told no! They were experiencing how very unpredictable kids' feelings can be, and how hard it is for anyone, even a parent, to know in advance what makes blending a happy transition and when it triggers pain or anxiety.

The ultimate solution to this situation was that the 8-year-old was promised that she would have a new dress for her mother's wedding, just like her little sister would, but that she did not have to do a single "job" at the wedding unless she decided she wanted to. That satisfied her, although she then proceeded to ask if her father would be there and whether she could sit with him. When told, "No, Daddy isn't being invited," she got teary but managed to ask them who she could sit with then.

As we had planned in advance of this conversation, they turned the question around to her, and she immediately knew that her second choice was to sit with her 16-year-old cousin. To everyone's surprise, their acceding to that request made her instantly happy again, and soon after, she began to be welcoming of Jonathan in some small ways.

What was being worked through at this stage of blending for Jonathan, Audrey, and her children was a loyalty issue (Boszormenyi-Nagy & Spark, 1984). The 8-year-old's question about "sitting with Daddy" was the earliest clue to the divided loyalties she was facing head on.

NEWER FORMS OF BLENDING FAMILIES

Blending takes on another form when one partner has had a child prior to the forthcoming marriage and that child was conceived or adopted outside of marriage. In many, but not all, of these cases, we see the mother as having the primary caretaking relationship with the child.

As she was turning 40, Lynne faced a somber reality. Her biological clock was ticking, and she was not in love. In fact, she hadn't been dating for about 4 months—and that was not by choice! She decided to turn to a sperm bank and become a mother, a single parent, hopefully before her 41st birthday.

Lynne was one of the lucky ones; she conceived with her second insemination and carried her pregnancy to term without any complications. She was healthy throughout the pregnancy, had a female friend who was happy to serve as a labor coach, and labor itself was uncomplicated as well. She gave birth to Donna, a 7-pound, 5-ounce girl, and felt fulfilled and happy at once and for years after the baby's birth.

With the help of her parents, who lived within 40 minutes of her apartment, and a flexible position as a senior editor that allowed her to work at home part of each week, Lynne managed to have child care in her home for Donna until she entered public school. She loved her daughter and never once regretted her decision to become a single parent.

When Donna was in first grade and Lynne was 47, the unexpected happened: She met a 49-year-old man whom she found very attractive and interesting. Divorced with one child of his own, a 10-year-old boy, Oscar was a college professor. He had a custody arrangement that allowed him to have Johnny live with him on alternate weeks and for half the summer.

This parenting plan allowed Oscar and Lynne to get to know each other rather well on an alternate-week basis, and they were extremely comfortable and happy together, much to their delight. After about 6 months of this dating pattern, Lynne asked Oscar to join her in one of her individual therapy sessions.

Both Oscar and Lynne had clear priorities: their children. When and how might they introduce them? Donna had met Oscar, but Lynne and Johnny had not been introduced in person, although they occasionally talked on the telephone.

I mentioned that there was no real need for them to meet each other's child until the relationship was serious and moving toward commitment. At first, they became shy and looked at each other, questioningly, with something like a smile on each of their faces. Then, almost simultaneously, there were two heads nodding.

I wondered, for a moment, if I should leave my own office! But I stayed and was witness to this committing on their part. We all were moved, and then they looked to me for "the next step," as Oscar phrased it.

"Have you just made a commitment to each other, about your intentions?" I asked.

"I have," Oscar answered quickly.

"Yes, me too," said Lynne, with tears in her eyes.

With that, our work blending these four lives together into a new and different family began.

Oscar's homework was to involve Johnny in planning to meet Lynne face to face. As it turned out, Johnny had a lot of questions about Lynne, and he suggested that they include Donna and spend a day at the zoo, having fun and getting to know "the faces behind the names," as he put it.

The introductions went well, and slowly, over the 8 months before the wedding, a blending of the two families took place. The kids led some of the movement with questions like "Are you and Lynne gonna get married?" (from Johnny) and "Can Oscar and Johnny come and live with us here?" (from Donna). Answers followed, with Lynne and Oscar coached to consistently keep the reins in their adult hands. The children's frequently enthusiastic questions simplified some of their steps, but they were never allowed to confuse who was actually in control and making the decisions. That job resided with the adults in the couple; period.

It was agreed that each biological parent retained ultimate authority about the standards and rules for his or her own child, but premarital sessions focused on parenting styles and issues. The couple's goal was to be on the same page as much as possible. They each knew what they wanted, both as individuals and as a couple, and they learned how to communicate the new set of expectations to their children.

A bimonthly family meeting (on alternate Sunday afternoons when Johnny was with them) was established once they were all living together. "How're we all doing this week?" was the topic, and candor with kindness was encouraged and modeled. Both children readily got the picture. Johnny even once told Lynne, "I don't think you know me well enough to love me yet, but I bet you'll be good at it before my bar mitzvah".

EVASIVE CLIENTS

It's appropriate to mention that among our least successful clients are couples who are evasive in session. They often have something to hide and find it difficult, or are unwilling, to bring whatever they are hiding out in the open. The question mentioned earlier—"What's it like to be married to me?"—often helps us ferret out such clients from the start. These challenging clients are likely to be disdainful of the question, and unwilling or incapable of thinking through an answer to it. These same couples may reject homework assignments or coaching from us, frequently fearing that these tasks might lead to revealing whatever it is that they're hiding. Julie and Edward were one such couple.

Julie and Edward initially presented like a couple that was solid. He was a self-declared "finance maven" from New York. She was from England, where she also had been involved in the finance industry, and now was in New York to pursue a Ph.D. in consumer marketing. When they came to see me early in the summer, they said it had been love at first sight. Both were in their 30s, neither previously married, and both were athletic and interested in writing, theater, "bizarre music," and food. They were also "loving their great sex life" together. I wondered why they were seeking premarital counseling.

When I asked them how they had met, they talked casually about "meeting through friends a scant 6 weeks ago." At some level, what they said was true. Each of them had been encouraged by several friends to become active on a dating website. But the perceived stigma they both attached to this method of meeting prevented them from speaking of it directly.

Because I suspected that their mutual denial of the way they actually met was apt to be in the way of their happiness together, I brought it up during our second session.

"What's it like to have this shared secret?" I asked.

"We don't care!" Edward pronounced for both of them, while Julie sat quietly, thoughtful.

"I do care," she said tentatively. "I wish we could be honest about how we met, but it's so embarrassing . . . and Edward says it makes us sound like we're losers. At home, people just mind their business so much more. America's so . . . I don't know exactly . . . it's just so hard to have privacy."

This couple's shared sense of embarrassment about the source of their meeting—plus their cultural differences and some level of excess impulsivity for each, but particularly on Edward's part—led me to move from my initial sense of confidence to one of concern. In addition to his impulsivity, Edward seemed excessively guarded. His

"We don't care" remark in response to my question about their secret seemed intended to keep me out of their feelings, and it set off a red flag that was hard for me to ignore.

In the end, I didn't have to worry very long about my assessment and treatment of this couple. They cancelled their third session and, instead of rescheduling, sent me an email from Edward's account. "Thanks for your help and understanding. We've decided to elope next weekend, and won't need your premarital services further."

I wished them good luck, and still do.

It is very hard for therapists to confront a premarital education or counseling situation in which their instincts say "This may be wrong" while the couple is intent upon going forward, sometimes in haste. Opinions vary on whether it's best for therapists to remain neutral or noncommital (at one extreme) or to fully divulge their perspective (at the other). Most of the time we're not as lucky as I was with Edward and Julie. Their decision to elope made it unnecessary for me to wrestle with the question of whether and how I might suggest that they backtrack before rushing helter-skelter into marriage. They rushed; I was dismissed. No more dilemma!

POWER IMBALANCES IN A COUPLE

Another type of premarital client with whom it's hard to be successful is the couple who denies an existing, significant power imbalance. In these cases, the therapist is frequently sought merely as an advocate for the stronger member of the couple, and any steps we take to redress the imbalances become a reason for the couple to abruptly stop the therapy. It is important to note that education and counseling are not the actual goals for these clients (or for those who are unwilling to reveal secrets), even though that is the pretext for their seeking therapy. Had Julie and Edward stayed in counseling longer, it may have become clear that Edward's financial assets created just such an imbalance in their relationship. From this vantage point, that's simply speculation, however.

It's helpful to establish a clear contract with premarital couples in the first session. As described earlier in this chapter, focusing on a contract for the therapy may help couples, as well as therapists, recognize the nature of the work early on. It will help rule out couples who are in the wrong place—couples whose needs will not be met in the therapeutic, educational environment of premarital counseling.

WHERE DO PREMARITAL CLIENTS COME FROM?

Our referral base is wide. What follows is a compendium of some of the most common or interesting avenues our couples have traveled on their way to our offices.

Preexisting and Returning Clients

This category consists of two groups of clients. The first is made up of preexisting clients, that is, people who are already in individual therapy with us and then "meet someone" and want to bring them in and do some premarital work together. Most of these people stay for as long as it takes to be ready to marry well.

The second group is returning clients, people with whom we have worked in an earlier time period, often during divorce or the illness of a spouse who ultimately dies, and they come back at a later date, having "met someone new." What these clients want is to do premarital counseling with the therapist they already know and trust,. They return to a clinician whom they feel knew them really well and can help them not repeat old patterns.

In either case, so long as a clinician can accept the premarital couple as the client, and a bias work without bias, both of these sets are interesting premarital couples with whom to move forward.

Word of Mouth or Internet

It is common for people to surf the Internet for purveyors of services, and therapy is no exception. The AAMFT provides a therapist network (AAMFT Therapist Locator) to help people learn about providers in their communities. Many therapists also have a personal Web site, which is easily accessed by surfers.

In addition, there are people who have heard or read that we do premarital education and counseling and call to meet with us once or twice, just to experience the process. Many of these people are guarded or shopping without commitment, and they often leave after the introductory session, unwilling to set ground rules for self-awareness and partner appreciation, or disappointed to hear that there's more to this "marrying well" than just hot sex.

Personal Referrals

Today, very few people—at least in metropolitan areas—feel ashamed to have "been in therapy." In fact, in our practices, we emphasize the belief that people who come to premarital counseling are courageous and wise, as well as generally healthy and curious.

Family members, friends, neighbors, or acquaintances of former or current clients often hear about us and are encouraged to give us a call. Many of them do, wondering if this premarital counseling and educational work might apply to them and be useful or at least interesting.

We've discovered through experience that when the couple has heard about us from their sibling or friend who trusts us, there's a high likelihood they'll call to schedule a first session and then choose to stay to do some work together. When their parents are the initial source of the referral, there's a reasonably good chance the (soon-to-be) engaged couple either will never make the call or, calling, will need to be referred elsewhere. It's harder to predict how referrals of this sort—in the event they actually show up—will work out!

When referrals come from a relative or personal friend of the clinician, however, for ethical reasons, the clinician will typically refer the couple to another therapist. It is important to model and keep clear boundaries, particularly with regard to our own professional versus personal relationships.

Referrals from Attorneys

People who have seen a lawyer, either individually or together, perhaps to draw up a prenuptial agreement or discuss estate-planning, frequently are referred to us for a taste of premarital education. Such couples are rarely getting ready for first marriages, and, already aware of some of the pitfalls of marriage, they are often willing to do whatever it takes to promote a lasting relationship.

Referrals from Physicians

Gynecologists, urologists, internists, general practitioners, and family physicians who treat one or both partners of a premarital couple and observe some fairly obvious symptoms, including anxiety, often will make a referral to us. These couples almost always call, come in, and stay to do some effective work. They have trust in the referring doctor, and they place that same trust in us as we embark on premarital education and counseling.

Often, the type of physician who is making the referral provides a clue to the type of work you will do with the couple, as the following case example illustrates.

> *Mark and Jenny were referred to me by Mark's urologist. Mark, 28, had been having significant urinary-tract infections and been treated by his urologist for nearly a year, during which time he and Jenny decided first to live together and then to marry. Our conversations frequently had to do with sex and performance anxieties. (Because I am trained to do sex therapy, these are topics I am comfortable with. Clinicians without the necessary education refer these cases out.) The referring urologist had recommended that the couple embark on premarital education to reduce Mark's anxieties, both about possible sexual dysfunction and about marital responsibilities in general. This urologist believed that the therapy would benefit both Mark and Jenny, and he emphasized that when he made the referral.*
>
> *We had a long premarital counseling relationship, working through the sexual issues and anxieties and moving on to the practical questions of where and when to hold the wedding, when to buy wedding rings, and how to prevent parents from destroying the harmony the couple was seeking. The referral from Mark's doctor was valuable to the couple on many levels.*

*Referrals from Therapists in Disciplines
Other than Marriage and Family Therapy*

MFT is a relatively new discipline, and not one in which all mental health professionals are comfortable. Thus, many referrals of premarital couples come to us from other professionals in the field who just don't want to work with more than one person in the office at a time.

When these referrals are unmarried couples, they usually develop rather easily into premarital education cases. Such couples have at least one member who is comfortable in therapy, and frequently both parties are able to be open and introspective.

Referrals from Clergy, Congregations, or Justices of the Peace

When one is asked to officiate at a wedding ceremony, there is often a period when approximately six meetings take place prior to the wedding, during which it is *marrying well*—not the catering, flowers, or music—that is considered. Some clergy go on to recommend a more in-depth kind of conversation, such as premarital counseling can offer. We appreciate these referrals, and we note that the premarital work is not always completed when the wedding ceremony takes place. Counseling, begun so close to the wedding, can expand from premarital to "early marital" sessions if needed.

Occasionally, a couple in our office is also doing work with a member of the clergy. It's important to remember that there is more than one perspective on the premarital (and marital) experience. It is our hope that couples find value in both secular and religious insights, and that clinicians will encourage and support that view. Marilyn and Al, introduced earlier in this chapter, had their own unique opinion after doing both secular and religious premarital counseling.

"There were lots of advantages, for us, to doing secular premarital educational counseling," Marilyn told me during our last session. "We did the Pre-Cana classes, but found that they focused on questions for people who have not lived together. The classes were a good enough experience, but superficial. They'd ask questions about stuff like: How will you plan your vacations after you're married? Will

vacations include going to church? Or: How much time do you think it's okay to spend away from your spouse each week?

Al added, *"As important as religion is in our lives, communication is more important right now, and so is learning about the role of children in the family. We needed tools for fair fights and how to listen and negotiate, not a big discussion of whether we'd go to church when we were away on vacation! We got much more of what we needed to learn about marrying in premarital education and counseling than at Pre-Cana."*

Speaking Engagements

We always carry marketing materials, including business cards, with us when we are invited to speak at meetings or conventions. People generally know *someone* who's engaged or about to be engaged, and premarital counseling is enticing. Referrals after speaking engagements are common. For example, during one of my classes, a pregnant woman in the room was so interested in what we mentioned about premarital education that she called her recently engaged twin sister during the first break and demanded she come to listen to the rest of the talk. The woman embarrassed us both by coming up with her sister at the end of the day and insisting that she schedule an appointment with me for premarital counseling, on the spot. I demurred and suggested instead that she take my card and call me after she'd discussed the idea with her fiancé, which, in fact, she did the next day.

Workshops

Libby, also introduced earlier in this chapter, is a good example of how workshops often produce results beyond the time spent in the group. As you may recall, Libby initially attended a workshop I conducted, then set about doing individual work with me, and ultimately, when the need developed, came back for premarital counseling.

Coincidence

When we have our checks and deposit slips printed, we include a line that says "Marriage and Family Therapist" above the address and under the name. Usually people just ignore that line. But sometimes they ask about it.

> *I had a cordial relationship with Sarah, a teller at my local bank, and we talked informally each time I had banking to do. One day she finally asked what a "marriage and family therapist" does. I explained, including a comment about premarital education. This prompted a conversation about her intention to do stomach surgery to lose over 100 pounds. I wished her good luck with the surgery before saying good-bye and leaving the bank.*
>
> *A few months later, Sarah was back at work. Surgery and initial recovery over, she now talked with pride whenever I saw her about having a fiancé and her plans for a wedding. All of these conversations were very brief. One day, however, it became obvious that she wanted to talk at greater length about her fiancé's mother, and she asked if she could meet with me in my office. Sarah and her fiancé came to premarital therapy for about eight sessions, and then married without further hesitation about family interferences.*
>
> *Self-referred after noticing the marketing line on my checks and deposit slips, Sarah demonstrated that clients may come via very low-cost advertising!*

Clients come to us from many resources, and they present a wide variety of issues.

Regardless of how clients come to your office and what issues they bring to therapy, as premarital therapists, we have the opportunity to witness the unfolding, for each of our clients, of one of life's major transitions: the movement from individual to partner in a couple. In addition, we may be able to demonstrate that there's more than "lies and pain and sorrow" to be derived from this experience, particularly when it is engaged in thoughtfully. In all of our work, it's incumbent upon the therapist to model some of the things we will encourage our clients to do: Listen with an open mind, accept each person who comes to your office or refer them elsewhere, model a safe, healthy relationship with each client, and be curious!

CHAPTER 5

Common Premarital Problems

Elena Lesser Bruun

I am human. Therefore, nothing human is alien
to me.

Terence (163 B.C.)

There are about a dozen issues that couples frequently bring to counseling that therapists must be prepared
to handle: differences in race or ethnicity; gender; finances;
values; goals and lifestyle; politics and religion; children and
family planning; sex, intimacy, and premarital affairs; relationship boundaries; sociability; readiness and commitment; communication; and/or emotional intelligence.

Sometimes these are issues couples thinking of long-term
relationships are aware of, know they need to discuss, are stuck
on, or have already been arguing about when they schedule a
first appointment. But just as often these same issues are hidden, lying just below the surface, too hot to acknowledge at
first, because premarital couples want desperately to hold onto
their positive feelings for each other and about the relation-

ship. If the couple does not somehow mention the elephant in the room very soon, it will be up to the therapist to inquire about it. Therefore, it is also imperative that we be comfortable dealing with any or all of these problems ourselves, and if any of them hit too close to home, work to resolve them in our own lives. We have to know our own Achilles heels and not "take a pass" by refusing to see a couple or automatically referring a couple out when we are initially uncomfortable or unfamiliar. I once heard a therapist at a national meeting unambivalently state that when she was contacted by a Muslim couple she simply referred them to a therapist who was "more familiar" with Muslim marriage.

One could argue for the validity of this decision, and many therapists would undoubtedly agree with it, thinking she was only trying to be eminently fair to the couple. But we believe this seemingly innocent action is indefensible. First, according to the MFT code of ethics, "Marriage and family therapists provide professional assistance to persons without discrimination on the basis of race, age, ethnicity, socioeconomic status, disability, gender, health status, religion, national origin, or sexual orientation" (AAMFT, 2001, p. 1). Second, her automatic refusal to treat reveals an underlying presumption about the couple's issues—when, in fact, we cannot know what a Muslim couple is coming in for until we have spent some time listening to them. Last but not least, there is something sad, and spiritually lacking, when we avoid differences or unfamiliarity rather than viewing them as learning opportunities. Ironically, most issues couples bring are largely universal, common to many, if not most, kinds of marriage.

If we are not comfortable with difference, we risk sowing seeds of intolerance or helping to perpetuate it. To combat a tendency to avoid, we have to take on the unknown and the unfamiliar, especially our prejudices, and struggle to overcome them. We do this by welcoming couples who bring new problems—the more unfamiliar the better—and finding common-ality, knowing that there is always something we can come to understand and enjoy in even the most unfamiliar or initially off-putting backgrounds. We have experienced these kinds of differences receding in importance and becoming second-ary to the couple's underlying problems, which we can always relate to. The challenge is for us to grow to the point where we can honestly say that "nothing human is alien."

The following is a case in point. Not long after I became a therapist, I was fortunate to be helped by a client to overcome a fear of, and knee-jerk negative reaction to, German accents and thus German people, stemming from my American Jewish childhood and having been born at the start of World War II. Renata was a non-Jewish German woman with a strong Ger-man accent. She had lived with Andre, a French Jewish man, for many years and had raised a son with him. Though she still loved Andre and considered herself married to him, she was extremely unhappy and wondered if she should finally leave.

> Renata had contemplated leaving Andre for many years, but ulti-mately she always felt sorry for him and couldn't walk out because he was "mentally ill." Recently, after a serious disagreement when Renata once again threatened divorce, Andre shot himself three times, took a prescription overdose, and was hospitalized. Over the years, Andre had often verbally abused her, though never physically, and had frequent one-night stands with other women, leaving his list of contacts around for Renata to see. He kept his rare gun collec-tion, which scared her, handily displayed in the glass-doored cabinet in their dining room, and would not store them elsewhere despite her protestations.

How could any sane woman live with this man? Well, as one might speculate, Renata had been physically abused herself by her German father, who had served in the German Army during World War II and singled his daughter out for "special" scapegoat treatment when she, a bright, spirited child, would occasionally disobey. Moreover, Andre at times treated her very well—much better than her father had—and always told her he loved her and would do anything to keep their relationship.

One reason for his dramatic suicide attempt was that Renata would not commit to getting married. She was the main bread-winner and primary parent, and her low self-esteem was at complete odds with her competence and character. She had no economic reason to stay. Now that their son had taken a job on the West Coast and was fully on his own, Andre panicked that Renata would finally leave.

This extreme illustration highlights two common problems therapists bring to the table: potentially contaminating preju-dices, and instances in which a couple's issue is so embedded and toxic that we feel a need to drop our usual neutrality and take a position. When there is potential danger to our client or the misery quotient is extremely high, are we not compelled to take a stand? To at least issue a warning by saying something akin to: "I'm worried about the possible danger to you. How much have you thought about this?" Renata used therapy to ponder her situation thoroughly, but in the end she decided to stay. She took heart in the fact that Andre now had psychiatric help and was vowing to be a better mate in the future. The crisis seemed to have brought all of their problems into the open, and I was able to refer them both for couple therapy. With a newer rela-tionship without such a long history together, Renata probably would have left and started anew. In any event, thanks to her I am cured of my fear of German accents and German people.

This is delicate maneuvering, just as it is with married cou-ples in extreme distress, but it's a little different in the premari-tal situation because there is usually more of a sense of relief on the part of the couple in having caught the problem in time— and more satisfaction for the therapist in having helped a couple prevent a more complicated and guilt-ridden separation or divorce. There are, of course, exceptions to these "rules," but in general it is possible and right for clinicians to consider taking *slightly* stronger stands with highly distressed premarital couples. Many of these couples are already questioning whether their relationships are meant for the long term.

RACE AND ETHNICITY

We are seeing increasing numbers of mixed couples—interracial or interethnic—combinations of Caucasian, African American, black African, South Asian, Chinese, Japanese, Korean, and Native American. These differences, however, were rarely if ever among the presenting problems, probably because these couples so often have had to push past a powerful common enemy to come together in the first place. The enemy was the dominant culture, which issued a clear "no" to many of these relationships in the past—and in some cases still does.

> *In high school in the mid-1950s, for example, Jeanne, a Caucasian girl, dated Harry, an African-American classmate whom she adored. After dating for several months, they went to a movie in Times Square. Forty years later she confides to her therapist that she can still feel the sharply disapproving staring eyes as they walked and held hands on the street. To this day she regrets her mortal embarrassment, which precipitated the breakup.*

For many years, interracial couples were particularly stigmatized, and whatever might be wrong inside the relationship was relatively unimportant compared to their joint fight to survive in the world. Interracial coupling has now become much more common compared to when I started practicing in the early 1980s, and I see these couples so often that it takes me a while to realize just how many I see. They now report less of a need

to fight outside rejection and are more aware of their own relationship problems apart from racial/ethnic difference. Perhaps they have more faith in therapists' acceptance now. In
any event, the problems these couples present with are about
ethnic cultural differences rather than skin color per se. It is
important to note how much progress has been made toward
acceptance of racial/ethnic difference and inter-racial/ethnic
marriage since the last miscegenation laws were struck down in
the 1960s. Before that, we were a society so obsessed with race
that Martin Luther King could only dream we would be able to
overcome it.

Annette and Daniel, the interracial couple introduced in
Chapter 2, illustrates how far we have come.

*Annette and David began having a series of relationship prob-
lems, and the threat of separation hung over their lives like a looming
storm. Nadine had become a serious handful and the couple could
not agree on how to contain her. Daniel clearly loved Nadine and
wanted to marry Annette and be Nadine's adoptive father. In the
course of counseling, Annette was persuaded that Daniel really did
love her, not just Nadine, and she agreed to marry in the hope that
this would help settle them and Nadine down. This is just some of
what drove Annette and Daniel to seek counseling; race was never
an issue.*

It is important that we not assume that if we identify a difference or a problem area, the problem must therefore exist.
In the end, it is only a problem if it is a problem to the couple.
We might be struck on first meeting by an interracial/ethnic
couple and red-flag racial/ethnic difference as an underlying
issue if the couple does not identify it at once. But race/ethnic-
ity might not be on their problem list at all.

While on the subject of race, it is worth mentioning another
problem that exists but is only tangentially on the minds of

interracial/ethnic couples, or couples of the same race/eth-
nicity with a therapist of a different race/ethnicity. With inter-
racial/ethnic couples in which one partner is Caucasian, I'll
sometimes ask if my skin-color likeness to the one member is
a concern. Admittedly, my sample is relatively small, and con-
founded by difficulty admitting it to a Caucasian therapist, who
they might worry would be biased toward the Caucasian member of the couple, but so far no one has said that it is a concern.
If the couple is the same race and ethnicity I am different, I
also inquire whether they have any concern starting out and
encourage them to tell me if they feel that our racial/ethnic
difference seems to interfere or become an issue at any point
along the way.

GENDER

Heterosexual couples rarely state gender differences as their
presenting problem. Usually they will say "we don't understand
each other" or "we have communication issues." Clearly men
and women do have certain problems communicating, and by
now most people are familiar with them thanks to bestselling
books such as *Men Are From Mars, Women Are From Venus* (Gray,
1992). Men complain that women beat a subject to death by
"rambling" and providing endless examples, whereas men
simply want to "get to the point" or "advance the narrative."
Women complain that men are too irritable, that what women
need is empathy and someone to listen. Women say they need
more expression of caring and appreciation before they can
open up sexually. Men want to cuddle and have foreplay, but
they express and experience love most easily through sex. Men
tend to value independence and attachment equally and thus
appreciate women who give them a long leash; women want
independence, but closeness and attachment more, with all the
romantic symbols of it that they can get (attention, romantic

dinners, flowers, jewelry, and so on). Yes, these are stereotypes, but for a reason—because they apply in most cases.

Are these differences innate? Perhaps to some degree, but they have also been socially prescribed and well-learned. Until recently, and in some cases even now, women have been reared to believe that they have less value if they are single. To be a fully recognized adult, a woman must be married—thus the premium women place on it. Many women still consider themselves a failure if not married by a certain age. Men can still get away with remaining single, though not as much now as in the past. Just think of the connotation of *spinster* versus *bachelor.* Clearly, if given a choice, one would rather be called the latter. A bachelor might be suspected of being gay, but his status as a fully mature adult stays intact.

These different expectations for men and women may be subtle, but they are nevertheless successfully instilled both at home and in school, so that young children are fully indoctrinated and able to assume their "proper" role by about age 5. Anyone who doubts this should consider the hyper-romanticized princess dolls who live to be discovered by a prince doll, and accoutrements marketed to and prized by girls of 5 and 6. Dora the Explorer is long forgotten by that age and what Naomi Weisstein said 40 years ago still holds true: "I don't know what immutable differences exist between men and women . . . perhaps there are some . . . but it is clear that until social expectations . . . are equal, our answers to this question will simply reflect our prejudices" (1970, p.220).

In any event, it is probably safe to assume that these differences will not evaporate completely in the near future. This also means that when therapists hear about them from a couple or spot them at the root of a communication problem, they can first normalize these differences as typical in gender-different relationships and then gradually help the couple make a course correction before locking themselves into an exaggerated or

extreme version of gender-separate roles that could jeopardize
their relationship. The following case illustrates this.

> *Wendy and Martin had a very good relationship until they got
> close to committing to marriage. They lived a half-hour away from
> each other at home with their parents, and they would often meet in
> between for dinner and a movie. Sometimes she would visit him at
> his house, or he would visit her. But once the couple began discuss-
> ing the possibility of marriage, it suddenly seemed that Wendy was
> asking Martin to court her "properly." She wanted him to pick her
> up at her house every time and drive her home; she would never
> "take the wheel" or meet him half way. Her parents' version of correct
> gender-role behavior had descended upon her and there was no turn-
> ing back. This was a test of Martin's love—a test that Martin felt
> he should not have to pass. Despite couple counseling, they broke up.
> Martin was upset that Wendy had changed the rules, and could not
> accept her idea of a very traditional marriage.*

It is often true that couples unconsciously become more traditional as they head into marriage, and the roles they assign
themselves may be artificially and unnecessarily confining.
When this appears to be the case, therapists need to point it
out and give the couple an opportunity to make conscious decisions instead.

Same-gender couples often, though not always, play and
present in similar roles as gender-opposite couples do. One
may be more "feminine" and the other more "masculine"—
and they will have many of the same communication problems.
Heterosexual therapists are less likely to see these couples
because gay couples still feel so beleaguered by the society at
large that they often will only trust their own—gay therapists—
and with good reason. Heterosexual therapists have had almost
as much difficulty accepting gay relationships and gay marriage
as the society at large. Even the AAMFT resisted a call from

some members who wanted it to support the legalization of gay marriage—though in its defense, the AAMFT did assume an educative role, making data available to show that gay marriages are equally or more solid than heterosexual ones.

Given that gay couples—many of whom informally "marry" in commitment ceremonies where they can't legally—are determined to lead full, open, out-of-the-closet lives, and need help coping with all the usual issues plus societal repression, they are increasingly looking for competent, welcoming therapists regardless of the therapist's sexual orientation. Notwithstanding the now-controversial estimate of homosexuality reported by Kinsey in 1948 and 1953 (10% of the male adult population and 4% of the female), the actual population of gays and lesbians, in the United States remains unknown. However, Gates' (2006) analysis of the 2000 and 2005 Census and along with the American Community Surveys suggests increasing numbers of individuals who report living as a same sex couples and with a growing number of states authorizing same sex marriage—as of this writing five states (Massachusetts, New Hampshire, Connecticut, Vermont, and Iowa) and others such as New York in the process (Goodnough, 2009)—the numbers and visibility of these couples will also increase. In turn, the numbers of these couples seeking assistance will surely increase.

Though some clinicians thought it impossible to accept interracial/ethnic relationships, we have not only adjusted, but now support the right of interracial/ethnic couples to marry, and we will undoubtedly do the same when it comes to same-sex marriage. Though it may take some time, we owe it to our clients and our own humanity to "stretch" and embrace it.

FINANCES

The most common issues around money are spending versus saving, disagreements over how to organize finances, disparities in income and resources, which partner is in charge, and secrecy versus transparency. Each of these issues may be intensified if the position taken is supported by the family of origin ("that's the way my parents did it and it worked for them"). This was the case with Inga and Kaarle.

Inga and Kaarle's new relationship was being threatened with frequent disagreements over how to use their money. They had decided to live together after the unexpected arrival of a now 6-month-old daughter whom they both adored. Inga was from the Midwest and had been raised in a large, frugal, tight-knit Scandinavian family; Kaarle was from Finland and came from a somewhat disengaged, but economically well-off entrepreneurial family where it was "every man for himself." Kaarle was unhappily distanced from his father and determined to re-ingratiate himself after his early 20s were misspent by too much alcohol. He took a janitorial job at a Ferrari dealership to get a foot in the door, and in a year had convinced the owner to let him try selling. Sell he did, and he was enormously proud of his success, openly expressing his dreams of their family's future wealth. He was earning close to six figures when Inga dragged him to therapy for buying a $2000 suit without telling her. There was no way she was going to marry someone so extravagant and whose values were so shallow. His offer to buy her an equivalent outfit did not help his cause at all. Happily, they were able to explore various options to accommodate both their needs, and they worked out a compromise whereby they would put 10% of his earnings into savings and work out a budget to allow him some luxury spending she would not denigrate.

My suggestion was that they also consider making room for her humanitarian impulses, with an understanding that should they accumulate substantial wealth, she would be allowed to devote a portion of it to charities. Kaarle understood when it was explained that Inga's background might make her uncomfortable with his success, that saving some portion of their money was a good idea, and that allowing her to contribute money to good causes would enable her to champion him. Inga came to see that Kaarle needed to be financially successful to earn his father's respect.

Ethan and April were living a "folie a deux." They both believed their arrangement was "fair," agreeing they each should contribute equally to the common "pot." But they still argued about money constantly, because she never had enough for her share and didn't seem sufficiently concerned about it. The problem as that Ethan was the owner of a successful small printing business, had an income he could reasonably rely on, whereas April was a struggling actress who sometimes had work and sometimes did not. Other than establishing their 50/50 deal, they never sat down to discuss their plight or what they might do about it. In therapy, where they were coached to discuss the matter calmly and slowly, they realized that Ethan actually earned four times what April did in a given year, and that she could not realistically commit to being an equal financial partner. In rethinking the issue, the couple decided that the same percentage, but not same amount, of income would go into the common pot, and that 75% of what each of them earned would cover their expenses. The remaining 25% would be for savings and vacations. Happy ending.

Things didn't work out as well for Ted, a corporate attorney, and his fiancée, Karen, a schoolteacher. The "each according to his means" principle that Ethan and April adopted did not satisfy Ted, who insisted no matter what, that Karen should contribute the same amount as he to their expenses. His point was that she could have been a high earner in a more lucrative profession and that her career choice did not absolve her of an equal obligation to the relationship. Karen suggested they find ways to cut expenses so that she could afford her half of the obligation, but Ted still would not budge. His resistance to looking for other solutions stemmed from his family-of-origin experience, in which his stepmother had "extorted" money from his father in a divorce. The economic power struggle took over the relationship and the engagement was broken.

We suggest, especially in cases with money issues, telling couples (particularly married couples) that they are "the CEOs of their marital corporation." They must each be comfortable with the decisions they make, and the decisions must be good for the corporation (i.e., the relationship). As equal partners, they may have different jobs or roles, but decision-making is collaborative.

Another problem that can crop up when one partner earns a significantly higher income is competition. This played out in the following case.

> *Dennis and Carolyn met in graduate school, where they both were pursuing doctorates in astronomy. Dennis had entered a subfield that was considered "hot," whereas Carolyn's specialization was not. After completing his dissertation, Dennis was offered a plum job with NASA in another state, and he asked Carolyn to join him. She got a good position close to where they lived, but her salary was half his. Having been the better student in graduate school, Carolyn began to resent the recognition and increased rewards Dennis was receiving. The salary difference was eroding the mutually supportive relationship they had in graduate school and they were starting to feel competitive. All of this put a strain on their relationship until they finally aired the problem in counseling and worked it through.*

When relationships become competitive in this way, it is important to point this out. Helping the couple trace this competitive struggle back to family-of-origin parent or sibling relationships and make distinctions between past and present is often necessary.

Other problems crop up when it is the woman who has the higher salary or greater means through inheritance. In the past, societies soothed the male ego by stipulating that he control marital money whatever the source. That is in good measure what the dowry was about. Although few men today would say they "mind" their wives having or earning more, it is a problem that often brews just below the surface and breaks open after marriage. That is why we want to inquire about this if the couple does not raise it in sessions. There are men who truly can handle their wives earning more and are comfortable even as house-husbands earning no direct income themselves. But they are rare. Those who think they can do it often find their identity becomes shaky without a "real" occupation, so it is better to work out feelings on this score beforehand and especially to insure that the man is settled on and happy in what he has chosen to do *and* has the self-respect and respect of his spouse before charging ahead with the wedding.

Judy had a demanding fast-track job in advertising that she loved. Bob's last paid job was as an office manager for a busy plastic surgeons' group practice. He did not like the medical environment, was let go, and had lost confidence in himself. When the couple came for therapy, Bob had been out of work for a year and a half and was only going through the motions of a search. Judy was frustrated and angry at his seeming lack of motivation and afraid that if or when they got married she would have to "carry the ball alone." As they began to discuss matters in therapy, it was apparent that she conveyed more criticism than worry and more disrespect than fear— when worry and fear were actually at the heart of it for her. Judy reassured Bob that she would not mind if he earned less than she, as long as he was happy and contributed in some way financially to their lives. With "permission" to cast a wider net, Bob decided to look for a position in the not-for-profit sector related to education, which was his passion. He found a job in university administration very quickly, did well at it, and the relationship improved markedly.

Another case shows how money can be a hidden issue.

Eileen and Tim were living together and planning to be married shortly. But Tim had been behaving strangely: coming home very late from work, disappearing on weekends for hours without explanation, and lying around listlessly. Sometimes it almost seemed as if he were in a stupor. Then Eileen discovered an empty pill bottle that had contained medicine originally prescribed for his knee surgery, and she realized over the course of a few days that he was hooked on prescription drugs. She quickly demanded that he get professional help to withdraw, which he did. At the same time they started couple therapy, realizing that they were arguing way too much. Lo and behold, Tim's self-medication was a way of trying to control upset over the fact that Eileen's mother had bought the house they were living in. His mother-in-law and Eileen were co-owners. Though Eileen tried not to take advantage of the situation, her mother seemed ever present in their lives. Eileen also knew her mother would supplement their incomes anytime Eileen asked. Both Eileen and Tim agreed that the extra money was good because the couple had less financial strain than many others, but it also was not good because it kept Eileen very tied to her mother's apron strings and undermined Eric's wish to feel like "I was really going to be taking care of my family."

VALUES, GOALS, AND LIFESTYLE

Values, goals and lifestyle issues sometimes seem insignificant in the very beginning of a relationship, but are incredibly important because they relate to a couple's future and the direction each member of the couple wants to take in life. Over time, they loom larger. Romantic love is blind to these issues, and although differences may actually add to the initial intrigue and attractiveness of the partner, gradually the differences become magnified and frustrating. This was what happened with the following couple.

Joe and Cynthia met in college. It was not love at first sight, but close to it. Cynthia knew she was "gone" when she overheard one of Joe's friends ask him what he was doing outside last night in the snowstorm. Joe explained that he was shaking the ice off a tree near the dorm because he was afraid the limbs would snap. Cynthia had never heard of anyone doing anything like that before, and was touched. Joe was sweet, smart, and witty, like her father, and she was idealistic and outgoing like his mother. What they didn't take into account was that Joe was shy and had come from an unpretentious middle class family that idealized the "simple country life." They distrusted cities and all the grit, greed, and unbridled ambition they represented to them. Cynthia, on the other hand, grew up in a family that did espouse certain humanitarian values, but also aspired to an upper-class high life, including beautiful homes, beautiful objects, and beautiful art. Eventually, Joe's negative view of Cynthia's aspirations made Cynthia feel thwarted and judged. And Joe could feel her frustration and impatience with his shyness, perceived complacency, and lack of ambition. Clearly, their goals were evolving in different directions and the relationship eventually crumbled.

Richard and Bettina, on the other hand, caught the problem in time. Bettina, a beautiful young woman in her late 20s, was from Argentina. She had moved to the United States 5 years before for a job as a museum curator, intending to return to Argentina in a few years. She, like Cynthia, came from an ambitious, upwardly mobile family. In New York, she met Richard and fell in love. He was a talented writer in his early 30s working for a pittance at a commercial trade magazine. He came from a well-established family and had never had to worry about money. He knew he would inherit a substantial amount of money someday, and in the meantime he was happy with a very modest lifestyle. His dream was to freelance and write the great American novel. He was serious about his craft, but he had no concept of 9 to 5, and was also very scared to strike out on his own. Conversely, Bettina was a "make it big on your own" kind of person, very committed to her career. She pushed Richard to quit his job and "get to work on his novel." But he would respond by procrastinating, staying put at the magazine. Bettina was growing increasingly irritated with him.

At the time they came for counseling, Richard was suffering from colitis and insomnia. Bettina was at her wits' end and ready to end the relationship. In counseling, they clarified their positions. He confessed to being scared and feeling pressured to act by Bettina; she confessed to feeling lonely in a country not her own and needing him around more than she might otherwise. She also wanted him to succeed on his own—to release his creativity and be happier with his life. She had definite ideas about how he should proceed and a timetable. He agreed to proceed and she agreed to back off and let him do it in his own way. He quit his job, rented a small studio, went there every day, and completed his first novel in eighteen months.

POLITICS AND RELIGION

Knowing the religious heritage or upbringing of a couple doesn't necessarily tell you very much. There are so many levels and kinds of observance these days that the therapist has to be very careful not to make assumptions based on broad religious categories. We've seen couples presenting with irreconcilable differences in their allegiances to two Protestant denominations, differences in the strictness with which partners interpret or choose to follow the exact same religion, and, of course, the more familiar problem of two completely different religions and what to do about raising the children. We've seen an engaged Jewish couple argue about whether a Christmas tree was pagan or Christian, and two Catholics by birth, one an atheist and the other a believer, run into trouble because the atheist could not tolerate his prospective wife's belief in God! These differences remind us of the old marital standoff:

"If you really loved me you would change your religion for me," and the counterargument, "if you really loved *me*, you wouldn't ask!"

Religious issues, like many of the issues couples raise, are so linked to basic values and also to inherited values from past generations that it is very hard for people to bend for the sake of the relationship. Yet, that is what must happen for a couple to resolve these things. We ask them where their values about religion came from, and then how strongly they themselves feel. Are any of their religious values modifiable or can they in any way start anew to create a new set of values together? Obviously, if their different values go back generations and each partner feels strongly about what he or she believes—more strongly than he or she feels about the relationship—then the relationship is stuck and cannot go on. That said, we have seen couples with radically different political and religious convictions have satisfying, lifelong marriages, so we know it must be possible!

Linda and Don, the couple we introduced in Chapter 2 who were buffeted about by Linda's parents had another serious underlying problem.

Don believed and resented that Linda "let" her parents have their way and that although she denied it and did make an effort to stand her ground, she could not sustain it. Her mother was still, in her words, "my best friend" and the parents never backed off. We could say that this family was caught between the old (parents decide who their daughter will marry) and the new (daughter decides). But it is also true that Linda, when push came to shove, was very ambivalent about marrying out of her faith, and couldn't bring herself to own it. Finally, this case was amazing because it turned out that Linda's mother was an unacknowledged convert to Judaism and had never disclosed it even to her daughter! Linda "knew" but could never be sure. Some cases are simple, but many that seem simple at first are

multilayered and multi-factorial, posing endless challenges to the
therapist. Suffice it to say, though I do not know for sure, I believe
this couple did not make it to the altar.

Religion is often a stand-in for another basic issue—namely
how much difference, separateness, and individuality each
member of a couple can tolerate in the other. Some couples
are able to bridge religious and political differences by simply
agreeing to disagree and understanding that toleration of difference might be a very good thing when it comes to providing a
parental model for children. One couple understood this after
months of haggling over religion and began to picture helping
their children understand, experience, and appreciate "Mommy's religion" and "Daddy's religion," letting the children also
explore other religions and then make their own choices.

Political differences are no different. Couples can compromise, one can "convert" to the other's party or persuasion, or
they can rethink their political convictions, agreeing to disagree, arguing with fervor, forever energizing the relationship.
One young woman described to me the benefit she derived
from having politically opposed parents.

"When I was young, my dad was Democrat and my mom Republi-
can. During a presidential election when I was about 8, I asked them
whom they were voting for, which led to an intense discussion about
their different political views. They let me make up my own mind
about what I believed, and I decided I was a Democrat. It was the
first important, independent decision I made about my identity and
I recognize it now as being probably my first step toward becoming an
adult. Just goes to show how differences between the parents can be
very healthy for the child!"

James Carville, the Democratic pundit and strategist, and
Mary Matalin, Republican strategist, met on the campaign trail

and have been married with children for many years now, each keeping their diametrically opposing views. They are the best example of a politically risky relationship that turned out well. Perhaps the way to think about them is that although they differ in their beliefs, they are birds of a feather in their extremely passionate devotion to their causes! Neither spouse could—or, at the end of the day, would *want* to—win the battle or convince the other to change, because the fun would be over.

The essence of our job in these instances is to try to lighten the discussion, which sometimes can seem like life and death. The therapist can convey a sense that the couple can be creative in how they attack and solve these problems. One couple was asked to brainstorm all the possible solutions to their political-difference problem. One was for Obama, the other was for McCain. Their first solution was to never discuss politics with each other, which they quickly realized would be impossible. The second was never to discuss politics in the bedroom, and the third was to get better educated together to see if "really" knowing the other's position made them more sympathetic to it. Fourth, they agreed to have a "stop talking" signal that they would use if they were discussing politics in public and one was getting too annoyed with the other. They settled on these last three ideas, and the problem receded into the realm of the relatively unimportant.

CHILDREN AND FAMILY-PLANNING

A number of issues revolving around the question of children should be brought to light in premarital counseling. Believe it or not, some couples never discuss whether or when they want to have children. There are those who simply do not want to have children under any circumstance, and others who are simply not sure. Some discuss it only superficially, and others use not wanting children as an unconscious way to express ambivalence or some other dissatisfaction, with the relationship. Still other couples who cannot decide whether the relationship should go forward end up getting pregnant to make the decision for them.

Finally, there are still some people who consciously or unconsciously use the age-old tactic of getting pregnant to lure their partner into a commitment. That was the issue for Jim.

> *Jim and Rena had a close but stormy relationship. Both sets of parents were divorced and the couple thought the experience they lived through as children would make them immune to the mistakes their parents made. They had a lot more in common than their parents did—music, friendships, travel, doctoral degrees—and they were headed for lives as diplomats serving abroad. When they married at 26, after 5 years of dating, there was still no mention of whether or when to have children. When she turned 29, Rena felt it was probably "time," and with hormones raging and the clock ticking, she convinced Jim they should try. Jim wanted to be much more cautious and not rush into it, but he gave in to her anyway. She got pregnant right away, and the day it was confirmed, she rushed from the doctor's office to tell Jim, who was working late in the library stacks. Excitedly, she told him "I'm pregnant!" His cross response—"Shh, someone might hear you"—still echoed in her mind years later, becoming the "first nail in the coffin" of their marriage.*

Fortunately, things turned out different for the following couple, who took the time to discuss the issue of children before getting pregnant.

> *Seth, 50, and Maxine, 40, had been dating for a year and were planning to marry, but the issue of children was standing in the way. Maxine desperately wanted children; Seth was unsure. He "wanted to want" to have a child "for Maxine," but he was afraid he would not be a good parent and that he would resent Maxine for pressuring*

him into it. Underneath Seth's hesitation was an old family-of-origin issue. He had an older sister who had seriously abused him, and his parents had not protected him from the abuse. He feared having a daughter himself more than anything. Moreover, he was the only boy grandchild among seven in his generation and the only boy in his nuclear family. Maxine had two sisters and no brothers. Seth believed the likelihood of girls was very high.

Seth could imagine adopting a boy, but he was not entirely comfortable with adoption either. Intensifying Maxine's powerful desire for a biological child was the fact that she had had a full ovary and part of the other removed in a series of operations as a young teenager and wanted a biological child to "finally feel normal." She had no objection to adoption, but first wanted to try for a biological child.

Happily for this couple, they were able to understand and empathize with each other. Maxine took the pressure off, and Seth was finally able to find a way to move ahead. Through therapy, Seth was helped to realize that though his parents had not protected him, he would be a good parent and wanted the experience of raising a child.

Ben, 40, and Rebecca, 32, were another story. Master communicators, they could discuss anything civilly and respectfully—except the issue of children.

They had been together 4 years when they entered therapy, but much of that time had actually been spent apart because of Ben's work as a foreign correspondent. Rebecca could not travel with him because her job required her to be at home. The plan from the start of their relationship was that after 3 years living apart, Ben would take a job that did not require travel they would get married and have a family.

After 3 months living together, however, Ben informed Rebecca that he could not go through with the plan. Marriage he could envision, but although he had promised they would start a family, he could no longer say he wanted children for sure. Rebecca was hurt and angry at his broken promise and felt she could not trust him anymore.

At the same time, Rebecca learned of a brief affair Ben had while they were apart. The affair itself was not a serious threat to the relationship, but Ben's lingering guilt about it and Rebecca's criticism were a starting point for discussing other issues in the relationship. Ben felt she was too judgmental and made him feel "like a little boy," which he had had "too much of" in his family of origin. Their lifestyles and personalities were also different: Ben was a slow-moving, philosophical, somewhat self-preoccupied type. He worked best from 4 p.m. to midnight, slept late into the day, and wanted to go out for drinks once a week with his correspondent buddies whose workday also ended late. Rebecca was a highly organized, nondrinking, greet-the-dawn type whose job required her to be at work at 8 a.m.

Further complicating things was that Ben had delibitating problems with his back and worried about whether he could be a consistent giving parent. Although Rebecca was sympathetic, she didn't understand why he wasn't reassured by the fact that they could rely on relatives and friends who lived nearby if he was feeling "down" or ever incapacitated. When they could not resolve the issue of children, they separated and simultaneously left therapy, leaving me to wonder whether Ben's changing his mind about children was his way of saying he thought the relationship was not going to work.

These two cases are alike in that they involve two men who were hesitant about having children with women who clearly did want to have them. But they differ in that one primarily involved a family-of-origin problem and the other a problem largely in the relationship itself. Also, Maxine and Seth knew from the start that they had a problem, whereas Ben changed his mind after a promise was made.

One lesson to be drawn from these stories is that couples need to have the discussion about children early on and certainly before an engagement. If a couple does not bring it up, the therapist should. Also, therapists who believe by dint of training or life experience that not wanting biological children is abnormal in some way should think twice. It is not necessarily unhealthy to refuse parenthood. As Eric Erikson once pointed out, there are many ways to fulfill the life stage in which we give to the next generation. Biological parenting is one of them. Adopting, teaching, and mentoring are some other very meaningful ways. For couples debating whether to have children, it is reasonable to propose that in making their decision they consider the world around them and their possible social responsibility to it, given our current "hot, flat, and crowded" planet (Friedman, 2008). The biblical admonition to "be fruitful and multiply" may not always apply.

Along with a discussion of whether or when to have children, the couple's attitude toward contraception (and abortion in the case of an unplanned or problematic pregnancy) needs to be addressed and if they differ, worked through. These are instances in which therapists' often firmly held opinions need to be kept to themselves, out of the discussion entirely. As long as the couple can live with their actions and are prepared to handle the consequences of them, and as long as what they are doing serves their relationship and *their* values, the therapist should be satisfied.

SEX, INTIMACY, AND PREMARITAL AFFAIRS

Most premarital couples report having had a good—or great—sexual relationship in the beginning, but most also report deterioration as other problems cropped up. Many say that they now have intercourse rarely (once a month or less) or not at all when they finally they come in for therapy. Problems in the sexual relationship are not always a presenting problem, however, so a therapist may have to inquire about it after other presenting problems have been aired. "How have the problems that brought you here affected your sex life?" is usually sufficient to start the conversation. Some clients will ask if we "do" sex

therapy. We say, "Family therapists are like primary-care practitioners in this domain. So we can explore how sexual intimacy
works or doesn't work for you together, and if it becomes clear
that a sex therapy specialist would be advisable, I'll be happy to
refer you."

We mostly see couples whose desire has waned, and who,
when queried, are able to have satisfactory sex alone—mas-
turbating. Thus we know there are no serious anatomical or
physiological problems. Mostly, our couples are either sexually inhibited and have trouble expressing what they want and
need to each other, or have underlying resentments that are
indirectly expressed by loss of attraction and lack of desire.
The sexual relationship often returns when the underlying
relationship problems are addressed, as it did with Gabriel and
Hannah.

> *Gabriel had lost his desire for Hannah. Hannah still "wanted"
> Gabe, but less than before. It seemed they were in a struggle over the
> future of their relationship. He wanted to get married; she was still
> unsure. As she kept avoiding the subject, he felt less sexual interest
> in her. She started to look different to him. Instead of looking like a
> slim "supermodel," she began to look "too tall and too skinny." And
> instead of the "great girl" who was just as happy at "Dirty Dick's
> diner" as at the best restaurant in town, she began to insist that they
> eat only at "white tablecloth" places. He began to feel he was spend-
> ing his savings on someone who really did not care about him, which
> was a huge turnoff. He wondered if he could ever get his attraction
> back.*
>
> *In therapy, Gabriel realized that he placed too much importance
> on weight. He had watched his mother wither away from cancer; also
> he was angry at Hannah for not helping him feel secure and plan
> for their future. Simultaneously, Hannah was coming to realize what
> he was struggling with and her own reasons for shying away from
> marriage. Soon, all the things that drew them together in the first*

place came rushing back. In his eyes, she was beautiful again and Hannah minded a whole lot less dining at Dirty Dick's.

Much has changed since the 1950s, when premarital sex was prohibited. Most therapists no longer think twice about whether it is okay for a couple to engage in premarital sex or live together prior to marriage. In the sexual revolution of the 1960s, and with the advent of birth control, the rule changed. First, for women, the rule changed to: "Although it is still not okay to have intercourse before marriage, all will be forgiven if the relationship is serious and you wind up getting married." Then it became acceptable for a young woman to have sex with her prospective mate to make sure they were compatible. Even today, a young woman's simply enjoying premarital sex with no thought to the future is seen as not quite appropriate, and relatively few women manage it well.

Of course, the rules are different for young men, who are advised to get as much experience and have as much fun as possible before marriage so as to avoid extramarital problems in the future. Cheating, these days, becomes an issue pretty early in a relationship, as soon as a couple has progressed from "hooking up," to casual dating, and then agreeing to date exclusively. So on the one hand, whereas women seem generally to need exclusivity pretty much as soon as they have intercourse, men have permission to have a certain degree of sexual latitude up to marriage and, as we have seen, and some would still say, forever.

Lucy and Ned were married. Both reported a wonderful relationship prior to and through the first few months, until Lucy learned that Ned had "lap-danced" with a colleague during his bachelor party. He thought nothing of it; she was beside herself. This was the issue that brought them to therapy and it took months for them to resolve it. To Ned it was an innocent last night out and he didn't

want to hurt the other girl's feelings by turning her down; to Lucy it
was a sign of disrespect to her and their relationship—virtual cheat-
ing, clear and simple. There was, of course, more to the story in that
Ned did have a close friendship with the lap-dance girl, but to him it
was "brother-sister"; to Lucy no explanation made it right.

In spite of the fact that there is still a double standard, women do cheat, although not as often as men. We see instances of women's affairs in our practices regularly. For the most part, men's reactions are similar to women's—feeling hurt, betrayed, angry, confused about whether the relationship can or should continue, and/or at a loss to understand how it could have happened.

> *Anita and Jerry, in their late 30s, were living together quite hap-*
> *pily until Jerry wanted to get married. Anita came to therapy by her-*
> *self because she wasn't sure she wanted to marry him. She loved him,*
> *but she also loved Noah—passionately. There was good old reliable*
> *Jerry, and then there was wild, exciting Noah, whom she was sure she*
> *could never really tame and didn't really want to. She had met Noah,*
> *a career mountaineer with two trips up Everest under his belt, many*
> *years ago when he was her expedition leader, and she had numerous*
> *subsequent rendezvous with him in other parts of the world, as she*
> *was in the travel business and could easily get away. About to marry*
> *Jerry, she poured her heart out in a farewell letter to Noah, which*
> *Jerry then happened upon. Though devastated, Jerry was willing to*
> *forget what had happened. Anita and Jerry kept their wedding date,*
> *but Anita was having serious difficulty keeping her vow. Two years*
> *later she came back to therapy again, because she had heard from*
> *Noah, who missed her and was now ready to settle down.*

Both of these premarital affair cases posed problems for me as the therapist. With Ned and Lucy, the challenge was to empa-thize with Lucy, because it seemed that the lap dance was just a mild form of cheating in a relatively safe predictable moment that posed no serious threat. Ned clearly loved her and gave every sign of becoming a responsible husband. My problem as therapist with Anita, Jerry, and Noah was that though the client was Anita, my empathy more naturally fell to Jerry, the underdog who was being abandoned. Anita married Jerry when she was truly in love with someone else—and with her eyes open. I felt that, at 38, she "should have known." In both cases, I had to dig deep.

I managed to restore empathy for Lucy by remembering that her background was very traditional; her family would have been horrified as well. The family pressures on Lucy to have a "perfect" partner and relationship were great. I also had to remember that the definition of cheating is in the eye of the beholder—the one cheated on—not the cheater and not the therapist. At the same time, it was important for Lucy to realize that objectively, a bachelor-party lap-dance is not a long-term affair. My ability to empathize coupled with the objective data did help to calm Lucy down and the couple completed therapy with a repaired relationship. A 2-year follow-up found them happy and about to have a baby.

In the second case, although I initially had difficulty empathizing with Anita, I was fortunate to sense it in myself and correct for it. I realized that Noah was not a realistic option for Anita when they first met, that Anita knew she was not getting younger and had simply tried to make a realistic accommodation for herself in marrying Jerry. At the end of the day, I found myself actually envying Anita's passion and freespiritedness, despite her own ethical qualms about leaving Jerry. I would not have felt comfortable in Anita's shoes and though I wondered if she might be making a mistake, we did thoroughly discuss how she would feel if the relationship with Noah did not last. I also had to help Anita feel less guilty about her decisions, explaining that if she did not really want to be with Jerry, he

would have a chance at a better life without her. Perhaps need-
less to say, Anita went off with Noah and I never found out what
became of them.

Premarital affairs happen every day with the same jealousy
and powerful sense of betrayal as if the couple had already tied
the proverbial knot. The challenge is to help couples make the
rules beforehand, and for the therapist to take the stand that,
given human nature, it is probably better to avoid an affair if
possible and to accept, certainly in marriage, that if one is constantly tempted, it is time to discuss problems in the marriage
before doing anything else. On the other hand, affairs, as we
know, happen anyway, and it is good to know that couples can
and do survive them. We believe that if a member of a couple is
on the verge of going outside the relationship, he or she should
probably consider at least a temporary separation rather than
try to keep a festering secret or rub salt on an open wound. A
mature couple is able to agree on this possibility ahead of time
as part of a written or unwritten contract.

RELATIONSHIP BOUNDARIES

Every new couple has to negotiate the issue of how, when, and
where to place boundaries. Each member of the couple needs
a certain amount of privacy and autonomy within the relationship. And each couple has to place a boundary around their
relationship to protect it from too much outside interference.
The boundaries in both cases need to be semi-permeable so
that one member of the couple does not relinquish his or her
own identity completely, and so that friends and family are able
to provide nourishment, variety, support, and perspective without encroaching. It is like what nations do in establishing rights
of individual citizens and families, as well as their own sover-
eignty in relation to other countries.

For the individuals in a couple, boundary issues come up

around time together and time apart. Each couple has to decide what is reasonable to ask or expect of the other. Tom needs a lot of time alone. Nora needs time alone too, but not nearly as much as he does. Nora wants more "quality time" with Tom, and he seems to resist it. If Len wants to spend his one free day a week playing tennis and having a few beers with the guys before taking Sandy out for dinner, is Sandy within her rights to complain?

> *When Beverly and Stuart first became a couple, they spent every evening and weekend together, all day both days. They shopped together, did laundry together, went to the gym together, made dinner together, saw friends together, went to church together, and slept together in a single bed. When they found they were arguing a lot, they came for counseling. Their problem was that they had no "alone time," no breathing room, and they also felt they had no time to accomplish individual things that were important to them. They were trying to merge into one. In therapy, as they described how they spent a typical day, both quickly realized that they had each come from enmeshed families and wanted to have a different kind of marriage in which they did not feel "joined at the hip."*

Issues may also come up around division of labor. If Fran never had to keep house before she met Josh, why should she have to now? She doesn't mind a messy living room and resents his badgering her to pick up.

These are problems mainly *in* the couple, although family-of-origin "ghosts" may be present as well, as they were with Beverly and Stuart. Perhaps Len's father spent his free days on his own; Fran's parents probably had a housekeeper. In every case, the therapist's challenge is to help the couple understand where their ideas of coupling come from and to decide how to best structure their relationship, recognizing the importance of a good balance between together and apart.

This process can be more difficult when it comes to perceived or actual threats posed by third parties and the intense jealousy that can result. This was evident in the following case.

Alyssa's fiancé, Keith, wanted to spend every Saturday with his father, who had been "lonely" since Keith's mother had died 2 years ago. Alyssa loved her father-in-law, but one weekend when Dad walked into their house without knocking, it was the last straw for her. She wanted to "draw a line." Fortunately, Keith agreed, and he spoke with his father, who understood.

In this couple, the issue was easily resolved. But other situations can be more complicated. Is it okay for Luke to have a regular lunch appointment with an attractive female colleague? How about a regular dinner meeting? Is it okay for Luke's girlfriend to expect him to stop having a work relationship with a woman he previously dated? Is it okay to ask him not to go to national business meetings where he will certainly see someone he had a premarital affair with?

In all of these instances, the couple has to dig deep to understand what each of them as individuals can tolerate, and pull back from extreme stands. And although it may be hard, the therapist also has to keep his or her own opinions out of the arena, except to urge the couple to make decisions based on what is best for the relationship. One very smart client came to terms with her jealousy saying, "So the relationship is like another entity. There's you and me, and the relationship is a third thing we have to take care of! If I'm thinking of the relationship, I should probably stop checking your email and voice messages." And she did.

In the end, it comes down to a willingness or ability to trust, or in the case of a misstep, willingness or ability to forgive and trust again. It may take time, but if trust does not reappear, the relationship is probably over. Sometimes, if the couple does not come to it on its own, the therapist can suggest that should a third party ever become a serious threat, each member of the couple promise to disclose, discuss and possibly separate instead of transgressing. It is also worth stating that the best hedge against outside interference is making the current relationship as strong and satisfying as possible.

SOCIABILITY

Marty loves company and having friends and family around. Cathy is friendly but needs her privacy. She is not interested in his friends or family but doesn't resent his going off to be with them. He, on the other hand, wishes she were more outgoing and wonders if she is the right life partner for him. Eric and Mary have the same issue with one key difference: Eric doesn't mind going to parties and events by himself and doesn't care that Mary is shy and not always up to accompanying him.

Differences in sociability are probably connected to basic temperament, which is not subject to change, and to an individual's degree of social comfort, which can change, sometimes with an accommodation by the spouse. For example, Joyce and Arthur realized that their opposite social behavior stemmed from the same source: they were both uncomfortable in social situations. But he talked too much and she too little. They decided to recalibrate their behavior accordingly; he would speak less, she would talk more, and neither would criticize the other's efforts. This pact increased their team feeling and their popularity!

READINESS AND COMMITMENT

In the case of readiness, timing and prior experience make all the difference. For a marriage to have the best chance of succeeding, it is best if both partners have had prior relation-

ship experience and feel ready to "settle down." The number
of teenage children whose marriages last a lifetime is relatively
small. The older the partners are, the better the chance the
marriage will last.

But perhaps even more important than prior relationship
experience and chronological age is perceived readiness and
desire to be married. I see many young couples where one or
occasionally both partners succumb to parental pressure to
marry, couples who feel pressured into marrying because their
friends are getting married, and women in their 30s (and men
in their 40s) who feel that they are "supposed" to be married by
that age. Rushing into marriage because one feels pressure of
any kind is a mistake, as the following case shows.

> *Sammy and Lorraine, both 22, became engaged soon after Sammy*
> *tried to end the relationship. Lorraine was his first serious girlfriend,*
> *and he did not feel ready for such a big commitment. Lorraine became*
> *extremely distraught and threatened suicide. Sammy concluded that*
> *if she loved him "that much," it would be enough to justify his get-*
> *ting married, and enough to make a marriage work. Sadly, he went*
> *ahead, but he ever after felt manipulated and harbored a lot of resent-*
> *ment toward her. The couple went on to have three children, and*
> *although Sammy was a devoted father, he never formed a deep attach-*
> *ment to Lorraine. At 42, he begged his wife to go to couple therapy,*
> *but she refused, saying it was too late. She had already found another*
> *relationship where she felt "really" loved. If Sammy and Lorraine*
> *had had the benefit of premarital therapy, they might never have got-*
> *ten married in the first place.*

If either partner in a couple indicates that he or she is not
ready for marriage, the therapist should help the other take
it to heart. Sometimes it is simply a matter of maturity; other
times it is that the individual senses that the relationship is not
quite right. In either case, if lack of readiness is not openly

presented by the couple, I screw up my courage and broach the subject by saying something akin to "I could be wrong, but I wonder if part of either of you feels like you're not ready." If the answer is in the affirmative, I then go on to probe whether there is anything that could be done, by the partner or for the relationship in therapy, that could change that feeling. Sometimes I'll suggest a few changes they could try, but when nothing comes of the probe, when someone is not ready, there's a feeling of lethargy in the room, and I start to accept that the relationship probably needs to end.

COMMUNICATION

Communication is a code word for just about anything a couple is distressed about. But it is also how couples try to explain the trouble they have discussing and resolving the inevitable differences that arise between them. When a difference of opinion is sensed, some couples try to push it aside, either telling themselves they'll deal with it later or hoping that it will go away on its own. They tacitly agree not to communicate about it. Like Phyliss and Joel, who we'll meet in Chapter 8, these couples tell the therapist "we never fight" but that they feel distant, that their sex life has diminished, that they don't feel as close as they once did. At the other extreme are couples who say they fight constantly over the smallest issues and never seem to find peace or resolution. Neither "approach" serves the relationship well. In the first instance, the couple is afraid of conflict; they believe it will somehow ruin the relationship. In the second instance, they know too much fighting isn't good, but believe they'll somehow "lose" if they give in. When a couple cites "communication issues" as the problem, I simply ask them what they mean by the phrase.

Helping couples learn to express, manage, and resolve either open or covert conflict takes years for therapists to learn and can only be hinted at here. Suffice it to say that there is little difference between premarital and marital conflict and little difference in the techniques that can be employed to facilitate the process. Still, I can try to give the flavor of what I aim for in the first few sessions.

I try to be myself in the room. No affectation, no profes- sional bull—my best self, that is. I provide three basic rules: try not to interrupt or speak too long when you have the floor, please tell me if you feel I am not hearing you, and let me know if I appear to be siding with the other person. I tell the couple that my interest is helping their relationship, not judging what is wrong with it or wrong with them. I try to hear what each member of the couple is saying and trying to say, mentally flag- ging anything that strikes me as important to return to later. I try to model the kind of patience, respect, and attention I want them to show to each other. I also ask if they've see a therapist before and, if it was a good experience, what made it good, and if it was not, why not? That way, I explain, we can at least try to avoid repeating something that did not go well and build on what did work. I try to engender a collaborative egalitarian spirit "we're all in this together." As part of this spirit, I encour- age the couple to ask me questions about myself, my family, my views and if, and whenever, they are curious. I will answer any question except in an unusual circumstance where I sense it would not be in couple's interest at the time.

If a couple still has trouble opening up, I encourage them to start anywhere, using the expression "all roads lead to Rome." If the couple can't stop pointing fingers, I try to calm them down by reassuring them that we have time, and that by slow- ing down we'll actually accomplish a whole lot more. I've never studied hypnosis and do not much like the idea, but I some- times feel as if that is what I am doing especially with nervous, high-strung couples. Once I "have them," which means that I sense they trust me enough to let me help them, I will adapt one or a combination of the approaches described in Chapter 2 to suit their issues and who they are, or I will come up with something on my own.

EMOTIONAL INTELLIGENCE

"Emotional intelligence" is a phrase coined by Daniel Goleman in the book by the same name (2005). It refers to the brain's capacity for self-monitoring, self-soothing, and self-control. It is this learned ability that enables people, and in this case, couples, to use reason and not get "emotionally hijacked" when trying to work through conflict. When one or both members of a couple state that the other one "has a temper," a complaint often lodged in counseling, it is likely that someone's amydala has overtaken their frontal cortex, to use neuroscience terminology, and that nothing positive is likely to occur until the person calms down. Every therapist knows this, and Gottman made his name by graphically documenting it in the therapy hour. "I can't talk to her because she blows up the minute I start." "He jumps down my throat as soon as I open my mouth." These are the giveaway phrases. When one or both partners appears to lack basic emotional intelligence, there also may be other critical issues the couple has, but which they do not volunteer or cannot begin to acknowledge. We refer here to suspicions we might have about drugs or alcohol, obsessive jealousy, suicidal ideation or attempts, physical or sexual abuse. Further, there may be serious mental illnesses that might not be immediately apparent such as bi-polar or borderline personality disorder. Untreated, either of these issues could unhinge a relationship.

It is often hard to accept that even new young premarital couples may have these problems, or hard to inquire about them if suspected, but we have to. It also means that where we uncover something beyond our scope of practice, we need to consult with or refer to other appropriate resources, such as psychiatrists, drug and alcohol addiction specialists, or Alcoholics Anonymous, to name just a few. We will discuss another aspect of these issues in Chapter 7, but the basic point here is that the clinician's job is to calm the waters, and create enough safety and structure for the couple to be able to engage in productive dialogue. If the presenting problems still do not budge, the clinician then has to help the couple go beneath the surface to more fragile feelings and vulnerabilities to help each member of the couple feel more empathic, closer to the other, and more disposed to risk opening up again.

CHAPTER 6

What Predicts a Satisfying Marriage: Individual Factors

Anne F. Ziff

We shall not cease from exploration
And the end of all our exploring
Will be to arrive where we started
And know the place for the first time.
                    T. S. Eliot, *Little Gidding* (1942)

As we acknowledged in Chapter 1, marriage is a risky venture. It offers odds that no reasonable hedge fund manager would choose to assume—hedge fund managers like to have the odds *at least* 60% in their favor, we are told!

Amplifying this risk are the census figures of 2007. They report that the divorce rate in the United States—which appears to have reached its peak in the 1980s—is currently "only" 40 to 60% for first marriages, and 10% higher for remarriages. We anticipate that a general increase in the number of couples engaging in premarital counseling will provide a frame within which more satisfying, lasting relationships can develop.

TOWARD SATISFYING, LASTING MARRIAGES

As we noted in chapter 3, data are becoming available on a wide sample of couples who marry after participating in premarital couple counseling and education. But these early studies do not yet address long-term effects. We anticipate that premaritally counseled couples will have marriage outcome numbers that differ (favorably) from their cohort couples in the general, married population.

How will we know this? As premarital counseling becomes more widespread, it is reasonable to anticipate that meaningful clinical statistics representing the premaritally counseled population will be collected. To some extent we will have to wait for this, and see. However, until that happens, we recommend that individual clinicians track the 5-, 10-, and 20-year outcomes of couples who have participated in premarital counseling with them, with an eye to publishing, or at least discussing, these findings.

With the intention of fostering movement away from divorce and toward lasting, satisfying marriages, in this chapter we will discuss how to recognize the key individual predictors of satisfying marriage. Chapter 7 will be focused on couple predictors of marital satisfaction and stability. What, you may ask, are the differences between these sets? Individual factors look primarily at the readiness of each partner to approach and participate in the formation of a successful couple and the satisfying marriage that is likely to follow. In contrast, couple predictors of marital success speak about qualities that develop within the couple, promoting the likelihood of a long and satisfying marriage.

INDIVIDUAL PREDICTORS
OF MARITAL SATISFACTION

Risks in forming a marital union of any kind certainly exist. It is our belief that all couples, making educated decisions about themselves and their relationship, can increase the statistical outcome in favor of lasting, satisfying marriages, and this is worth the time and effort that are warranted.

Following are 10 key individual predictors of marital satisfaction. Because they appear in no predetermined sequence in real life, we have ordered them alphabetically here, rather than ranking them according to prevalence or perceived importance.

- A sense of good humor
- Commitment
- Communication skills
- Determination
- Education
- Fair fighting
- Flexibility
- Loyalty, which includes prioritizing the couple as number one
- Respect for differences
- Trust

Before we describe these predictors in depth however, a brief discussion of assessment and certain information-gathering will be helpful.

Assessment and Information-Gathering

We find it is useful, as we mentioned in Chapter 4, to begin to focus our initial intake session with a genogram, originally a Bowenian technique. (See *Genograms in Family Assessment,* by

Monica McGoldrick and Randy Gerson, 1985, for detailed information on the genogram technique. If this is a new technique
for you, you might consider creating a genogram of your own
family to learn just how fascinating and informative it is.) We use
the initial, intake genogram to create a quick, graphic represen-
tation of information about each member of the couple, as well
as of their parents' and grandparents' generations when such
information can be found, and any children, when a partner is a
parent. A three-generation genogram provides the clinician with
an easy guide to marital models in both families of origin and in
each partner's history, and it quickly reveals underlying patterns
in one or both partners' original families as well.

Using a genogram, the clinician can see basic multigenera-
tional information: family and individual patterns, triangles,
distance and closeness, ethnicities, values, health issues, and
more. This information allows us to recognize, and perhaps to
understand, some of the experiences and expectations in the
hearts and minds of the people who come to us for premarital
work. Recognizing patterns in each family of origin also helps
to alert us to the possible presence or absence of key individual
predictors of marital satisfaction.

As we talk in session about information to include in the
genogram, both members of the couple begin to reveal things
about themselves either to, or simply in the presence of, their
future spouse. It's useful also to keep track of how much of the
information actually is new to the listening partner, and how
many of the answers come easily and quickly to the speaker
versus how many seem to provoke a high degree of emotion
(in either partner).

KEY QUESTIONS TO ASK PARTNERS
In identifying the key individual predictors of marital satisfaction and creating a genogram, there are many different ques-

tions we turn to for exploration, particularly in the early sessions when we are assessing partners and identifying the contract for our work. Some of the questions we ask, primarily focused on the couple's relational models, we have described earlier (Chapter 4). The following are also early assessment questions, and these are focused more specifically on the individuals in the premarital couple:

- **"Has either of you ever been married before?"** If the answer is "yes," ask for details about what that marriage was like and why it ended. For example: "How old were you when you met, when you married? What motivated the marriage? What was it like? Are there children?" (If so, complicating data may arise as you learn about the children, including how they responded to the divorce and to this new relationship, what the custody arrangements are and how they affect the new couple, and so on.)
- **"What were your earlier relationships like, and with whom did you talk about how you were feeling?"** We want to encourage the partners to explore in some depth both their strengths in communicating, and the things they may have done that jeopardized the earlier, significant relationships.
- **"What kind of marriage have you been thinking of entering into?"** For example: traditional, egalitarian, romantic, companionate, and so on.
- **"Have you talked with each other, before this session, about the way you picture this marriage?** If so, are there any areas of disagreement? What are the areas of agreement?" If the couple has *not* previously talked about this, invite them to take some time now to fantasize about their marriage: "Both long-term and daily, what will it be like, do you suppose?"
- Addressing one partner: **"Ask yourself this question: What**

do I think it will be like to be married to me?" (Dunne, 1991.)
Follow this by asking the same of the other partner. This is a
key, provocative question and it is imperative that each partner answer it for him and her self. (Potentially, answers to
this question, plus the cross conversation it can stimulate,
will be time consuming. When possible, we will start a session
with the question, to provide the maximum available time.)

- We now either review or initiate questions about relational
  models. Our goal is to have each partner in the couple
  begin collecting ideas for an ideal model (Assagioli, 1965
  and 1974) marriage.

- **"What kinds of marriages do or did others in each of your
  families have?** Your parents? Grandparents? Siblings?"

- **"Are you hoping to have a marriage that is 'just like' (or
  very much like) someone else's?** What about it, and you,
  makes you want to emulate this particular marriage?"

- **"Are there any aspects of other esteemed marriages that
  you would not like to see in your own?"**

- **"Tell me a little about the 'ideal model' marriage you'd
  most like to have yourselves.** How do you picture specific
  things, like:

- Where you will live?

- How you will pay for your home?

- Whether you will move into a new home or into a home
  one of you already lives in?

- How you will budget finances?

- How you will budget household responsibilities (i.e., chores)

- What the small, daily stuff will be like—for example, who
  will make meals and which meals you will eat together versus separately?"

- "Will you both be going off to work? Will either of you
  work from home?"

- "Do you plan to have children? If so, when? How many? Will
  that change any work and financial plans for either of you?"

- **"What will you do—what do you do—when you disagree emphatically about something?"** This may also be a useful time to introduce the concept of "fair fighting," which is discussed in more detail later in this chapter. (p. 157)

These questions—as well as those mentioned in the Intake section of chapter 4, and others that may come to mind spontaneously—are an effective way for clinicians to begin gaining an understanding of their clients. They serve to educate the partners about themselves as well as about each other, at the same time. As we discuss the issues that come up, and map patterns on the genogram, we like to also listen for the individual predictors of marital satisfaction, described in the following sections. We will explore the ideal model concept in greater detail at the end of this chapter,

A Sense of Good Humor

To some extent, maintaining a "sense of good humor" speaks of "being funny," but the key to this good humor is in not turning the "funniness" on another person as a distraction or attack. A sense of good humor refers to recognizing humor in oneself, or in the things one has done or failed to do, or things another has done or failed to do, and then relating that to life or to others in such a way that kindness, not acerbity, prevails. One especially valuable aspect of a sense of good humor is demonstrated at times of stress; it can be very helpful in reducing conflicts and re-establishing equilibrium, in individuals as well as in the couple.

Commitment

Once a person is involved in a relationship that feels special and valuable, the kind that might move into "forever," the time for playing games is over. Commitments begin. Initially the commitment might be to forego dating other people, or to be sexually monogamous, or to save some number of nights each week to be together. But ultimately commitment has to do with offering to each other a sense of safety in being oneself and knowing that anger, sadness, or any other intense emotion will not destroy the foundation of the relationship. A committed relationship has room for growth and change, but it is anchored in each partner's intention to recognize and work through the inevitable problems, thus allowing the relationship to endure—with both partners continuing to be satisfied because they value being in this relationship.

Communication Skills

These include each person's capacity for listening and speaking truthfully and clearly—without subterfuge or hidden agendas. That goes way beyond simple honesty. Speaking truthfully, in this context at least, has to do with saying aloud the things that are in your heart or mind, and doing so in a way that is neither hard to understand nor inflammatory. It also has to do with only saying what you mean and meaning what you say. No threats! When we each communicate with skill, when we listen and speak with truth, clarity, and understanding, we create a safe environment in which both the individual and the relationship can thrive, and neither will be jeopardized.

Determination

Determination in this context has to do with each partner's individual intention to succeed in the quest for a satisfying, healthy, long-term relationship, and to nurture it, when possible and desirable, into a marriage. Determination of this sort does not have anything to do with being pig-headed or inflexible! It is our belief that individuals who first make *educated* decisions about themselves and their relationship and second are *determined* to continue to hold spouse and marriage as a high priority, can increase both the personal and statistical outcomes in favor of lasting, satisfying marital relationships.

Education

When we speak of "education" as an individual predictor of marital success, we are talking about people who have taken the time to become educated about themselves –to learn about, and be accepting of, their characteristics. This education in self-discovery might take place in a class of some sort, or occur just through life experience, earlier therapy, or journaling. The education is in knowing oneself from the inside, and the likelihood of marital success increases when one looks for a partner who is similarly aware, or "educated."

Fair Fighting

We believe that the skill of fair fighting is essential for couples. (It can turn out to be particularly useful to introduce to couples who remain irritated, but have decided to enter into a prenuptial agreement, discussed at length in Chapter 8, stage 6.) The "fair fighting" method we suggest to couples involves five relatively simple steps:

1. *Say what you are feeling,* without hiding your emotion (e.g., "I am angry").
2. *Say why you are feeling that way,* and use full affect when you speak (e.g., in a voice louder than usually used indoors, "I am angry because you never told me you were married before, and I feel blindsided now").
3. *Take a slow, deep breath.* The deep breath allows you to

move from an emotional high pitch to a more focused, rational state from which you take the next step. Further, it is possible that this breath releases serotonin, which affects the central nervous system by calming it. For the purposes of this fair fighting exercise, the deep breath is simply very helpful.

4. *Present an option* ("Here's what I'd like to do about it"). Perhaps you need some time to think further. Perhaps your partner does. Name what's needed (e.g., "I want to go for a walk to clear my head and then come back in 30 minutes, and let's talk this through").

5. *Ask, "What do you think about that?"* Once you've gotten your thoughts out, give your partner a chance to respond. The negotiating now begins.

And thus fair fighting is underway—no name-calling or pejoratives allowed, no threats, no disappearing acts. Conversation is the tool to use, primarily speaking from the perspective of "I" statements. And sometimes it is necessary and helpful to agree that there's an issue on which you disagree.

Flexibility

On the surface, flexibility, or willingness and ability to change, appears to be almost the polar opposite of determination. But the two do not actually contradict each other at all. Being determined, as described earlier, has to do with the strenghth of an intention, not rigidity in holding it. Flexibility, in turn, speaks of being able to accept changes on the road of relationship, and the ability to move off the dime in order to reach a goal. For example, if Marty values annual vacations more than Sophie does and he is "determined" to have one this year despite the economic downturn, perhaps it's wise and flexible for him to ask Sophie to meet him halfway—if she'll agree to have this annual vacation, she can be the one to choose what it is, whether it involves a spa, a ranch, camping, a big city, a visit to family, et cetera.

Loyalty

In this context, we are examining the tremendously important, sometimes difficult, sense of "you and me against the world." As we have seen before, and learn from Nagy (1984), old loyalties—whether to a parent, sibling, or best friend—shift positions as a couple forms. Each partner still loves and respects those with whom he or she had previous, primary loyalties, but it is the soon-to-be spouse who must be moved into "first place." It's very important that loyalty priorities be established within the couple.

Respect for Differences

No one is 100% like any other person, and although sometimes we wish it were otherwise, usually this is a very good thing. It does keep life interesting. If one partner, for example, loves mysteries of all kinds, and the other hates mysteries but really enjoys sports, how do we respect the differences and compromise? Spend half the month reading and watching mysteries and the other half in the thrall of sports? Although this may be possible, it's not usually going to work effectively. A better option might be to simply acknowledge and then respect the differences and make room for them in the relationship. How? Well, the mystery lover might read a book while the sports devotee watches the tennis matches on the weekend. Sports-versus-mysteries is, of course, a relatively minor issue. Things get more complicated when couples are dealing with, for example, differences regarding readiness to have children. But, as the case story of Doris and Frank (introduced later in this chapter) illustrates, the ability to respect differences between members of a couple, while always important, is frequently difficult.

Trust

Trust is a significantly important individual predictor of marital satisfaction.

Trust, by which we mean the implicit understanding that your partner will recognize your needs as well as his or her own and treat them as equally important most of the time, is an essential element of an enduring and safe relationship. We will see a moment of Trust in action in the case of Bernie and Bonnie, towards the end of this chapter, in the Ideal Marriage discussion. This moment came at the point they decided to move their relationship forward to marriage, trusting, despite knowing that their feelings of love were not matched equally. What they each were able to trust was their mutual capacity to recognize one another's needs and treat them as important. The ability to trust that quality as present and enduring in each of them, allowed this couple to agree to marry.

THE INDIVIDUAL PREDICTORS IN ACTION: TWO CASE STORIES

We will be looking at a number of individual factors in the following case stories. First we'll follow the case, and then review some of the predictors. Doris and Frank's story lets us see key indicators including education, flexibility, respect for differences, trust, and communication.

Doris and Frank said they were good communicators even before coming to therapy; they had talked a fair amount together about what they each hoped their marriage would be like. Neither had been married before.

"I love my work,"Doris explained after the couple sat down in my office. "I'm not at all sure I can stop working, even when we have children. And I do want to have children. Two, right?" she asked, looking at Frank.

"Yeah, we want two kids," Frank said, "and Doris not wanting to stop working to raise them before they go to school . . . that's our biggest problem, I think."

Will one of them turn out to be flexible about this? I wondered as they spoke. Who, and how?

"Some of our friends said the same thing though," Frank continued, "and after the first baby was born you couldn't tear the mom away from the baby. No more work for mommy! Remember Dani?" he turned to Doris.

They both smiled. Doris nodded, with a thoughtful expression.

"I'm afraid he's counting on me doing the same thing, though, and what if I don't want to? I don't want that to make me a bad mother and a disappointing wife."

I emphasized that we didn't need anyone to make a permanent decision today—or get stuck in judgmental indictments, ever! We had just entered a thorny area, and we had all learned some things that needed to be resolved in time, but not on the spot. They agreed to wait, but each was visiblky emotional about the parenting issue.

In my mind, the decision about parenting itself (the content) was not what was primarily important right now. It was the revelation of the discrepancy in the hopes and dreams within the couple, and the development of self-knowledge around this issue, that seemed therapeutically most imperative (the process). As a premarital couple, Doris and Frank would benefit most from the process of acknowledging this issue (which had happened) and then from the outcome of their ensuing conversations. It was important, in terms of premarital counseling, that we learn many things about this couple: Can they disagree and survive? How? When the disagreement is over a subject that each considers important, is either partner, or both, able to demonstrate flexibility? How deep is their trust when disagreements

present themselves? Where is either partner's respect for the other when
they disagree? Most important, probably, is how effectively can each
partner simply communicate to the other "what is going on for me"?
The work to be done, if Doris and Frank were capable of it, had to do
with effectively blending their possibly disparate individual goals in
the service of the couple. I believed it was essential that we emphasized
process in this premarital case at this stage, rather than risk becoming
bogged down in the specific (and tempting) issues of content.

Education, of course, factors into this situation, and cases
like it. As partners learn about themselves and each other, they
grow in their understanding of their idealized, "fantasy" couple. That's the one in which the house is always magically clean,
dinner is on time and delicious, great sex happens all the time,
and there are no body odors, no garbage to get rid of, no disagreements, no anxieties—no problems at all! Slowly, reality
intrudes as we explore these idealizations and give thought to
the real marriages the members of a couple think they know
best: those of parents, siblings, and close friends (as well as
their own previous relationships).

Ultimately partners in a couple are able to differentiate
themselves and their own relationship from the relationships
they have been closest to or have participated in previously.
Both members of the premarital couple become able to identify and establish personal and shared values and goals. While
this work is completed, a trustable and solid couple is forming, and the premarital coaching and education changes as the
work begins to focus on the couple itself and the predictors of
its ultimate marital satisfaction.

At about this point, the predictor of *determination* enters or
reenters the premarital counseling process. Once the couple
has defined the marriage they will live and grow in—with the
qualities of acceptance, trust, intimacy, compassion, humor,
and security that so often are included—the work develops,

and it's outcome depends significantly on the determination of each partner. We benefit here from reviewing, and perhaps elaborating on, the earlier question, "What will it be like to be married to me?"

Obstacles to the determined outcome or goal come in all sizes both before and during marriages. However, once a person's mind is made up and he or she focuses on the (determined) truth "I want us to be life partners, and I will do the things in my power to help make that happen!" issues like whether the wedding trip ends in 8 days or 10, or the bride's mother's refusal to wear the same color dress as the bridesmaids, become less important. (Finding one's lost sense of good humor around now can be extremely valuable—and equally difficult!)

In the next case story, with Brad and Helene, watch for the key indicators of a sense of good humor, flexibility, determination, and education, among others.

Brad and Helene, both in their mid-30s and neither married previously, came to see me because so many problems had arisen after their engagement that they were becoming afraid they'd made a mistake in deciding to marry. And yet, as they told me quickly and emphatically in my office, they loved one another very much and didn't want to end the relationship. Clearly they were determined to "be together," but they were now unsure about whether marrying was a necessary component of this decision.

The couple had met 2 years earlier at a mutual friend's dinner party, and they had begun an intense relationship, moving in together within 4 months of their first meeting. They lived in New York City, where both worked in finance—which meant that they worked hard and they worked long hours. Often after work, they would meet for dinner with friends from one office or another (unless they just "went home and crashed"). Their relationship was based on good sex, companionship, excellent conversation (espe-

cially about work-related topics), and mutual hobbies including tennis, hiking, sailing, and reading.

On the second anniversary of their first date, during a late summer's dinner at one of their favorite restaurants, Brad asked Helene if she would like him to propose to her. "I wasn't sure I'd heard him properly!" Helene recounted. "Propose? I thought. Is that what he really said?"

In case it was, she answered him honestly: "No, I don't think you need to do that, to propose to me."

"But I do want us to get married, Helene," Brad had persisted. "I want you to be in my life forever. And maybe even for us to have children. . . ."

"I just didn't know what to say," Helene said, turning to me. "But I did agree with him about being together forever, so I looked him in the eye and said, very softly, 'okay.' And before I knew it, I had tears in my eyes and was crying. Right?" she asked, now of Brad.

He nodded, encouraging her to go on. When she remained quiet, he looked back to me and continued, "I was determined to make this work, and it seemed to me it had to happen right. For me, that meant the whole wedding circus, families and all, and then our lives together would be blessed and we'd just go along like we always do, unless there was a kid. . . ." He drifted into what seemed like uncertainty.

Helene picked up the story again. "So we just sat there, and suddenly, he's on one knee in front of me, holds my hand, and asks me to be his wife! I laughed out loud. And then I said, 'Yeah, of course I will. If you swear to remember to put the toilet seat down 'til death do us part.'

"And he said yes, and got back into his chair. I thought that was that; we were engaged now. And then he pulled out one of those jewelry pouches, and handed it to me—and inside was a diamond ring!" She extended her left hand toward me. "This diamond ring!"

Brad, it seemed to me, was a model of determination; Helene, of flexibility. First he asked if she'd like him to propose; when she hesitated, he persuaded her of the value of his proposition, and by the end of dinner, it turned out that he'd already bought the engagement ring for her! But they had come to my office because they were reconsidering the plan.

Even determination in combination with flexibility cannot "single-handedly" do the job of creating a satisfying marriage. Although Brad and Helene were reconsidering marrying, the issue that brought them in to see me was not concern about making a commitment to each other. Their desire to do that was clear to each of them, and I believed them as well. As we talked, Brad and Helene began to reflect on what had been happening, to consider what they were hoping for in their marriage, and discuss whether a big, late-spring wedding, scheduled 8 months from now, was going to help them make that happen. I introduced them to the predictors of flexibility, trust, and determination.

"Well, Brad certainly demonstrated flexibility!" Helene said with a smile. "He got down on one knee and proposed to me right in that restaurant!" At this, they both started laughing, demonstrating very clearly that a sense of good humor was alive and well in this couple.

Humor not withstanding, I did question the degree of flexibility for each of them. Let me explain.

Once Brad and Helene had agreed to marry, the wedding ceremony almost automatically upstaged everything else that was going on. But although this happens for almost every couple at this stage, and is something they survive, for Brad and Helene the shift in focus was very much not to their liking.

It had suddenly become very difficult for them to demonstrate flexibility in meshing their parents' goals and dreams into their picture of their wedding. And this was causing a huge problem for them. I began our next session, therefore, by passing some questions to them.

I began our next session, therefore, by posing some questions to them.

"Please think about this before you respond," I began. "As I understand your concerns, what you want me to help you with has to do with feeling overwhelmed about what has followed your engagement decision, now that you've agreed to marry. Is that much correct?"

Two heads nodded yes, looking expectant.

I continued, "And marrying each other remains your goal?"

Again, two affirmative nods.

"Can you identify the troublesome parts, and will you also give some thought about which of these thorny aspects relating to a wedding ceremony and celebration you might be able to do without?"

There were several moments of silence before Helene looked at Brad and said, "I think I hear her asking when and where we're willing to say: 'I don't!'"

They had a short laugh (more good humor; helpful!) and then the silence continued. Brad broke it, noting, "I'd say 'I don't' to a lot. I don't want flowers and music and color coordination of our parents and our attendants, and hoopla. That's it! I do not want hoopla. I want to marry you, Helene, and I want an 'event' that focuses on us marrying. I don't want most of what we're struggling with just to please our families!

"And by the way, I do want our parents and families to be with us when this happens. Just no 3-ring circus.

"Wow," Brad continued, "I hadn't known any of this until right this second! I hope it's not too big a surprise for you?" and he looked directly at Helene, concern on his face.

He was panicking; would she be able to be flexible enough to understand what he had just heard himself say? And what would happen now?

Another silence.

Finally, Helene responded, slowly at first, "Well, it is a surprise that you feel like this. I really hadn't realized. I mean, you're the one who initiated the change from our living together to our marrying

. . . but 'too big'? No, I don't think so. I mean, I think we can handle it." She paused. "

Do you want to call it off, though?" she asked.

"Not at all!" Brad said quickly. "I think what I really want to do is tone it down!"

A negotiation followed throughout the next several sessions, demonstrating unexpected and admirable flexibility in each member of the couple. In terms of their wedding ceremony, some examples of this communication and flexibility and negotiating included: jettisoning the flower girls and ring bearer, as well as all music other than chamber music while guests assembled. For the ceremony's music, they ultimately agreed on Helene's preference, Mendelssohn's wedding march. Brad really wanted to stand and watch Helene walk down the aisle to him; she, initially quite willing to blow off the whole "here comes the bride thing," agreed to do that, mainly for his sake, although it pleased her parents, as well.

The need to respect differences between themselves and their families of origin was easy enough, since most of the differences they faced were matters of style. The number of guests was pared down from 250 to 90, and anguish from both sets of parents was eventually assuaged with the promise of a large party at the end of the summer. Both mothers became totally involved with the caterer and invitations for that party, and left the wedding where it truly belonged—to their children, the actual bride and groom.

The focus for Brad and Helene became the ceremony. The celebration afterwards was going to be cut back to a "lovely, tasteful" sit-down meal in the hotel where the ceremony was taking place, and there'd be no dancing and no "hoopla." Although their parents wanted to participate differently in the ceremony, it was easy enough to accommodate the requests. Brad's parents chose to be seated, unobtrusively, when the guests came in. Both of Helene's parents wanted to participate in walking her down the aisle, "giving her away" so to speak. The choices were readily understood by the bride and groom and agreed to.

Helene and Brad ultimately decided to meet with the woman who'd
be performing their marriage, in addition to continuing premarital
counseling with me, until they felt on solid ground again about the
actual ceremony for their marrying.

I was pleased with the outcome, particularly because it
allowed me to recognize the presence of other key individual
predictors of marital satisfaction that were now discernable in
this couple. These included respect for differences and communication, particularly the ability to truthfully express their
own feelings without making "killer statements." Concurrently,
they could each hear their partner's feelings in a spirit of understanding, without becoming reactive or adversarial.

The work with Brad and Helene also clearly emphasized the
importance of loyalty, as they showed readiness and then demonstrated the ability to prioritize each other ahead of family
and friends.

I am happy to report that the reliability of these predictors was borne out in this couple. Brad and Helene have been
married successfully for over 10 years and have two children.
Helene changed career paths and decided to stay home and
pursue graduate school while raising them. She is now back
in the workforce full time, and Brad is considering a second
career of his own.

CREATING AN "IDEAL MODEL MARRIAGE"

As an outgrowth of our work with the individual predictors of
marital satisfaction, when time allows, we often ask couples to
work for at least two sessions on creating an "ideal model marriage." When creating an ideal model, the picture in your mind
is of what your *marriage*, in this instance, can become (Assagioli,
1965, 1974). There are many variations. Initially, we, encour-

age both parties in the couple to accept some homework assignments.

Task #1: "Who Do You Want to Be in Your Marriage?"

The first task is for each person to create a 3-column list of who he or she is now, thinks they are seen by others as, and, finally, hopes to be, or hopes to be *able* to be, in their marriage. (While discussing these hopes, it's useful to think about Dunne's question, cited earlier: "What will it be like to be married to me?") Qualities might include: I am smart and fun-loving. My friends at work think I'm a nerd. In my marriage, I hope to be loving, loyal, devoted, independent, friendly, and financially secure. At my not-so-good times, I might be grumpy, tired, anxious, withdrawn, and so on. There are many options for what will be included on this list, and, except for the fact that honesty must be counted on in the answers, there is absolutely no right or wrong!

This exercise allows the two members of the couple to create the picture that they anticipate will be both true to themselves and accepted by their partner. We ask them to actually picture (see, imagine, or feel) themselves in the ways they would like to live and be known after their marriage, and then to make notes about how that "peek into the future" looks.

Next, we ask the members of the couple to take turns describing this picture to their partner. We encourage careful listening initially (including taking notes if desired) and then questions and conversation in session after the descriptions have been heard. With some couples, as Bernie and Bonnie whose story follows, we introduce the ideal marriage model in the early weeks of therapy. I did so here to navigate an impasse.

Bernie and Bonnie were referred to me by Bernie's college roommate and his wife, with whom I had worked before their wedding a year earlier. Bonnie, a teacher, and Bernie, an attorney with an office in New York City, were both 27 when they sought premarital counseling. They had been dating exclusively for nearly 5 years, although not living together, and very recently had decided to marry. They were not yet officially engaged, however. It seemed to me that this indicated the presence of some obstacle, but the couple was not at all forthcoming about what it might be.

Initially, it was difficult for me to understand what they were hoping for from our work. By the third session, I was really stymied. And so, genogram completed, I asked them, in session, to take 5 minutes and picture how their ideal marriage would look, and then to describe that marriage aloud. What would the marriage be like, and what would they each be like as participants?

I was hoping this exercise would shed some light on who each partner was and help us move toward assessing each of them in terms of key predictors of marital satisfaction. It did.

Bonnie finished first and asked to speak first. Bernie nodded, and she began.

"I'd be loyal, of course, and a really good wife. I'd cook and clean in addition to my work teaching, and I'd love to have children in the next couple of years. I'd be a really terrific mother—very loving, would teach the kids to read early and keep them on a nice schedule so Bernie could bring work home like I think he would want to do. . . . It would be quiet, so he'd be glad to be home with us all, and he could go into his study—we'd have a house and there would be a library or study for him—and just concentrate after dinner."

That seemed to me like a brave start, and revealing, so I asked Bernie to give us a description of his ideal marriage and his role in it.

"Imagining isn't what I do very well," he began. "I prefer to be concrete and evidence-based. But . . . I'd leave for work early, by 6 a.m., from a house we'd live in—with a garden—in one of the suburbs outside the city. I'd get home around 7 or so, and be very tired. I guess we'd eat dinner at home and after, I'd want to read a paper

or prepare for the next day, and then get to bed pretty early. Not much social life in the picture, except family. I wouldn't have time for it, and really, I'm not very social anyway. I keep to myself quite a lot; I don't think that will change."

"Children?" I inquired.

"I suppose . . ." Bernie answered, sounding truly unenthused at the prospect, and he drifted off without saying more.

"How did you two meet?" I interjected, for no particular reason except that they clearly were stuck here.

Bonnie looked pained, hearing my question. Bernie made the first warm or kind gesture I'd seen in the couple; he patted her shoulder. And then he said, "We were introduced by a mutual friend."

Bonnie became teary-eyed. "His ex-girlfriend. She rejected him and then passed him on to me. We used to be friends . . ."

Then she turned to face Bernie and said directly to him, "I know I'm not who you really want. I'm not even sure you love me. But I think we can make a scomfortable life together, and that things will work out in time. I really think I know how to be a good wife to you, and I'm willing to take the chance to find out. Are you?"

Bernie looked rather stricken. After a period of silence, he responded slowly, still pained. "I'm sorry you know that. And I really appreciate that you're willing to take this chance with me. I don't think I can promise you much more than that I'll take good care of you, and of our children if we have them, and perhaps love will grow over time. I just don't know. . . ."

I realized that they were no longer stuck, and that was good. I wasn't entirely certain which way they were going to go, although my instincts told me they had years of experience of one another, and of mutual trust, and they would choose to marry. I was not going to cheerlead for them to go in one direction rather than another. Instead, I suggested that we end for the day (10 minutes before the end of the session) and meet the following week, when they would tell me what they had decided to do. They agreed.

To my surprise, they came back asking to write a prenup with me, and then to take a month off from sessions. They were going to be married in 3 weeks in their rabbi's study with just immediate family, and then travel for 10 days in Spain. When they returned, they hoped we could continue our sessions (education sought) as they house-hunted and tried to get their family started. They felt confident they would make a go of this (showing determination, flexibility, and trust). I agreed.

That was 21 years ago. Today, this couple remains married. The ideal model Bonnie pictured was really quite accurate. Bernie acknowledges that he has grown to love Bonnie, slowly, but in ways that she recognizes and they both appreciate. Her love for him and trust in their future have flourished. Their children are in college, and she looks toward retirement eagerly. He's a workaholic, they agree, and will probably never retire. They'll work that out, too, they expect.

My work with Bonnie and Bernie took a turn that made it unrealistic to complete the planned exploration of an ideal model marriage. When that happens, the best thing, in our opinion, is to just go with the flow, so to speak. In premarital counseling, as with so many other situations, the Scottish poet Robert Burns's words apply: "The best laid schemes o' mice an' men/ Gang aft agley" (go oft awry).

Task #2: "What Do You Hope for From Your Spouse?"

In most situations, after listening to the partners' pictures of their ideal marriage and their own ways of being in the marriage, we present an additonal task: the creation of yet another list, this one identifying what the partners hope for from their spouse. Here again, after the lists are created, we encourage the partners to give them thought and then explore the information in session.

Task #3: Ranking Marriage Pitfalls

Alternatively or additionally, we sometimes give the partners the following list of possible marital pitfalls and ask them to rank the items "in order of their importance to you."

- Children
- Communication
- Control (power)
- Isms: alcoholism, chauvinism, workaholism, etc
- Loyalties (previous versus present)
- Money
- Neurosis
- Religion
- Sex
- Trust

After the members of the couple have ranked the items, we ask them to each write two or three sentences about their thoughts on each item and its possible role in the forthcoming marriage.

As with so much of our work, when we set up these "ideal model marriage" exercises, we cannot possibly know where they will take us. But based on experience, we know that some doors will open and each member of the couple will be stronger for the experience. If and when this is not the case, we all have to face the possibility that marriage is not the right step for these two people at this time.

CHAPTER 7

Couple Predictors of Marital Satisfaction and Stability

Elena Lesser Bruun

"It is tough to make predictions, especially about the future."

Yogi Berra

Yogi's admonition notwithstanding, this chapter describes over 20 characteristics found in successful long-term marriages, consistent with what the growing body of outcomes research suggests is predictive of marital satisfaction and staying power (e.g Holman, 2001). Some of this material overlaps with topics presented in Chapters 3, 5, 6 (on research, and common issues and individual predictors), in order to expand upon or emphasize important concepts. As we saw in Chapter 5, some couples intuit that the issues they have could threaten their relationship, and they are usually right. Thus, couples who seek counseling before marriage have a golden opportunity not just to fix the issues that trouble them but also to do broader preventive work to safeguard their relationship for the future. The aim is to help them understand that building a soul-satisfying marriage is hard work, and to enlist their energy and enthusiasm for the effort.

Some couples have been tutored by excellent parent role models. Ample research shows that children of parents who married well, our first predictor, are at an advantage when it comes to marriage (Holman, 2001). These couples may not need premarital education. But for others not so lucky, the presenting problem is the tip of the iceberg, and the therapist can explain the benefits of investing time assessing and strengthening their relationship in preparation for their future. The couple may believe in their relationship and hope that their love will triumph over every adversity, but not know what makes a satisfying marriage.

The other predictors discussed in this chapter are:

- openness; belief in the other's goodwill;
- age;
- similar backgrounds or appreciation of differences;
- life goals, values, and lifestyle;
- prioritizing the relationship;
- absence of addiction;
- extended family and friendships;
- managing conflict;
- emotional compatibility
- balance of individual and couple needs;
- sexual intimacy;
- common interests;
- humor and creativity;
- balancing power and willingness to be influenced;
- emotional connection;
- division of labor;
- couple-esteem;
- knowledge of couple life stages and changing needs;
- friendship;

- financial security;
- emotional compatibility.

A lack of the knowledge, skills, willingness or ability to alter one's stance toward any of these items does not necessarily spell disaster for the couple—but it is also probably true that the more items on the list a couple has trouble with and remain unresolved, the less likely the relationship will be to last.

The reader may have already noticed that romantic love is not on the list. As we've discussed in Chapter 2, romantic love is only a recent phenomenon in marriage and has not, to our knowledge, been shown to predict long-term happiness. Our list consists of what must either accompany romantic love to keep it going, or hopefully remain after the mist of romantic love clears.

We use this list with our couples whenever they show the slightest interest in what keeps a relationship going over the long term, and we help them self-assess as they read and work their way through it. We suggest using it with couples "individually" or in a small group of three or four couples. We find it as effective as any of the paper-and-pencil tests listed in Chapter 3 and it is a relaxed, informal approach that couples seem to like. We also suggest that they keep the list and look at it at least once a year to stimulate discussion of "how're we doing."

OPENNESS

Sharing information and being open about one's past and one's actions, background, health status, religion, ethnicity, finances, socioeconomic status, country of origin, and level of education are of supreme importance for couples. Possibly the most important thing in a marriage is the ongoing experience of being fully known and appreciated for who one really is. Partners without that deep knowledge of each other start out at a disadvantage.

At the same time, we all have limits and need both boundaries and a zone of personal privacy that not even a mate should be able to penetrate uninvited. Additionally, openness is an especially tall order for those who have family or personal secrets they are embarrassed about, or are afraid that if revealed would drive the other person away. Still other times, the truth is too hurtful to share. The criteria must be whether it is important for the other person to know. Whatever is in the service of the relationship should be shared, so that both partners are playing with a full deck.

Some corrosive secrets would include drinking or using drugs on the sly, keeping money in a separate account when separate accounts have not been agreed upon, and certainly, having an affair. Keeping the fact that one is a recovering addict from the partner, failing to disclose that one will (or will not) inherit this or that, failing to tell a prospective spouse that one has children from a prior relationship and are or are not supporting them, or that a child was given up for adoption—all are examples of past behavior that could affect a marriage. Medical issues such as having a sexually transmitted disease, HIV, or a potential genetic disease are obviously important too, as is holding back information about one's religious beliefs or background, ethnicity, or nationality (by saying, for example, that a deceased grandparent was "different" in some way—Jewish, Irish, African American—or that one is or is not a pure this or that). All of these make for potential problems in the future should—or more likely when—they come to light.

For example, one of our clients claimed to be of French ancestry and didn't know how to tell his fiancée it was not true. Another told his fiancée he had two previous marriages when it was really three. When the truth came to light, his explanation that the third marriage was too brief and insignificant to count was unconvincing, and the wedding was cancelled. Had he been totally honest from the start, she might

have decided to risk being wife number four. Another client, Lori, had
had extensive chemotherapy for a life-threatening childhood cancer and
hesitated to tell her fiancé she might not be able to conceive.

A good secret for a client to keep from his partner would be
that a friend of his thinks she is "not the brightest bulb." Or
that her deceased father, whom he knew as a child, groped her
teenage cousin. Or that her mother confided to him that her
daughter, his fiancée, was not her favorite child. What point
would revelation serve in these instances? It would only hurt
the partner, who could do nothing about it.

There are endless examples of these kinds of situations, and
the therapist has to work gingerly to help one member of a
couple decide how, how much, or when to reveal an important secret to the partner. The therapist has to walk the fine
line between helping the secret holder prepare to reveal (by
say allowing an individual meeting with the secret holder) and
creating an unholy alliance if the secret holder was still unable
to open up.

Most of the time, simple encouragement during a joint session will enable the secret holder to open up. If the joint session does not suffice, in those rare instances, the secret holder
usually requests an individual session to discuss the matter. I
will then ask if the partner would mind my meeting individually
to help the secret holder overcome their discomfort and that
the individual session would in all likelihood be a rehearsal for
disclosure to the partner. This is exactly what happened with
Maureen and Eric.

Eric was afraid to tell Maureen that he had fathered a child out of
wedlock before he met Maureen, and had been supporting this son, who
was now seven, since birth. When he was finally able to tell Maureen,
he felt relieved and she was able, though not right away, to come to
terms with it.

For a thorough discussion of secrets and how to handle them, see Imber-Black's book, *The secret life of families* (1999).

BELIEF IN THE OTHER'S GOODWILL

This is perhaps the core of all good relationships. If a couple cannot rely on each other to be motivated by goodwill—by fundamental caring—there is little else to sustain them. If either feels the partner does not have the other's interests at heart or care enough about the relationship, all seems lost. Partners can tolerate stupid, thoughtless, and even desperate behavior, but not behavior that is detached or malevolent.

Common breaches of trust are premarital affairs, one partner consistently allying with a third person against the other partner, and gambling away (or otherwise recklessly spending) honeymoon savings—all of which we've seen. It is hard to see how any of these behaviors are caring of the partner, but in many instances they *were* intended as such—albeit ultimately very ineffective. The job of the therapist is to trace the thought process behind the behavior back to its source, and then to reframe and reinterpret the behavior away from malevolent to a "not good" solution to a problem.

> *For example, one of our clients, Jack, did not know what to do about his fiancée Tammy's claim that intercourse was painful. The couple did have intercourse occasionally, but she would always say it hurt. He could not bear to hurt her, and could not relax when they did try to make love. He thought that by having intercourse with someone else, he could stop pressuring her and be less frustrated himself. One could almost say, he had an affair to help his relationship with Tammy. Obviously, having an affair was a terrible solution to the problem of painful sex, but once Jack's fiancée was helped to understand that Jack did not intend to hurt her physically or emo-*

*tionally, she restored her faith in his goodwill toward her. They were
then able to effectively collaborate and resolved the problem together.*

Another example:

*Gordon's mother and his fiancée, Robin, often felt slighted by
the other, and they would complain bitterly about it to Gordon, who
felt stuck in the middle. Although he kept quiet when the three were
together, afterward he would try to explain to Robin that his mother
only wanted the best for them. Robin felt unsupported and distanced
from Gordon, and she would retaliate by openly "wondering" whether
this was the right relationship for her. In therapy, Gordon admitted
that he was siding with his mother, but as the couple explored how
this pattern got established, he realized that it was only because he
thought his wife was the more self-confident of the two women in his
life, and that Robin could afford to defer to his mother. He believed
Robin knew how much he cared for her and was just being unreason-
able. In fact, Robin was not confident at all and needed Gordon's
support. When Gordon realized the position he had taken and its
effect on Robin, he began to give her more support, and Robin started
to feel better. She recognized her oversensitivity to perceived slights,
and she was able to be friendlier to her mother-in-law. Robin saw
Gordon's high regard for her and understood that although he was
mistaken in his approach, his intentions were not malevolent.*

*Similarly, Lori, mentioned briefly in the previous section, did ulti-
mately tell her fiancé about her childhood chemotherapy treatment
and the possibility that she would be unable to conceive. Henry was
first taken aback and angry, which led them to see a therapist. In
the safety of the office, Lori explained that part of her fear was that
he would leave her and also that talking about it made it more real
and therefore more painful. Henry's response was perfect. He quickly
regrouped, having understood why she withheld before, and stated
that if she could not conceive, he would gladly adopt. He stopped, in*

essence, taking her lack of initial trust personally and realized that she had a problem too.

AGE AND EDUCATION

We know that chronological age when a couple gets married makes a difference. The younger a couple is, the more years of marriage they face, the more incomplete their emotional and intellectual growth is likely to be, the less education they have, the harder it will be for them to earn a decent living, more likely they will be to change their needs and preferences individually and collectively, and the harder it will be to be satisfied and stay married. Generally speaking, the better educated and older a couple is at the time they get married, the more realistic they are likely to be, and the better their chances of staying married. High-school sweetheart marriages only sometimes make it in the long run. Young couples, especially those who have never lived singly first, tend to idealize marriage out of proportion to what it can deliver, and missing that crucial individual stage of development can put young couples at a disadvantage.

SIMILAR BACKGROUNDS OR APPRECIATION OF DIFFERENCES

It is certainly easier starting out if the partners' backgrounds are the same or similar. There is a comfort level and a sense of safety, familiarity, and belonging together. It is about having a past in common. But there are also instances in which differences in background and a break from family of origin can be a strong positive in a marriage. The value of difference in background is most evident when the background of one member of the couple has been very limiting or abusive, or if somehow the members of the couple feel they never really fit in their family of origin.

This happened with Amy, who was adopted into a small-town Southern family—good, kind people, but not very ambitious and not very bright. Amy moved to New York, married a guy on Wall Street, and never looked back. Similarly, Rochelle felt confined in her parochial New York Jewish family and longed to travel and learn all she could about other places and people. She met a handsome French Catholic man on a trip to Europe; they fell in love at first sight, married, and settled in Europe. Peter, a White Episcopalian with lineage back to Charlemagne, was abandoned by his mother before he was 2. He married an Asian-American woman who had strong ties to her family of origin, and they are still happily married.

While couples who meet when they are older have definite advantages, it can be hard for them to bridge differences. That is why some of the best remarriages are between people who knew each other in high school and reconnect later on. When we are young, the mate we choose completes unfinished parts of ourselves. We may also pick someone radically different as a form of rebellion. By midlife, most people want a soul mate.

As we have said elsewhere, for differences in background to keep being a source of strength, the couple must understand that they have to continue working hard to respect and admire what each has brought to the relationship and be creative in developing or changing rituals and ceremonial occasions to meet both their needs.

GOALS, VALUES, LIFESTYLE

It is amazing how many couples do not discuss the future before marriage, assuming that because they are in love, they will always be in agreement. It is also true that goals, values, lifestyle, and even desires such as that for children can change over time. It is important that couples not only discuss these matters and come to understandings before getting married but also commit to having these discussions *throughout* their marriage.

> *For example, Sheila and Adam had no difficulty agreeing on life goals, expectations for their relationship, finances, lifestyle, and children. But Sheila didn't fully realize just how important her career was to her and how much time she would want to devote to it. Adam had once told her that he rejected the idea of dating a woman he had once met because "she was too involved in her career." Sheila thought "uh, oh" to herself, but said nothing, figuring they would work that out later. Clearly, all of these projections—life goals, expectations of marriage, children, lifestyle, and finances—are interrelated and affect each other, so once they were married, Sheila and Adam had big problems balancing their needs as Sheila's career needs began to interfere.*

> *Lenore and Andrew were perfectly suited for each other. They had met hiking in the Rockies several years earlier, and they had similar backgrounds and sets of values. Both wanted children and a strong family life. Shortly after their engagement, however, Andrew realized how important it was to him to live in Greece, where he was born and had lived the first 5 years of his life. Lenore, on the other hand, had recently lost her sister and father, and she was adamant about not moving away from her mother, the only remaining family member she had. Amazingly, they had never discussed where they would live beforehand.*

> *Because I knew the marriage was essentially viable, I was able to treat their dilemma with a certain amount of humor, suggesting they consider living in Iceland, where neither of them knew anyone or wanted to be. Ultimately, they resolved the issue by agreeing to live in Greece but devoting a sizable percentage of income to traveling back to the States regularly. Lenore went with Andrew willingly, but from time to time in other stressful periods, his after-the-fact revelation would once again become a source of bitterness.*

Many couples are afraid to disclose these things, fearing it will cost them the relationship, but this approach is short-sighted and a therapist is well advised to help the couple broach discussion of their future and what they want it to look like while they are in a counseling mode. In some cases, this means compromise on the part of both partners; in others, it means one partner must defer to the other.

Madeline was one of my braver clients. She told Brett in no uncertain terms that she did not want to have children. She had been the eldest of many children in her family of origin, drafted to help raise the younger ones. She had already had her fill of "parenting" and was happy at the thought of being an aunt to a bevy of nieces and nephews. Brett did want children, but he wanted Madeline more. They have one of the best marriages I know.

PRIORITIZING THE RELATIONSHIP

This is a very simple concept, but also an extremely important one. We see many couples who have made a commitment to marry and have a wedding date but who still are not fully cognizant of the emotional shift involved in being married. The notion that the marriage partner comes first, before all others, in one's thoughts, consideration, and actions is actually difficult to grasp. There are so many other allegiances, to family of origin, friends, bosses, work, and eventually to one's children. It is not always clear where one's primary loyalty belongs. As we discussed in Chapter 2, in the past, allegiances to one's family of origin were often expected to be stronger than to one's spouse. That was when marriage was not about intimacy, or even love, but about enhancing the economic and social position of the inter-generational family. Today, it is different, and well-trained therapists know that a dead giveaway for future marital unhappiness is when one or both halves of the couple deposit their emotional eggs elsewhere. This was the case with Keith and Andrea.

> *Keith and Andrea had been dating for 3 months when Keith revealed that he had a 13-year-old daughter from a previous relationship. Though he had never married the mother, now that she was ill, he felt responsible for her and for his daughter. As a child, Andrea had felt sidelined in her family of origin when her aunt and uncle died in a plane crash and her cousin came to live with Andrea's family. At age 6, she suddenly had a new "brother" exactly her age who needed all kinds of attention after the loss of his parents. Now Andrea wanted a committed relationship leading to marriage, and she felt thwarted again. Keith's daughter was now clearly the top priority in his life, and Andrea could not bear the competition. So despite a good-faith effort on both their parts, the relationship broke up.*

Some very young couples have difficulty prioritizing their relationship because they have not yet fully transitioned from being a child of their parents to adult couplehood. That was in some measure William and Adele's problem.

> *At one point in therapy, William, a Brit who had moved to New York with his new wife, Adele, turned to me and casually offered that "there is nothing I would rather do than have a cup of tea with my mom." In that instant, it was clear that there was no hope for his relationship with Adele.*

Often, too, the failure to prioritize the partner is the result of unspoken problems in the relationship—disappointments, unresolved issues, hurt feelings, and so on. Or it can be caused by a man's belief that he will be less masculine if he gives his relationship top priority. Alternatively, he, or the woman, may have been overshadowed by someone in their family of origin and unconsciously and now "overreact" by downplaying the importance of his/her partner. In any event, the therapist's job is to help couples pinpoint the cause and see the importance of prioritizing the relationship.

A partner may also assign priority to a thing or an activity, to an avocation or an interest. This was humorously illustrated in a wonderful cartoon I once saw, where a husband, about to turn on the television, asks his wife, "Is there anything you would like to say before the baseball season begins?"

ABSENCE OF ADDICTION

Serious addiction is a major cause of failure to prioritize one's relationship and deserving of its own section in this chapter. We could write a book—and others have—on the negative impact addictions have on families, and particularly on marriage. A serious addiction, whether to alcohol, drugs, gambling or food, forces a person to care about something else more than their mate. Very simply, there is no reasoning with someone while he or she is using under the influence, and no way he will or she will even be *capable* of putting the mate first. Twelve-step programs recognize this by asking recovering alcoholics to make amends for bad behavior or neglect while they were addicted. If a therapist has any clue that addictions are involved, there is an obligation to inquire and make the case for dealing with it prior to marriage.

Lydia and Barry came for premarital counseling because he seemed to put everything else before her. He played squash, went snowboarding, hung out with his best friend from college, and spent endless hours at work. He claimed to love Lydia but did little to show it. She craved his attention and hoped that once they were married things would change because at least she would see him at the end of the day. Sadly, after marriage it got worse, and their sex life plummeted as well. Barry was also very tired from his "long commute to and from work," and he would sometimes come close to dozing off in sessions. I asked what was wrong, but got no response.

Then, one day during a session, Lydia revealed not only that she knew Barry "sometimes took prescription painkillers when he could get his hands on them," but also that she had discovered he'd been taking the medicines she had been prescribed for chronic endometriosis and a series of root-canal surgeries. He had literally finished them all, and there were none left for her when she had a bad pain bout. That convinced her that his priority was the pills and not her wellbeing, and that the truth had to come out. Had they dealt with this before marrying, far less anger and distrust would have ensued and relationship damage would have been avoided. Luckily, once the addiction was aired, Barry was motivated to seek treatment and the marriage improved dramatically.

EXTENDED FAMILY AND FRIENDSHIPS

For a marriage or any long-term intimate relationship to survive and thrive, a partner almost always has to be willing to be part of the family of origin and extended family of the other. We have given several examples in earlier chapters of couples who came for therapy with thorny, damaging presenting problems concerning in-laws. In general, we take the position that each member of the couple needs to minimize or control his or her issues with the others' family members for the sake of the relationship. This is another special case of prioritizing the relationship and the partner—putting the couple's need for smooth relations with the outside world above one's own perceived or actual slights. At the same time, the one who controls or sacrifices the desire to distance or avoid the other's extended family or friends needs a strong show of support and appreciation from the spouse.

Sometimes it is the prospective in-laws who precipitate the problem, as we saw with Don and Linda. Here we include newly married Stephanie, whose mother-in-law went with the couple on their honeymoon cruise and insisted on having the first dance with her son-in-law. Another client's mother-in-law would call her son for financial advice without ever asking about or asking to speak with her new daughter-in-law. And then there was the engaged, prospective daughter-in-law whose own parents lived far away and who asked her mother-in-law-to-be to help her pick out a wedding dress. The soon-to-be-mother-in-law made a date but then cancelled it, saying she was "too busy" to reschedule. In these cases it is incumbent on the child of the parent to speak with the parent about his or her behavior. If the child resists the idea, it says something about how the marriage will go and where the child's allegiance mainly is.

When the family is willing, having joint sessions with prospective in-laws and the couple can be very helpful. These are usually educational rather than therapeutic in nature, and the therapist can discuss life-stage transitions, new roles, new obligations, and the need for families to widen the circle to truly include the prospective new member.

MANAGING CONFLICT

At the thought of conflict, distressed couples either overreact or try to avoid. We see both with premarital couples, but more conflict avoidance than overreaction, especially in the early stages of a relationship. Living together, whether it is a family, a commune, a couple, or just roommates, inevitably involves differences of opinion and the clashing of needs. Couples in an intense emotional, financial, and sexual relationship not only have to expect conflict, but also be prepared to learn a set of skills to minimize and work conflict through to mutually satisfactory conclusion.

High-conflict couples usually fight frequently, and they seem to have the same fight over and over again. They have unproductive, distressing, time-consuming "discussions" and rarely reach an understanding or resolution. The fights may or may not start civilly, but regardless, they escalate out of control and end with one partner yelling, name-calling, refusing to talk, getting physical, or leaving the other one in the lurch or both in a funk, frustrated, exhausted, and anxious, with their connection seeming more frazzled and unworkable than before the argument started.

In the office, the role of the therapist is to help the couple preserve what goodwill they still have and to contain or minimize the arguing until they know how to do it better. We've never had a couple refuse to accept some minimal containment rules, such as do not interrupt each other, and make your points as quickly as possible. Picking a specified time to discuss relationship issues can help, as can limiting the amount of time spent discussing them (15 to 30 minutes). If the discussion becomes heated, one person can call a halt, but only by promising to continue at a later agreed-upon specific time (within a day). I use some variant of the speaker-listener technique to slow the process down with couples who cannot have productive dialogue without it.

As discussed earlier, destructive arguing will usually wreck a relationship and lead to divorce. Following Gottman's example, I keep an old school bell on my coffee table and jokingly threaten to tap it if arguments seem to be going nowhere or in an ugly direction. Couples know it is there (because they usually notice it and ask), and I almost never have to remind them! Incidentally, the only other gimmicks I have are a child's magic wand (in case we need more positive power) and a magic eight ball (in case we can't figure something out). Humor and humility never hurt.

I do not use humor, however, when serious violence is suspected or reported. In private practice, I try to refer couples where serious violence has occurred or when it is in the air because I do not have the capacity to assist in every emergency. Inevitably though, I cannot always screen this issue out. Suffice it to say that I probe as best as possible, help the couple develop a plan to avoid violence, and draw in other family members, friends for assistance as needed. Clearly, violence in a premarital situation does not auger well for a couple, but, especially in a new relationship, there is most hope for couples who can learn to deescalate.

Conflict-avoidant couples present a united front that somehow seems unreal and forced. They tell the therapist that they never fight and agree on everything, except the "tiny" issue that brings them in. What happens here is that conflict is shoved under the proverbial rug. And it is so frightening to the couple that they bury it rather than attempt to deal with it. With these couples, that can be very difficult to engage, the therapist almost has to agree that they have just one tiny issue, and then work slowly on that tiny presenting problem until their trust is gained and they see some progress being made. It does no good to inform the couple that they are avoiding conflict. If the therapist is patient, the couple will soon open their Pandora's box.

Successful couples are neither high-conflict nor conflict-avoidant. They trust their relationship to tolerate fights, but most importantly they know that some conflict is inevitable and they develop their own rules to manage it. They know how to argue well and are conflict-ready, pure and simple.

EMOTIONAL COMPATIBILITY

In Chapter 5, we discussed how if even one partner in a relationship lacks emotional intelligence, the relationship may be strained enough to cause a couple to seek counseling. Here we are concerned with simple emotional compatibility, what happens when each of the partners has a serious problem that does not mesh well with the others,' when their problems in fact clash. A sad but humorous example follows:

Noel, engaged to Suzanne, announced in session that he was breaking off the engagement because he realized he was in love with someone else. Devastated, Suzanne fought back, with "I know who she is, and she has just as many problems as I do. You just like her problems better than my problems!" Noel had to admit it was true.

Either on their own, or with competent help, couples can and do change their dynamic. But, when a long standing problem or aspect of someone's basic personality rubs up against an important aspect of the another's basic personality, a couple's most valiant effort may be in vain. This was certainly true of Simon and Claire.

Whenever Claire, already diagnosed as having borderline personality disorder, was angry with Simon, she would threaten to leave and would sometimes disappear for days. Simon in turn suffered from "generalized anxiety disorder," stemming at least in part from the fact that his mother had left him with his disinterested father and a series of nannies when he was three. Claire's threats would render him sleepless at night and panicky, unable to function during the day. She considered his reaction "weak," and would respond with contempt, making Simon more anxious than ever.

This pattern is only an extreme example of what goes on with any numbers of couples. In cases where the pattern is deeply rooted in individual pathology, a couple's behavior and interaction may not be significantly modifiable.

BALANCE OF INDIVIDUAL AND COUPLE NEEDS

For a marriage to succeed today, each person in the couple must attend to his or her individual needs, the needs of the other, and the needs of the relationship. All three are important and none can be neglected. In the past, women were often expected to sacrifice themselves for family, as we discussed earlier. This also happens to men, though less often. This was the case with Neil.

> *Neil resisted setting a wedding date with Lily. They had been together 8 years, living together for 2. Both were 35. There were many issues with this couple, but the predominant one that brought them in was that Neil thought he might be in love with someone else. In the first meeting, the sheer size of Lily's engagement ring provided a good window in to their relationship, because it turned out that Neil had felt he could not afford it. But Lily had been dreaming of a three-carat diamond and Neil was afraid to disappoint her.*
>
> *Underneath, Neil also was unsure that the two of them were a good match. Lily was often critical of him or angry "at something or other," and he could never seem to do anything right. She never wanted him to see his friends, and he had a hard time holding onto his once-a-month poker night with friends. He felt he was losing himself in the relationship, but rather than assert his needs, he slowly withdrew. The more he backed away, the more she would pursue him, until he literally backed out the door. Had Neil been able to assert himself and his own needs earlier in the relationship, Lily might have been able to understand, and they could have survived.*

SEXUAL INTIMACY

The sexual aspect of the relationship is a sensitive, private topic for most couples, and it is most revealing about the relationship as a whole to the therapist. A "rarely" or "never" response to a questionnaire inquiring about frequency of intercourse is not a good sign. Occasionally, a couple does present with a sexual problem or disagreement in an initial session, but not often. Sexual issues usually lie just beneath the presenting problem, waiting to be aired. If a couple does not bring up the topic, the therapist can, once the presenting story has been told and witnessed, giving the couple a bit of relief for the telling. I do not ask, "How is your sex life?," but "How has your sex life changed since the problem you came in with surfaced?" This way of inquiring helps the couple to talk because they do not have to answer categorically that their sex life is "bad" or "good." Rather, they can talk about it in relative terms as "better" or "worse."

There are some couples whose sex life appears to thrive or does not seem to suffer, when other things go wrong. But they are in the minority, though some of couples seem to have great sex only after a fight. For most, when conflict heats up or too much potential conflict is avoided, sex is the ground on which the battle is silently fought. The member of the couple who feels most misunderstood or mistreated loses sexual desire, The other member of the couple becomes tired or resentful "being the one" to initiate all the time. They withdraw, and sex happens less and less often.

We also know there are differences in levels of desire, and if a couple is mismatched with one always wanting it more, they have to be able to discuss it and reach a compromise. Level of desire may also be intertwined with the technique and prowess of the partner, with a low-desire partner potentially wanting sex more if the high-desire partner's approach or technique was more suitable, varied or respectful. I have had more than one woman client confess to wanting more sex when her husband did more housework! There are many things that can spark desire, the most obvious, of course, being able to discuss what matters and what each person likes and will respond to.

Too many therapists still suffer from this country's puritanical past and avoid opening up the question of a couple's sex life. Although it may not be easy, family therapists and others who work with couples are primary-care practitioners when it comes to sex. There is always the option to refer a couple to a sex therapist, but we do not need to refer at the first mention of the word—only if the problem seems unusual or if the couple earnestly asks for it. The fact of the matter is that fewer people are being trained in sex therapy today, so the referral may be to a gynecologist or urologist, neither of whom is necessarily trained or comfortable discussing the intimate aspects of sex.

COMMON INTERESTS

If a couple has a strong interest or passion in common, they are indeed lucky, as having interests together is one of the things that helps bind a relationship over time. When this is the case, the couple only has to be careful not to get over-involved in the interest and fail to develop or attend to other parts of the relationship. The following vignette illustrates one couple's creative solution to such a problem.

Gloria and Ralph, both in their 30s, had met on a film set where she was the director, he an actor. They married shortly thereafter. They loved their careers, had many friends and a large extended family, and figured they would have a great life. But they failed to predict something on their horizon: golf.

Ralph had never been interested in golf before, but after being invited by a friend to watch a tournament one weekend, he was hooked. Soon he was spending all his free time playing the game, and when he wasn't on the golf course himself, he was watching the sport on TV. Gloria gradually saw less and less of her husband and didn't know what to do. When a friend suggested they see a therapist, she scheduled an appointment.

In the process of coming to terms with Ralph's new passion and generating ideas about how to address the distance that had crept into the relationship, the couple decided that Gloria would take up golf and Ralph would forego watching the sport on TV. They were both delighted to find that Gloria enjoyed the game, and as she grew better at it, it became a genuine interest the two of them shared.

If therapists encouraged more couples to join forces and try things their mates love to do, or start a new activity together instead of wasting time battling over who gets to do what with their free time, their lives could be enriched.

HUMOR AND CREATIVITY

It has been said that to succeed in life, one needs a "keen sense of the absurd." And, if it is true of life in general, it is certainly true of marriage. We all take marriage, ourselves, and our partners too seriously. Laughter provides relief from relationship tension and helps us cope. At the end of the day, it is the impossibility of fully understanding or fundamentally changing another human being and at least temporarily abandoning the effort that allows us to loosen up, sometimes even embrace something we thought we could not tolerate, and try again. Good long-term relationships have that kind of humorous, long-suffering but loving aspect to them. The song "I've Grown Accustomed to Her Face" from the Broadway musical *My Fair Lady* (Levin, 1964) says it well. A couple who can channel anger and laugh about it is way ahead of the game.

For example, Doug and Olivia both came from families in which putdowns were an everyday occurrence, used both as way of expressing anger and as a way of expressing affection, like "roasts" to "honor" friends. Early in their relationship, when Doug would state something he was sure of, Olivia would challenge him with "How do you know?" to convey her disbelief that he could possibly know something like that. Doug would get defensive and they would argue. In therapy, Olivia heard how insulting this was to Doug, and she stopped using the retort as an attack. She still used it to tease him, however, and it became a source of humor—a joke, their joke.

Making a joke or a game out of a problem is a great way to safeguard goodwill in a relationship. Shifting from dead seriousness to humor can defuse many a marital fight, yielding creative solutions to otherwise deadlocked conflicts. This is part of what Gottman observed with successful couples able to make "repair attempts." (1999)

One couple came up with a particularly creative solution to defusing martial arguments.

Before their wedding, Jacqueline and Norman had decided not to register for wedding gifts, agreeing the idea was crass. A problem arose when they started receiving gifts neither of them liked, along with duplicates and items they could not return. They wound up with a large assortment of mismatched, ugly dishware, none of which could be exchanged. This, of course, was not why they sought counseling, but somehow in discussing the china problem, they came up with a solution. They placed the unwanted pieces on top of an old boiler in the kitchen, and whenever they had a big disagreement, the one who felt most aggrieved could grab a piece and smash it on the floor; the other one would simply get out the broom and sweep it up! It was their private game—one that tickled them and the friends who happened to see the china on the boiler and inquire about it.

Sometimes couples use "inside" jokes or putdowns of others to cement their good feelings about each other. One couple discovered they were both hyper-observant about other peoples' noses, and they got a kick out of pointing out, say, an "amazing" nose at the next table in a restaurant. Another couple used to argue because the husband would not want to drive more than a short distance to visit their friends. Their therapist asked them each to write down a list of their friends and how far they would theoretically be willing to drive to see them. This exaggeration of the problem brought home the absurdity of the issue, and the couple began to discuss what they could do on longer trips to make them more tolerable for the husband.

Clearly, therapists must have a sense of humor and be able to appreciate the couples' own brand of humor to help them expand their repertoire. A word of caution, however: though I gave examples of the use of light teasing and putdowns, this is delicate ground that must be treaded on lightly. There is a scene in *Diary of a Mad Housewife* (Perry, 1970), for example, in which the husband walks into a room in their apartment with his young children. His wife (the children's mother) is standing in the room. Her eyes are red and puffy, and although she's clearly been crying, she is trying to smile. See-ing her, the husband says to the children, "Look, children, isn't Mommy funny?!" Putdowns can also be excruciatingly unfunny.

Although our couples can gingerly use putdowns in the ser-vice of good humor, therapists have to be careful. It rarely works for us to put clients down even in lighthearted fashion, though we've clearly seen sarcasm used to good effect. One oft-repeated example in the therapy field comes from a thera-pist, his name now long forgotten, whose young, single client had gotten pregnant again after multiple abortions. He said in commiseration, "Well, maybe we could enter you in the *Guinness Book of World Records!*" This actually helped the client, because it was truly funny, spoke to the absurdity of the problem, and was a positive reframe of a terrible problem. In general, however, it is better for us to take the one-down position, showing our own vulnerability, than to contribute to clients' own sense of theirs.

BALANCING POWER AND WILLINGNESS TO BE INFLUENCED

Willingness to be influenced does not mean giving in or "accommodating" just to make peace. It means recognizing what the other person has to contribute to a discussion or a solution and being willing to change something, learn something new from the other person, or adjust one's behavior or thinking in deference to the partner's wishes or better idea.

Because men historically have been expected to have the power in relationships with women, it can be hard for them to understand what it means to women for them to relinquish some of it. It is difficult enough for many men to compromise in their dealings with women, but respecting a woman enough to give in or accept her influence is going a step further.

Both members of a couple have to be ready to accept influence, but most women already do it naturally. Women learn from the cradle to be hypersensitive to the needs of others and tend to defer rather quickly if the other person, particularly an authority figure or a male partner, asserts himself. For many men—and some self-confident women—a "no" from the other person is just the opening gambit. For most women, however, "no" means "no" and that is the end of it.

As we mentioned earlier, there is also data to suggest that unwillingness to be influenced is an important predictor of marital dissatisfaction and divorce (Gottman & Silver 1999, p. 100). We point this out to couples in our practice and encourage the men to practice taking the risk. Those who do often report feeling relieved that they don't always have to be right or wise.

EMOTIONAL CONNECTION

Most theories of couple therapy emphasize the importance of an emotional connection between the partners. In the past, as noted in Chapter 2, people did not expect this kind of connection in marriage, but today, an emotional connection is the essence of what keeps most couples together. The feeling of connectedness is so important that when it is frayed, couples will either seek help or look outside the marriage. When the connection is broken, the marriage dissolves. Therefore, it is not hard to see that a strong connection would predict marital satisfaction.

The therapist's office and the therapist him- or herself create a sense of safety that allows the couple to open up, explore, and reach back to the insult, hurt, betrayal, or sense of not being cared about that is the root of most couples' disagreements, problems, and gripes. As discussed earlier, Susan Johnson (2004) has cast research light on this area, giving these moments of disconnectedness the therapeutic prominence they deserve and teaching many of us to shepherd our couples back to those places to listen, hear, empathize, and finally heal. The importance of doing this sooner rather than later in the relationship is illustrated by the following case story.

Hillel and Dahlia's 30-year marriage was crumbling. Both in their mid-50s, they had tried therapy before but found it unhelpful. Just as they were about to give up again, Hillel burst out with "Dahlia will never forgive me for not wanting more children." This opened the door for a frank discussion of the couple's underlying problem.

"Hillel is right," Dahlia said. "I love our daughter Leah, but I always wanted a big family—especially after my brother died in the

Six Day War and it was just my parents and me. I just felt so lonely."
Additionally, most of the Orthodox Jews the couple knew in Israel
had large families, and it was embarrassing to visit them with just
one daughter, adorable though she was. "I just don't think I'll ever be
able to forgive him for being so selfish," Dahlia added.

Over the years, Dahlia's resentment had, caused her to pull back
emotionally and avoid sex. This had frustrated Hillel and prompted
angry tirades, which, in turn, had only made Dahlia pull away
more. As they discussed this cycle, Hillel explained how uncomfort-
able with and afraid of children he had been. Believing he would be
a terrible father, he had dreaded the birth of Leah, and he was afraid
of not being able to support more children should Dahlia become preg-
nant again. On top of that, he feared losing his connection to Dahlia
because of her complete devotion to Leah. "I'm so sorry," Hillel said
as he looked at Dahlia. "I wish we could go back in time and do
things differently, understand each other better. Maybe we could have
had more children." It was hard for Dahlia, however, to forgive him,
because the wall she had erected from years of vicious-cycle arguing
was, as she put it, "as high as the one separating Israelis and the
Palestinians on the West Bank."

If, in premarital counseling, this couple had learned to
expect a certain amount of hurt, to understand that it would
be unintentional for the most part, and to speak out at the time
and help each other "get past it" with empathy and soothing
rather than defending the offence, they would have been better prepared for married life.

DIVISION OF LABOR

Therapists can help couples get off on the right foot by encouraging discussion of how they plan to divide up tasks. Many
hidden resentments—or open disagreements—can arise over
who does what, making this a hot-button issue. Even misper-

ceived unfairness can lead to an overall feeling of marital dissatisfaction.

This section is not about how a couple decides what will be done, but rather who winds up doing what. It is more about precedent and falling into jobs than intention. Some couples resist having to spell out who does what, and others do well sharing or dividing up tasks evenly just by feel. Most couples, though, need the structure that a carefully thought-through division of labor can yield.

Owing to historical precedent and family tradition, it is often still true that women do more than half the housework, bills, errands, and childcare even when they also work outside the home. Whenever this issue comes up (and if it doesn't, I usually bring it up), I encourage couples to look at how true this cultural imbalance is of their relationship. When one partner has a much more demanding career or is immersed in all-consuming schooling, he or she will not be able to do "their fare share"—certainly not while the intense work or school load is in progress. However, he or she can think of fairness or balance over a life time and commit to rebalancing as needed.

Many couples feel overburdened by the work it takes to run a household and start to blame each other for not doing enough instead of thinking creatively about how to remove some of the stress. It is important that they be clear with each other about their needs and expectations. To give a simple example, when Simon and Corrine got married, they decided to handle housekeeping tasks by taking turns cleaning the whole apartment. It was a good idea, but they found themselves procrastinating, getting frustrated with each other, and accomplishing little. When they analyzed the situation, they realized that Corrine avoided her turn because although she didn't mind doing dishes or cleaning the bathroom, she hated vacuuming. Simon rather liked vacuuming but hated washing dishes and cleaning the bathroom. Figuring out a new plan was easy once they worked to understand the problem.

If they are not careful, couples can slip into roles their parents played. They can easily slip, for instance, into a male bread-winner marriage, not by choice, but by having grown up with it, although it may not fit their needs. One couple fought a lot about housework and who should be responsible for what. She didn't like housework (her family had a housekeeper), and wanted him to at least share chores evenly. He expected her to do most of the housework (as his mother had), but figured he would "help her out" by doing the laundry. They couldn't understand why their place never looked "shipshape," the way their parents' homes did. Finally, they realized it was because neither of them really cared enough to put a supreme effort into it. They decided they could clean a lot less often than they thought they had to, and live for the day when they could afford household help.

COUPLE-ESTEEM

When couples need help, especially early in their relationship, they are apt to feel somewhat ashamed, embarrassed, and "less than" the hypothetical ideal couple they measure themselves against. To counteract any tendency to put themselves down, I inject a dose of confidence as soon as possible by asking them about what is going well for them, or sharing what I observe.

> *Ray and Anna, for example, started their first session stating that they were not getting along well and were surprised that they had somehow managed to have a good vacation recently. Anna then mused that "of course every couple has a good time on vacation." I know this to be not at all true, and told her so. Some couples dread vacations and forced together time; other couples can't agree on where to go, what to do, or how much money to spend on vacations; still others worry about what is being missed at home or work and can't*

enjoy time away. I corrected their misperception and labeled their
smooth vacations a marital strength, which they were happy to hear.

This same couple had a solid commitment to their relationship, a good sex life, and common interests. In addition, Ray would "always bring flowers after a fight," and Anna could "always make [Ray] laugh." I highlighted all of these strengths to boost Ray and Anna's couple-esteem. Helping a couple like this re-experience their strengths enables them to start discussing problems more readily and also helps them realize how much they do have together that they can rely on in tough times.

KNOWLEDGE OF COUPLE LIFE STAGES AND CHANGING NEEDS

Whether to keep or divorce one's husband was a common debate in consciousness-raising groups spawned by the women's movement in the 1970s. Women in their 30s and 40s took solace with their "sisters" in their common disappointment that husbands were simply not the soul mates they had yearned for. Men of the same age did not have a place to express it, but also felt deprived of a soul mate. Surely we all always want to feel close—emotionally connected—to our mates, but there are other predictable relationship needs that compete with or even outweigh the need for intense closeness in different periods of our lives.

If we marry, say, in our 20s, we tend to choose someone different from ourselves—someone whom we admire, who has talents different from ours, who complements us. We are still incomplete, and the mate compensates for our missing parts. There are many examples. The minister all about mercy marries the litigator who is all about justice. The socially apprehensive librarian marries the used-car salesman. The concert pianist with a knack for languages marries the biologist with a tin ear.

By midlife, a time in which many get divorced, we have evolved. We begin to appreciate ourselves, and start to want someone just like us! So we seek a soul mate. The shift feels so natural that it is easy to forget how much we looked up to the spouse we married in our 20s.

In later life, we somehow either give up finding the perfect soul mate or no longer have such an intense need for one. We feel whole in ourselves. If we are in a couple, the good feeling is more like "Here we are, two separate human beings who came together in love but who can now stand together, each being who we are, helping each other have the lives we want to have." Finally, and hopefully by the time one of the partners dies, the remaining person is ready to stand alone—connected perhaps to one's children, grandchildren, or other people in the community, but alone.

When a couple starts out knowing about these more or less predictable but changing relationship needs, they can weather many a storm. For example, if a couple can stay together past midlife, the period in which the soul-mate desire is strongest, sanity may prevail and a couple is more likely to make it through. "The declining divorce probabilities at each year of marriage would suggest that this is so" (Stevenson & Wolfers, (2007, p. 29).

FRIENDSHIP

Martha was a very bright, successful administrator in a government-run institute of science, and an unusually beautiful woman. According to one of her lifelong women friends, she could have had almost any man she wanted. When she was young she fell in love with Roy, a handsome neurosurgeon who was careful in the operating room, but a bit rough around the edges at home. Roy constantly put Martha down, but she could not resist him sexually. They married, had two children, moved to the suburbs, and had the big house, the fancy car, and the rewarding jobs, but they were unhappy together.

Martha gradually lost respect for Roy, disillusioned by his rudeness and the way he treated her, their children, and their friends. She left him when they were both around 40 and spent several years dating different men, settling for none. Finally she met Stuart, a neuroscientist with a kind, gentle disposition. She quickly bonded with Stuart and knew very soon that she wanted to marry him. She was the pursuer for the first time in her life. The relationship had a sexual component, but that was not what excited her. This man was someone she greatly admired for his character, his emotional intelligence, and the way he treated her, her family, and their friends. "I want to be with him because I hold him in such high regard—and because he treats me so well," she would say. "We enjoy each other's company and always have interesting things to talk about."

Martha was experiencing was what the ancient Greeks termed "agape," a nonromantic, nonsexual love that is primarily spiritual. Agape and sexual love can coexist, but whereas many marriages survive without sex after a time, without agape, respect, and admiration, they eventually die.

FINANCIAL SECURITY

The data are clear: Low income and poverty do not bode well for marriage (Bramler & Mosher, 2002; Larson & Holman, 1994; Ooms & Wilson, 2004). Of course, being well off does not necessarily guarantee marital happiness; we have all known or read about wealthy couples and their mega-million-dollar divorce settlements. Perhaps both ends of the financial spectrum pose problems. But poverty is guaranteed to put a severe strain on marriages, as does unexpected job loss. It is important for therapists to know that although couples and families will or have to pull together during the crisis, such as happened in the 1929 depression when the divorce arte actually dipped, marital collapse often occurs after the crisis has passed (Cherlin, 2009a, b).

I am not talking here about the differences partners have in their financial thinking and behavior. I am referring to the simple fact of what it takes to have a minimally comfortable life, to live above the poverty line. When counseling premarital couples, discussing these matters can save them a lot of heartache later. Therapists must help couples that are financially naïve understand that it matters to be able to afford rent, perhaps to buy a house or car, and to have enough of a cushion to know they can feed and support the children they want to have, and weather an unexpected job loss, economic downturn or medical crisis.

Danielle and Travis are a happy way to end this chapter.

> They met relatively late, when both were close to 40. Danielle was a single mother with two children, 7 and 3. Her former husband was paying child support, but when Danielle met Travis, the payments stopped coming regularly and Danielle had to go back and forth to court. She became highly anxious when she realized she was pregnant, but she and Travis were planning to marry anyway, and they wanted this baby so that Travis could have a child of his own.
>
> With a new baby and Danielle's two other young children, no extended family help, and no way to afford professional childcare, Danielle, with only 2 years of college and no real profession, could not find remunerative work. Travis, an unlicensed plumber who had many jobs with licensed contractors until the economic downturn of 2008, was now unable to find work at all. He finally took a minimum-wage job in a hardware store and began working "ridiculously long hours." Luckily, he and Danielle were resilient enough not to crumble under the pressure. They felt "lucky with each other," though they barely made ends meet. They had the foresight to understand that once all the children were in school, Danielle would be able to work, and life would get better. Few could have predicted that this couple would make it, but they beat the odds.

CHAPTER 8

Eight Premarital Stages

Anne F. Ziff

thou to me
Art all things under Heav'n, all places thou
        —John Milton, *Paradise Lost* (1667)

You may have noticed—and possibly wondered why—
we did not identify and discuss love as one of the individual
predictors of marital satisfaction in Chapter 6. That omission
was not accidental. We will look for and at love—its presence
and absences— in our exploration in this chapter, of eight
premarital stages. The eight stages described in this chapter
form a paradigm which, in our clinical work, has been see to
describe premarital movement and developments as clients
progress from single status to member of a married couple. We
recognize and acknowledge the already well-known individual,
couple, and family developmental stages of theorists including
Erikson, Kübler-Ross, Piaget, and Carter and McGoldrick.

Engagement—when one partner proposes marriage to the
other partner and he or she says yes—has typically been considered the "official" premarital stage, leading directly to the marriage. In our experience, however, there are several more stages

that precede the wedding ceremony, five of which come before a proposal of marriage and two that follow it. Successfully identifying and negotiating all eight premarital stages is useful for both clinicians and couples, although the order of stages is not static, and some couples may skip a stage altogether. For clinicians, these eight stages help identify and focus on the type of premarital counseling that will benefit each couple. Premarital couples, recognizing their own positions in the stages, are able to gain perspective on their progress and develop skills to handle the inevitable conflicts that can occur both before and after marriage.

Let us be very clear: We are not saying that premarital counseling will eliminate marital conflict. We are, however, suggesting that during the course of premarital counseling, clinicians present opportunities for the partners to know themselves individually, know each other, know the things that are most important for each of them, know how to disagree safely, and know how to compromise effectively. Premarital counseling also encourages couples to keep their sense of good humor alive—a crucial part of maintaining a healthy relationship and a valuable tool for minimizing the experiences of painful conflicts.

In this chapter, we identify the stages of premarital relationship that we have observed two people go through as they move from dating to marriage. For the sake of organization, we identify and discuss these stages in a particular order. However, in real life, the stages are more mobile and do not follow a rigid continuum. The eight premarital stages we see as typical are:

1. The search for a partner
2. Dating and learning
3. Delirious happiness
4. Putting the cart before the horse
5. Foundation-building

6. Engagement
7. Acceptance
8. Hope

In premarital counseling, therapists find it useful to identify the stage in which they meet a couple and then guide them accordingly. As some of the case studies in this chapter demonstrate, however, the two members of a couple may not actually be in the same stage at the same time. It is also possible that a stage will be skipped. It is the clinician's responsibility, upon meeting a premarital couple, to assess the stage of each member of the couple, as well as that of the couple itself, and then to proceed with the premarital counseling with this flexible continuum in mind.

STAGE #1: THE SEARCH FOR A PARTNER

These days, partners may meet each other through a wide variety of viable means, a sampling of which are listed here:

- Through work, school, or leisure activities (including cultural, religious, athletic, or political events)
- Via introductions by friends or family members
- On-line, serendipitously or intentionally, through social networking sites (Facebook, LinkedIn, Twitter, MySpace, et cetera), and connections to high school or college classmates
- Though in-person or online dating services (eHarmony. com, Match.com or J Date, among others) or special interest sites, or meet-and-greet events
- Through classes, conferences, retreats,
- Accidentally, such as meeting at a library, coffee shop, supermarket, restaurant, or book or department stores, as well as while waiting for a bus or subway or asking directions, or even co-ed roommates.

When two people meet (regardless of how that happens) while they may decide to date, some couples begin simply by hooking up (having sex) with no thoughts of also dating. They rarely show up in our offices for premarital counseling! If two people choose to begin to date and find out more about each other, mature love is still not a component of what's happening. They are participating in stage 1, in which we generally acknowledge *an absence of love.* Even so, both reports and memory remind us that stage 1 feels "really exciting" and, sometimes, "excruciatingly painful."

Despite an absence of love, this first stage does contain the exciting, possible beginning of friendship. Friendship is a critically important element in a relationship and is potentially a precursor to the growth of actual affection that develops into love.

For "young" people particularly (those under 35 or so) this first premarital stage, the search, includes looking not only for someone they find attractive but also for someone who is different from them (or from one or both of their parents). The search is (unconsciously) for a person who supplies characteristics the searching person lacks and likes. Completion is the goal, and romance (frequently identified with good sex) is an essential ingredient. Gretchen's search follows.

> *Gretchen was a 29-year-old nurse already in her second career. She had begun working as an elementary school teacher but decided she didn't really like that field. She moved on, attended nursing school, and easily found a labor and delivery job in a teaching hospital near her home. She was fun-loving and bright, and she explained in therapy that she hoped to marry but wanted to be sure her marriage would last "forever," as her parent's divorce had deeply surprised and hurt her. She also reported that she had had to parent her distraught elder sibling through that tough family transition period—an additional unwelcome burden, and one that this parentified child recognized as such.*
>
> *Through an introduction by a mutual friend, Gretchen met Brett,*

*a 35-year-old established, successful attorney, the eldest of three chil-
dren in an intact family. He was serious, bright, and responsible.
Gretchen found him sexy because he represented the security she had
been unconsciously searching for in the men she dated, and Brett
appreciated the long-missing sparkle Gretchen brought to his world.
These opposites attracted—and fared very well together.*

With older couples—loosely speaking, those 40 and older—
the search for opposites is replaced by a desire for acceptance,
emotional intimacy, and companionship, notably a shared set of
values. These "older" relationships are apt to include romance
but the predominant characteristic is their companionate nature
and willingness (plus ability, in many cases) to sustain emotional
intimacy. By this age and stage, members of the developing couple know themselves—their strengths and their deficits, likes
and dislikes, degrees of flexibility, and so on—and compromise
is not anathema to them. Acceptance (which we explore in stage
7) is a goal in older couples not an afterthought.

*Jill was a rabbi who worked with a progressive congregation in
Manhattan. Now 48, she had given up the search for a mate but
secretly still hoped to someday meet a man who could accept her accom-
plishments without feeling competitive. Her "sense of self" included
being a talented, attractive woman, bright, insightful, spiritual, and
with a growing reputation as a scholar. She was aware also, at some
deep level, of feeling lonely.*

*One Friday evening, David, a 50-year-old single man, walked
past her synagogue just before services were to begin. Exhausted from
his work week (he was a free-lance writer who had just met a book
deadline), and feeling generally depleted, he impulsively went in to
attend services.*

*He was, in his words, "blown away" by the spiritual, congenial ser-
vice, but in particular by the rabbi. She "didn't look like a rabbi" and
her voice "replenished" him, he described to me one day. Not even think-*

ing about propriety, he lingered to speak with her after the service, and they quickly discovered a surprising number of commonalities, including their deep spirituality, love of music, Torah, and the law, and the sense of wanting to continue to talk to each other. Jill had responsibilities to guests for Shabbat and the weekend, but agreed that David could email her and they'd figure out a plan to meet again.

I met Jill and David in premarital counseling, so you can surmise where this sense of congruence took them!

STAGE #2: DATING AND LEARNING

In general, during early dating it is likely that a chemistry of some sort (either complementary or congruent) develops shortly after the early meetings, and although sexual chemistry is still not love, it usually propels the relationship into dating and learning, stage 2.

Although it may not be conscious, when you're dating someone, you're learning both about yourself and the other. This is a very propitious time for being honest about who you *are*, including the sometimes concealed parts about being silly, stubborn, sensitive, quick to anger, and so on. This is the time when people discover new things about each other: Do they like movies? Sports? Athletics? Concerts? Do they usually fix meals at home or eat out? Do they prefer talking on the phone or texting? Do they plan ahead or at the last minute? Are they punctual or typically late? What, if any, is their religious affiliation, and how important is it to them? And the very important question: Are they equally ready and willing to be monogamus?

It is also the time when partners figure out how to deal with differences. If one is punctual and the other is typically late, how does that get worked out? What if disagreements arise? How are disputes and resolutions navigated?

One client mentioned that, for her, stage 2 was a time when it was easy to overlook how important friends are and forget to make time for them, too. In the excitement of a new romance, friends and family too often get put on hold or dropped, and yet, if the romance fails, they're the ones you turn to and count on to get you through the hard days or nights.

Clinically, we think about this in terms of loyalties. We recommend that while a relationship is being explored and developed, both parties in the couple are wise and well-served to actively retain loyalties to the friends and family members with whom they've been accustomed to doing things. Be guided by the childhood lyric: "Make new friends, but keep the old / One is silver and the other gold." If the dating eventually progresses to stage 6, engagement, it will be appropriate for partners to shift 'old' primary loyalties from family and friends to the spouse-to-be. (Boszormenyi-Nagi & Spark, 1984).

STAGE #3: DELIRIOUS HAPPINESS

When the heat is still on after some dating, a couple begins to form. In other words, people who have been dating successfully for three weeks or more begin to think of themselves as "an item" or "a couple." Friends and family begin making plans to meet with *two* people for coffee, dinner, and so on, and a sense of "we-ness" evolves as the dating continues and intensifies.

Blending chemistry, friendship, and a continuing interest in getting to know more about each other, the couple moves into stage 3, displaying infatuation, delirious happiness, and limerence (Tennov, 1999), conditions frequently confused with love. This third stage is exciting and welcome, and even though it is not love, it is possible that it will serve as a precursor to a developing love.

Some of the qualities in this stage of delirious happiness include a kind of euphoria, the certain sense that he or she is "the one," a germinating belief that there's nothing the two of you cannot do if you choose to, and the unassailable proof:

When you meet for dinner, you're both wearing light blue sweaters!

While in stage 3 each person feels constantly on top of the world, although their stomach is often in their throat and they sport a silly, "Cheshire cat" smile. Stage 3 recalls the lyrics from the musical *My Fair Lady:* "I have often walked down this street before / but the pavement always stayed beneath my feet before / All at once am I several stories high / Knowing I'm on the street where you live." These lyrics capture the essence of that delirious happiness people experience in stage 3!

STAGE #4: PUTTING THE CART BEFORE THE HORSE

The problem with stage 3 is that it is often so delicious to finally be this deliriously happy that people leap to the assumption that they have fallen in love and immediately (prematurely) decide to marry. That brings us to the crucially important stage 4: putting the cart before the horse. Stage 4 is the time when, without a sufficiently solid foundation, the weight of the "structure"—that is, the relationship—collapses painfully for both people in the couple.

This fourth stage is also the time in relationships when projections are apt to be out of control. Either or both members of the couple tend to be blinded by excitement—which they prematurely deem to be love.

Discussing the fate of romance over time in his book *Can Love Last?,* Steven Mitchell (2002) contended:

> Authentic romance is hard to find and even harder to maintain. It easily degrades into something else. . . . Romance thrives on novelty, mystery and danger; it is dispersed by familiarity. Enduring love is therefore a contradiction in terms. (p. 27)

Agreeing with Mitchell, we contend that relationships that are formalized as engagements at the point of stage 4 tend to be ungrounded. They frequently face the risk of collapse in later years if they are embarked upon as is. For any clinician counseling such premarital couples, it's useful to be aware that, in stage 4, there are difficult decisions for the clinician to face. When does a clinician blow the whistle on a couple, and when should he or she remain silent?

Difficult Decisions for the Therapist

Early in my work with premarital couples, I realized I was probably going to need to recommend that a couple I was counseling *not* proceed with their marriage as planned. The prospect of this was troubling. What if my perceptions and assessments were wrong? And so, instead of making any recommendation, I decided to proceed with the therapeutic techniques of curiosity (asking many, varied questions), a good therapeutic rapport, and a bit of therapeutic impotence. (I find the latter is very useful in situations where therapeutic interventions may not be particularly welcome.) Here's the case.

> *Sharon and Joel met at work, where they were employed briefly by the same publishing company. Sharon, 32, had a history of anxiety and no long-term boyfriends; she had a large extended Irish family and was very close with her parents and siblings. Her career history was of working hard, being well-regarded by supervisors and coworkers, and making just enough money to live independently of her parents with little left over. She had worked with me in individual therapy intermittently for 2 years, reducing her panic attacks and increasing her initially wobbly self-esteem. She returned to therapy when she began to notice the new guy at her office—or, more accurately, when he began to notice her.*

"I need to talk," she admitted in her phone call, asking to schedule a session. "I'm afraid of making bad choices with another man, and repeating my old pattern."

Abused early in her teens by an older man, Sharon had described her social life to me earlier: "Any man I've ever dated for long turns out to be a raging bastard. The last guy I dated changed jobs and seriously wanted me to give up my entire life to be with him, and move away from my whole family. Forget that!"

The "new guy," Joel, was 33. His first marriage had been annulled, and the facts about it were shadowy. He was a short-term consultant at her company; he'd repeatedly asked her for rides home while his car was in the shop the previous week. According to Sharon, he acted "pretty flirty" toward her, and she wasn't sure how to respond, although she liked the attention.

After a month or so of both therapy and the flirtation, Sharon became less standoffish and invited Joel over for dinner at her apartment on a Friday. They read poetry together, watched a movie, and generally had a very good time. She remained nervous, however, feeling that something she couldn't put her finger on was wrong. But she pushed past the fear, labeling it irrational, and not wanting to be held back by her anxieties at this point in her life.

Before long, Sharon realized that she and Joel had become "an item" and people at work were aware of their connection. She was concerned about that, but Joel refused to keep a low profile, taking some apparent delight in flaunting their camaraderie and admonishing her when she expressed worry.

Sharon was sexually inexperienced, and she certainly was willing for that to change, but she was also afraid of getting dumped after allowing that "ultimate intimacy" (her perception of being sexually active). Yet she was "wild" about Joel, and from all she could discern, he was equally smitten with her. In fact, after 3 months of dating, he suggested that he move into her apartment so they could save money and see how it felt to live together. He said that he'd leave his con-

sulting job at Sharon's company and take something full-time in a
nearby town if she would say yes.

Convinced that he planned to stick around, Sharon agreed and
Joel moved in. He did indeed get a new job, and very quickly left
their mutual employer to start it. He was working late most of the
time, and when Sharon came in to tell me the news, she was less than
happy about their arrangement.

Let's observe what happened for this couple in terms of premarital stages. Sharon, at least, had not been actively engaged
in stage 1. She had not been searching for a partner, although
she was quite willing to have one find her. Joel and Sharon
dated (stage 2) after knowing each other from the office for
about a month. Their dating had lasted approximately 2 more
months before Joel initiated the idea that they consider themselves sufficiently well-suited to move closer. Possibly experiencing stage 3, delirious happiness, Joel asked to move in with
Sharon. They appeared on the surface to have common interests (poetry, food, and movies) and she reported that they had
a lot of fun together. There remained for her, however, some
vague sense that all was not right.

Sharon was moved to feeling very amorous, and Joel was a
patient, kind, and gentle sexual partner with her. But was it
wise to venture into living together, based on these indicators
alone? That was probably premature, especially considering
the fact that it was neither thought through in Sharon's mind
nor mentioned in her therapy. Instead, Sharon impulsively
agreed to Joel's premise that it would be good if they began
to live together, and afterward she regretted the decision. Further, she stated in therapy that she was afraid to disagree with
Joel. "We never fight!" she told me. "I think that's great, you
know? But actually, I don't really know how . . ." She trailed off.

This put us squarely in stage 4, I believed—putting the cart before the horse. Was the foundation of this relationship going to be able to support the weight of the couple's realities?

Despite the questions in my mind and in my case notes, I thought it was premature for me to identify my concerns for their relationship. There was the possibility that they would be able to reach stage 5, foundation-building, where changes could take place slowly and successfully.

So I encouraged Sharon to invite Joel to join her for some premarital counseling. Given her remark about not knowing how to fight, I hoped to be able to teach them about fair fighting, including how to disagree safely and how to compromise effectively. Joel had something else in mind, however, and attended only two sessions. In the first one, he enthused about their relationship, attempting to let me see it as positively as he did. In the second session, Joel was primarily withdrawn and quiet, except when he spoke with hostility about people outside the cocoon of their couple.

> In my office, during their first couple session, Joel referred to Sharon as his "soul mate" and talked readily about the future he wanted them to have together. Sharon glowed about half of the time, and appeared wrapped in anguish the other half.
>
> Joel quickly had lost the new job he'd taken after moving in with Sharon, and she was now supporting them while he looked for something else. Even so, he talked about "tying the knot" very soon.
>
> In their second premarital session, Sharon described herself as feeling trapped all of a sudden. She felt she'd "been alone long enough" but had no confidence in where this relationship with Joel really was going. Joel's body language spoke for him: he sat with tightly crossed arms, legs crossed knee over knee, and a scowling demeanor. At the end of this session, he turned to Sharon and said, "No one else can understand what we feel. Let's just go!"
>
> Joel stopped coming to counseling before a third session took place. First he said he was sick, and then he said he had job interviews.

*I didn't like what I was watching, but I was still reluctant to rec-
ommend slowing or ending the relationship. Instead, I intentionally
expressed curiosity and posed provocative questions to Sharon in our
now individual premarital sessions.*

*"Do you feel you know enough about Joel to continue supporting
and living with him?" (She did not feel confident about this.)*

*"How will you find out the things you need to know?" (This
was an instance of curiosity combined with therapeutic impotence.)
Sharon wanted to know more about his annulled marriage but was
afraid to ask him about it.*

*Suddenly, before we were able to construct a plan, a crisis occurred.
Joel told her, all in one evening, that he wanted to marry her, and he
gave her an engagement ring. She suggested a date 2 years in the future,
and, hesitantly, he concurred. But then, before she could call her family,
he said that he thought she'd want to know that he was declaring bankruptcy. Some people at the job he'd just lost were accusing him of losing
a very important account and were threatening to sue him.*

*Sharon was initially heartsick. She agreed to keep his bankruptcy
intentions secret from her family, but when she called her parents with
the "good news" she sounded more glum than excited. No one said
much about that to her directly, but in retrospect she was sure that
anyone talking to her could tell something was amiss.*

*Sharon cancelled therapy sessions after these events, for an entire
month. When she finally came back in, she showed me her ring and
burst into tears even before she "brought me up to date" on what had
been happening. As therapist, there was very little for me to do except
listen, and wonder if her anger would ever surface. She must have
really heard herself as she related her story to me, because she stopped
speaking for a moment, and then looked directly at me.*

*"Don't say a word!" she admonished. "You don't need to. I'll tell
him tonight that he needs to move out by the weekend. I'm truly not
desperate, and I really am more afraid to live with him than to go
back to being alone. You know, I think I'm furious! Wow, is he gonna
be surprised."*

And tell him she did. This "near-tragedy" as she described it, gal-
vanized Sharon, and she moved on in her life very purposefully. Dur-
ing the next 6 months Sharon succeeded in making a career change
as well (from publishing to academia). A determined young woman,
she worked very hard to not look back and become ensnared in what
she labeled "coulda, woulda, shoulda" thinking. Sharon was suc-
ceeding the last time we met, and she described herself as "lucky."

We began by assessing this couple in terms of premarital stages. It is useful to conclude these observations in the
same context. The "deliriously happy" and then "cart before
the horse" premarital relationship that Sharon and Joel were
enmeshed in (stages 3 and 4) was never able to make it to Stage
5, Foundation Building, which we will explore next.

STAGE #5: FOUNDATION-BUILDING

When a couple passes through the excitement and thrills of
stage 3 without marrying prematurely, and then still takes it slow
as they move through stage 4, their relationship has a chance
to develop into a lasting one, even into love. The two people
in the couple are taking the time to know each other now. The
romantic fog—which is initially delicious but not something
solid to build a life upon—has cleared. They are seeing themselves and their significant other quite clearly. Imperfections
are shown and known, and the ensuing disappointments are
only that: disappointing. They are neither grounds for closing
one's eyes in denial nor for abandoning the relationship. These
partners have built the strong foundation of desirable qualities
(including good chemistry and a deepening friendship) that is
hoped for and and often needs to be worked toward in stage 5,
foundation-building.

When treating couples in this fifth stage, clinicians have the
opportunity to prepare them to manage the virtually inevi-

table collisions of loyalties between families of origin and the new significant other. This is a time of delicate balancing and re-education. New loyalties have been identified and are not always welcome outside the couple. For example, where does the couple go for Thanksgiving—to her parents' house or his? If the couple is unable to choose just one family and disappoint the other, a possible option is to invite both families and make the dinner in the couple's own space. Another alternative could be to attend two Thanksgivings, or even for one set of parents to invite their possible future in-laws to spend the holiday at their home. Or, as a debilitating last resort, for them to "do" Thanksgiving separately and meet later or the next day.

But the real question is of loyalty, not where the couple goes for Thanksgiving. The issue is again one of process rather than content. How the couple decides, and how they explain that decision to their parents is much more important than what the actual decision is.

After identifying their new loyalties, the couple also will want to protect some of the closeness and ties they've each had within their families of origin, particularly with parents and siblings. To avoid power struggles, in stage 5 we teach couples how to talk through issues together, make decisions, and then communicate their jointly made decisions with family members. For example:

> *Alison was adopted at birth and had one sister, also adopted. She met and began seriously dating Marvin, an only child, when they were both 27. Their loyalty problems were exacerbated by the fact that Marvin was Jewish and Alison was Episcopalian.*
>
> *The spring they decided to begin living together, Passover and Easter fell on the same weekend. To Alison it was clear that they'd be with her family and do the "whole Easter thing"—church, egg hunt, and dinner. Marvin was equally sure that they'd be with his family for both Seders; how could he disappoint them? He was their only child.*

And they liked Alison so much. He couldn't wait to introduce her to this festival and his family's ways of celebrating.

A month ahead of the holidays, they came to my office, already in stage 5, for some guidance on the subject. We very quickly recognized that this was a good opportunity to work out some of the loyalty questions that were going to come up again and again if this couple moved forward. We talked about how important it was for their first loyalty to be to each other as they were forming a serious, committed premarital couple.

In view of that, I encouraged them to explore what parts of the holidays were meaningful to each of them. Marvin knew he loved the Seder ritual and having the immediate family join close friends, making it a big, ritual dinner party. Alison said that she felt the same way about Easter dinner. "It's not the religious part that means something to me," she explained. "It's the habit. We do the same thing, year after year. I just don't want to have to miss it! And I want Marvin to be there, too, this year. It's so fun!"

"How could you each have what you most want?" I asked.

After a pause, Marvin suggested that he would forego second Seder to be with Alison at Easter dinner if she would agree to do the first Seder on Saturday evening with him and his family. Alison immediately agreed and said she'd even ask her mother to make dinner later than usual so they wouldn't have to rush around quite so much.

I pointed out that they had automatically done something very important: Alison was planning to negotiate with her own family, and Marvin was planning to negotiate with his.

It's important—imperative, really—to keep the lines of communication clear in the way that Marvin and Alison were planning to, with each talking to the appropriate members of their own families of origin. Although in this instance it seemed obvious for both Marvin and Alison, often it is less clear.

Vertical loyalties to previous generations are strong even when they are invisible (Boszormenyi-Nagy & Spark, 1984). In creating a new relationship, particularly a long-term one such as marriage, it's very important to teach couples to negotiate sensitively but with a clear and expressed expectation: that the first and most compelling loyalty must be to the couple, a horizontal loyalty. And each partner, having established that understanding with his or her own family of origin, becomes free to love and respect and enjoy that original family and its members.

STAGE #6: THE ENGAGEMENT

The sixth of our 8 stages is signaled by the actual decision to marry, or the engagement. This stage is often long (3 months to a year or more in duration) and is almost always complicated. It again tests the strength and depth of the couple's bond (as stage 5 did), plus the couple's flexibility, determination, and ability to communicate both easy and hard thoughts or feelings. The outcome either is a strengthened couple or a weakened one. We'll discuss the many specific events set in motion by an engagement later in this section. First, let's look at the moment of becoming engaged itself, an event that is dreamed of and anticipated as joyous but often is a source of significant anxiety.

When a couple is ready to become engaged, the male partner is frequently the one "in charge." Fair or not, it is still usually he who decides when and how to "pop the question" and whether or not it will be a (big or little) surprise.

Kristen, 37, was a writer and teacher who had been seeing me for individual therapy. She had been dating Billy, 36, since he tasted the oatmeal-cranberry cookies she'd baked for a picnic with mutual friends about 15 months ago. Never previously married, Kristen spent a lot of time wondering if Billy, who was divorced, would ask her to marry him. She feared that he wouldn't ever decide to take a second chance on marriage. Billy knew this. Although it wasn't a

constant topic of conversation, Kristen was stressed about his inten-
tions despite the fact that they had discussed having a future together.

One spring afternoon, Billy called Kristen at work and asked if
she could meet him on Main Street for coffee around 6:30. He had
some errands to run and shopping to do, and he wanted her to help.
"Sure," she said. "I think the stores are all open late tonight."

They met at a coffee shop, talked about their workdays, finished
their drinks, and were about to leave when Billy looked at Kristen
from across the table and said, "I want to ask you something before
we take off from here."

Billy's question? "If you'll marry me, what do you say we go across
the street right now and pick out an engagement ring?"

Kristen reported being "totally blown away, taken by surprise, flab-
bergasted, and beyond excited!" After she stopped crying and laugh-
ing, she said "yes!" and off they went. In fact, after they chose a ring,
they went back across the street and into a store where they picked out
invitations for the wedding, which they had decided would take place
in about 10 months.

Billy and Kristen's story is representative of couples who
enter their engagements without a whole lot of commotion
although to hear them talk about it, there was absolutely nothing missing. In contrast, let's look at another kind of engagement, remembering there are no "right" or "wrong" ways to
become engaged so long as what transpires works for both
members of the couple.

Mort was a 37-year-old venture capitalist whose particular area
of interest was commodities, and he traveled frequently for business.
Lynn, 36, was a designer in the garment industry. They had moved
separately to New York from Montreal and Nova Scotia, respectively,
met through family friends, and begun dating.

In April, after they'd been dating seriously and very happily for
about 6 months, Mort suggested that Lynn meet him at the end of

his next business trip on the West Coast, and they'd have a spa week-end in California. They were to be joined by Mort's sister and brother-in-law, who lived in Vancouver and could easily meet them for a west coast weekend.

In the week leading up to his trip, Mort had a list of phone calls to make: one to his parents, and then to Lynn's father and mother, followed by calls to various siblings. As he felt was appropriate, Mort told all the family members about his intention to propose, express-ing his hope that they would be pleased by the decision. He was very sweet and open in the discussions and even admitted that he hoped he wouldn't be turned down!

He was not turned down. Lynn flew in the day before their guests, and several hours before their company was due to arrive, Mort took her for an exhausting late afternoon hike; he had the engagement ring in his pocket. They came back, hot and tired, and at Mort's suggestion stopped for a bottle of water in the spa's upscale lounge. They then walked out to a secluded and romantic spot overlooking the Pacific, where he proposed.

Lynn accepted happily without hesitation, and as the sun set, a bottle of champagne appeared magically at their table. About 2 hours later, family arrived as expected, and the engagement was celebrated again.

Once a couple embarks upon the sixth premarital stage of engagement, phone calls to family members and friends seem (and are) necessary. At the same time, they can feel like an intrusion on the couple's own private space, and can certainly affect the couple's ability to make decisions on their own. A newly engaged couple may be asked immediately, "When's the wedding?" Which often is followed by "Where will it be?" and "What about your attendants? What kind of music? Photogra-pher? Flowers?" and even "Who's paying?" or "Have you con-sidered eloping?"

If parents haven't put money away in anticipation of the

wedding, they are apt to distance themselves from the excitement (" . . . and we're planning to marry in 5 months!") in order to start calculating the expenses they'll be faced with. A parental withdrawal to regroup often feels like disapproval to the couple rather than realistic parental concerns about finances.

There *are* practical decisions that have to be made relatively soon after a couple decides to marry, particularly if there is not much time between the engagement and the wedding. Further, for good or for bad, almost all family members tend to think they have the right to express their opinions on these subjects. In fact, that may not be their right at all.

Issues of loyalty, linked also to stage 5, often reappear right after the decision to become engaged and marry. (This is just one instance of permeable boundaries between stages, which was mentioned earlier.) The "power" of these issues is frequently mitigated by the degree of autonomy of the engaged couple. Autonomy, in turn, frequently relates to the ages and finances of the couple.

I worked briefly with Tricia, the mother of a bride-to-be. Her daughter and her daughter's boyfriend, both 25, had spent part of a weekend at her home and were preparing to go to an informal event at their alma mater before returning to their apartment. "She just looked sloppy, getting ready to go out," Tricia told me, "and I was worried. What if he proposes on campus? That would be so romantic, and really, it would be just like him to make this a surprise."

So, "just in case," Tricia offered her daughter the use of one of her favorite cashmere sweaters to wear for the day. Her daughter happily accepted!

Tricia's intuition was 100% correct. At around 5 that evening, she got a phone call from her daughter and the man who would become her son-in-law announcing that they were engaged. Everyone was delighted.

Tricia's first question in therapy? "Now that she became engaged wearing my sweater, how do I get it back?!"

My answer: It's not your sweater anymore!

Had these "kids" been 10 years older, Tricia's role would have been less involved, and her sweater, too.

Parents often think ahead about child-related expenses after education, and weddings head that list. With young engaged couples, the parents often want to retain control of the use of their money. And so we see them participating emphatically in decisions about clergy, guests, location, food, flowers, music, photographers, dresses and shoes, wedding showers, rehearsal dinners, and so on.

Decisions about who pays for what, and who has the right to make the final choices, are individual in every situation—no matter what etiquette books or anyone else has to say. We are certainly not going to attempt to adjudicate those grounds—not in this book, nor in our offices. What we do emphasize, however, is the importance of process, the couple's talking to each other about the decisions that have to be made and the consequences of making them alone versus with family members (or anyone else).

These conversations, all part of stage 6, will lead us slowly into stage 7, acceptance. As we prepare to go there, however, let's not overlook the fact that "older couples" also need to discuss all of these premarital issues and be clear individually and as a couple about what and how they are planning. Age works in their favor, generally speaking. They are likely to be more autonomous, to have savings of their own and to participate in paying for the wedding, or, in some cases, to entirely pay for it. Either way, cash gifts from parents are always welcome, but only if they come without strings attached.

Older couples with children from previous unions must additionally consider the children. Remember the story of Audrey and Jonathan from Chapter 4, in which Audrey's 8-year-old daughter declined their invitation to serve as a flower girl. This couple had to deal with the children's needs as well as their own as their marriage approached. Did someone think courtship was an easy time in a couple's life?

Whether the couple is young or old, composed of opposites attracting or companionate in nature, it is essential, in our opinion, that the partners talk openly and plan thoughtfully, and then, where appropriate, share their decisions with the family and friends closest to them. In many instances, having little if anything to do with age and stage, we see couples who want to create a prenuptial agreement. For others, the very word "prenup" is polarizing. Before we go any further, let's be sure we have a reasonable understanding of prenuptial agreements.

Prenuptial Agreements

With certain exceptions (which we will specify shortly) we believe that premarital couples benefit from creating a prenuptial agreement ("prenup") prior to their marriage, either with a mediator, or with a therapist trained in the process, or a matrimonial attorney. We have seen, throughout the previous chapters, examples of couples working on or wanting a prenup. The goal of the couple during the prenup process is typically to create a thoughtful document which gives both members of a couple the opportunity to identify what it is that they hope for from their marriage in explicit, sometimes financial, terms. Prenups at their best, according to matrimonial attorney Jacalyn Barnett of Manhattan, go beyond anticipation of separation or divorce. They include questions about what each person hopes for from this marriage, and what a couple might do if:

- the marriage ceased to live up to their standards
- Financial circumstances changed radically

- Health (mental or physical) of a spouse changed radically
- Retirement became a relevant issue (What happens if, for example, he suddenly wants to retire in Arizona and she has always planned on Manhattan?).

We know the adage: "You're only as good as your plan B." A prenup is your personal, premarital plan B; when you write one, be sure it's good enough!

Who does not need a prenup? Attorney Gary Oberst of Connecticut, in a 2009 paper not yet published, identified people in the following premarital categories as unlikely to need a prenup:

- Couples without children prior to this relationship
- Couples without significant assets
- Couples with no realistic likelihood of inheriting significant assets
- Couples in which partners are of very similar ages
- Couples whose parents clearly will never need financial support.

Devising a prenup, and working it through to become a satisfying document, gives couples an advantage, we contend, that is well worth the time, effort, and cost. It gives premarital couples very practical experience with identifying problems, perhaps disagreeing and negotiating, expressing concerns, and encouraging flexibility, a sense of good humor, determination, and communication skills. Finally, the product, the plan B, will be one of the ways in which you protect and strengthen your marriage.

As clinicians doing premarital work with couples, it's important for us to remain aware that this period of stage 6 developing into stage 7 holds the greatest risk for losing sight of the goal: marrying well. Further, without consciousness, the pressures can overwhelm both bride and groom and damage, if not

destroy, the foundation of their couple. It is our responsibility
as clinicians to help couples maintain and safeguard the prominence of their goal, to marry well.

STAGE #7: ACCEPTANCE

Members of premarital couples entering stage 7 are committed
to the understanding that neither they nor their spouse-to-be is
perfect, nor do they always agree on things. And, even so, they
are still worth loving and marrying. This seventh stage is the
period of *acceptance* that forms the foundation for an enduring
and safe marriage.

Although imperfections will continue to exist in a partner,
once acceptance is experienced, they are no longer proba-
ble deal-breakers for couples. Both partners recognize that
it is safe enough to be imperfect, and safe enough to marry
someone who is also imperfect. Again, the foundation of the
couple relationship is strong enough by stage 7 to recognize
imperfection in both partners and expect that the couple
will survive. The case of Roberta and Michael, which follows,
presents an interesting twist on acceptance for clinicians to
ponder.

> Roberta, a fourth-year medical student, had just become engaged
> to Michael, an attorney. They had dated long-distance, spending
> most weekends together, and Skyping during the week, for nearly a
> year after meeting through friends at an engagement party in New
> York, where Roberta lived. Michael lived and worked in Portland,
> Maine, where they hoped to live together once Roberta graduated.
> They had flowed through the first 6 premarital stages with only one
> real glitch, and that's what brought Roberta to my office, alone, for a
> first premarital session.
>
> "I've thought a lot about what's worrying me," she began. "Michael
> and I are so very different in our backgrounds and families. . . . The

only thing we really have in common is how we've struggled to get where we are . . . and how much family matters, 'cause we each had so little family growing up.

"But he's such a wonderful guy! And I do love him, even though, sometimes . . . when he drinks a lot, that is . . . he scares me. His parents were both alcoholics."

As a therapist, listening to this, it was hard for me not to jump to a conclusion: Get out of this relationship! But I said nothing and listened as Roberta continued her monologue.

"He got scholarships to boarding school and then Princeton, and studied law at Yale, after that. Nothing gets in his way. I really respect that in him."

Curious about Roberta's education as well, I asked about it.

She responded through a sort of wry grin, saying, "My mother had a way with men; she really knew how to play them and get what she wanted. Except love, I guess." She sounded very sad, but quickly went on. "She'd remarry when a guy left her. She needed the money; I recognize that now. My two brothers and I all had different fathers, you see. I'm the eldest. I really wanted to go to college, and my grades were terrific. My little brother's dad got sick, and he said that if I'd go to medical school, he'd make it possible for me.

"That's exactly where I wanted to be, so we had a deal. And I came to New York because I got accepted at a college here.

"You know, I don't have a lot of time to party, or drink, or stuff like that. I hate it when Michael thinks he needs to go on a binge to unwind, even though it's mostly with his guy friends, not with me." She looked pensive.

I was curious to meet Michael and hear what he had to say about the issue of his drinking and its role in their relationship, so I asked Roberta to invite him to our next session. He was, to my surprise, very happy to come.

"I love Roberta," he told me after sitting down and being silent for a minute or two. I hate that anything I do worries her."

"Do you hate it enough to stop binge drinking?" Roberta jumped in.

Silence.

"I don't want to make a promise to you that I'm not sure I can keep," Michael said. I think both Roberta and I recognized instantly that another man in Michael's place might have made a facile promise to assuage his fiancée's worries. Michael had told her the truth.

And this brought the couple, rather quickly, I worried, to a moment of truth: Could Roberta accept, and choose to stay with Michael, knowing that he could not promise to stop his periodic binge drinking? Would that be healthy for her, and for the two of them as a couple? I wondered. Nothing else of major importance was discussed during the rest of the session, but they asked to schedule a premarital session again, as a couple, in 2 weeks.

At that time, Michael and Roberta arrived with a contract they had negotiated together since our last meeting. Because Michael was an attorney, they had begun to create a prenup by themselves to help them through this "difficult patch," as they called it. The document included agreements on many things that were likely to help them accept themselves and each other. They had rules to guide them about working late—for instance what to expect when one of them had to work late (a phone call), how often was too often (3 nights a week was the limit), and how to respond if one or the other overstepped these rules (see a therapist). They reported having begun to address the issue of Michael's binge drinking, but as of their most recent session, had not created any mutually satisfactory conclusive guidelines.

STAGE #8: HOPE

This brings us to the final premarital stage, *hope.* In the Greek myth of Pandora's box, Hope appeared last, demonstrating that despite our troubles, humans always have Hope to remind us of better times to come. In premarital counseling, we see many thorny problems arise between the engagement and the wedding. We name the eighth stage *Hope,* the quality that reminds couples of the good future they envision as they marry. Hope is based on both members of the couple having truly come to know themselves and each other. Hope is founded on a satisfying foundation of personal and relational trust and attachments, and the couple's expectation of a bright future. Hope is accompanied by, and exemplified by, the vows in the marriage ceremony. When our premaritally counseled couples reach the eighth premarital stage, they are appropriately hopeful. They are able to approach marrying as a celebration of their love, demonstrating a sense of trust in their ability, together, to face the inevitably difficult moments life will present them with, and to grow.

It is possible and likely at this point that couples have a sex life they consider excellent, but sex is not the only thing they cherish about being together. Couples who have walked through all eight premarital stages and reached the moment of marrying have a great deal to rejoice in. They love that they are able to disagree without fear of being wiped out or rejected. They love being able to laugh together and to have private moments of intense understanding. They love thinking about the future, of their feelings about becoming parents, about where they want to live and the work they want to do. These couples are able to write their vows tenderly, because they know who they are, have learned who the other is, and are accepting of what they know. Despite the possible disruptions of musicians, florists, photographers, and other last minute "catastrophes" on the way to the wedding, these premaritally counseled couples have well-grounded confidence that they are marrying well.

CHAPTER 9

Summary and a Not-So-Modest Proposal

Elena Lesser Bruun

If my ups and downs, our ups and downs in our marriage can help young couples . . . realize that good marriages take work . . . The image of a flawless relationship is the last thing that we want to project. It's unfair to the institution of marriage, and it's unfair for young people who are trying to build something, to project this perfection that doesn't exist.

Michelle Obama, *New York Times Magazine*

Writing this book has allowed us to explore aspects of marriage and premarital education in more depth than we had ever thought possible. In this final chapter we want to summarize what we found, concede that although we wish we knew what the future holds for marriage, the verdict is still out, and share with the reader the direction we hope the institution of marriage and premarital counceling will take in the future. We begin with a brief, chapter by chapter review of our thoughts on the subject of marriage and marrying well.

Chapter 1 served as a general guide to the book, which has

been written primarily to provide clinicians with the background, theory, tools and enthusiasm for the subject of premarital counseling. We outlined the book itself, delved into an
illustrative case study, and introduced the authors.

Chapter 2 discussed the various forms of marriage that have
appeared over the course of history (and "her-story"), argued
that these forms still exist in one guise or another today, and
that the 20th-century "invention" of love as the primary basis
for entering marriage is the one new thing that happened.
The institution of marriage has seen much change over centuries and will undoubtedly continue to oscillate back and forth.
Along with the love-based form, for example, we are seeing less
marriage again. We also have more cohabitation, single parenting by choice, plenty of marital dissolution and remarriage—
serial marriage—among those who do marry. Although none
of these current factors are new, many scholars worry that they
signal a shakiness of the foundations, and foresee an overall
decline, in the institution of marriage as the basis for family life
(Popenoe, 2007).

In Chapter 3 we saw that premarital education and therapy
took off in an effort to help couples manage their relationships
in this new love-based form and avoid their becoming casualty
statistics. These kinds of interventions appear to help most couples who have access to them. The research on effectiveness
is active and ongoing in terms of verifying what works, how,
and with whom, and we now have a good idea of what predicts
divorce, if not exactly how to prevent it. Neither premarital
programs nor couple therapy has been accessible to all, or to
many who need it most, and the research has not fully tested
the benefits of these interventions on the heretofore largely
omitted groups.

Chapter 4 discussed our clients. We covered who they are
and why they come to us for premarital counseling. Beginning
with some specific intake techniques, we went on to weave 5

case studies with theory in this chapter. In the final section, "Where do premarital clients come from?" we interspersed some practical practice marketing tips with answers to that question.

In Chapter 5, we delineated the set of issues premarital couples most frequently bring to counseling, as well as a few that therapists may perceive. Premarital couples often have a good idea of what they need to work on, and their concerns overlap considerably with what the research suggests will help them have a good chance of marital satisfaction. The clinician's role is to help them acquire skills and the right spirit to handle marital conflict, and to discover and implement their own skills to find creative solutions.

In Chapter 6, we introduced ten of the individual qualities that serve as predictors of marital satisfaction. These focus on the readiness of a partner to join another closely, permanently, to marry well. The key individual predictors included a sense of good humor, determination, flexibility, and loyalty. In addition, we described a method for "fair fighting," which we see as a necessary component of a safe and satisfying marriage.

In Chapter 7 we identified a set of couple predictors of marital satisfaction and stability. Almost all appear piecemeal elsewhere in the literature. Gathering them here, we are confident that the list is comprehensive enough to give clinicians a good idea of what to look for as they hear premarital couples tell their stories. If in the initial evaluation, the clinician can say, "This couple would probably say 'yes' to most items on the list," they are off to a great start. To review, the predictors are parents having married well; openness; belief in the other's goodwill; older time of marriage and higher education levels; similar background or appreciation of differences; similar goals, values, and lifestyle; prioritizing the relationship; absence of addiction; emotional compatibility; extended family and friendship support, ability to manage conflict; having balance of individual and couple needs; sexual intimacy; common interests; humor and creativity; balancing power and willingness to be influenced; emotional connection; division of labor; couple-esteem; knowledge of couple life stages and changing needs; friendship; financial security. That is a hefty list, but one couple we saw checked 19 of the 21!

In Chapter 8, we identified eight premarital stages that occur during coupling. They range from the search for a partner to hope and the wedding celebration. As clinicians, we educate the individuals in our premarital couples to know themselves, each other, the things that matter to each of them, how to safely disagree, and how to compromise effectively and to negotiate. "It's always something," as Gilda Radner of *Saturday Night Live* was famous for saying, and you can count on having discomfort in the midst of joy. We encourage partners to keep alive their sense of good humor, a sometimes daunting challenge. But with it, we can help our couples maintain perspective, so that the catastrophes around music, flowers, weather, etc. never dominate their goal: to marry well.

PREVENTIVE EDUCATION

Throughout the book, we have recognized that preventive education and therapy should consciously include discussion and exercises that allow full consideration of and support for backing away from a possible mate if and when that applies. The question of suitability and the issue of mate selection are not in the forefront of either researchers' or clinicians' minds these days, but perhaps they deserve to be given more consideration again. The most appropriate place for preparing young people for this would probably come *before* a mate has been selected, say in a high-school senior or college freshman course, probably as part of a course that addresses "how to have a happy life" or "what neuroscience teaches us about relationships" or "aspects of emotional intelligence" (Goleman, 2005).

A NOT-SO-MODEST PROPOSAL

Margaret Mead, speaking in the 1960s, believed that our society had it backwards—that it should be hard to get a marriage license and easy to get a divorce. Our vision—our not-so-modest proposal—starts there. Imagine this: a society in which people are not encouraged and do not expect to marry until they want to have children or until they know for certain that they do not. A society in which during young adulthood, everyone is single and there are no prohibitions regarding consensual sexual behavior. When ready to have a child, any couple—or any small group of people—could "marry," i.e. form a pact to last at least until the child is grown. The form or structure of marriage would not matter; what would be important would be the content and dynamics of the marriage, how people within it treat each other. Respect for one's mate(s) and responsibility for one's own behavior and for keeping the relationship intact would be the key forces binding partners, not love, though romantic love would never be prohibited! The marriage partnership would be legal and government-regulated, with the counseling, therapeutic and religious community providing extensive marriage preparation.

All prospective partners would be screened for red-flag problems such as addiction, violence, previous legal offenses, and so on. Most would take an in-depth, individualized premarital education and parentling course, and all would need to demonstrate a minimum level of couple competence, i.e., emotional intelligence, conflict resolution skills, parental coping skill, and economic wherewithal before a license to marry—have children—would be issued.

The minimum age for a marriage license would be about

25, and due to planetary overpopulation and strain on environmental resources, no family would have more than one biological child. Adoption would be strongly encouraged for the couples who want larger families. Each family would decide its own form of internal government and agree on a set of rules to govern daily life, including rules regarding intra- and extramarital relationships and the role of extended family, including grandparents. The legal marriage would expire when the youngest child reached 21, but could be renewed. Divorce would be discouraged, but easy to obtain in certain situations, and it would happen less often because of the automatic expiration of the marriage license.

In reality, since the 1960s we have had fewer people choosing to marry (Ooms & Wilson, 2004 p.441). According to Cherlin (2009b), "to some observers . . . marriage seemed to be fading away. It had become an optional life style" (p. 114). This proposal would undoubtedly result in fewer marriages still. But it would make the marriages that did take place stronger, and make the children happier. Marriage would become a greater sign of maturity, achievement, an earned status and a privilege rather than an automatic right.

We expect this proposal will strike some readers as absurd, unrealistic, or overregulated. But the point is not to argue its relative merits or plausibility so much as it is to propose a new blueprint for clinicians and others to react to, something that at least has heuristic value. Even in this collaboration, the two authors did not agree on all points articulated in the proposal! We also hasten to add that the marriage model we have now is not particularly well-suited to contemporary life and the possibilities for improvement are greater than most of us have dared to imagine. We can, in fact, consciously design a system that will work better than what is currently in effect. We challenge the reader to come up with other or better ideas.

We have come a long way from the days in which couples

were on their own, left to sink or swim. We know far more about what predicts dissolution and what a good marriage consists of, and there are many options to assist couples not only in keeping their marriage together, but also in making their relationship a satisfying, even life-enhancing adventure. We know that preventive work can help premarital couples beforehand and that therapy can help should problems arise after the fact. It seems that a common factors or integrated approach has already infused the practice of couple therapy, and integrated approaches drawing on knowledge gained from couple therapy have informed most preventive programs as well. All mental health practitioners should take account of this reality and begin to view the development of this two- or three-tiered system as a boon for couples and for marriage.

The issues going forward have to do with refinements—continuing the efficacy and effectiveness research on premarital therapy, assessment instruments, and prevention programs and including in this research more appropriately diverse samples; making continuous improvements in the programs and therapies we have; educating more mental health practitioners and marriage educators in "best practices" (Halford, Markman, Kline, Stanley, 2003); extending marriage-education benefits to more couples; tailoring approaches to meet different needs and changing couple needs over the life span; addressing the issue of the one third of clients who do not improve even with help, and the issue of relapse; and finally answering the question of how involved the government should be in promoting or regulating marriage and in what ways.

Premarital courses have simply been too timid and need beefing up. Issues surrounding sex, violence, infidelity, and the tension between the competing needs for a stable primary attachment and for the freedom and variety that change offers need to be freely discussed, as does the obligation for couples to keep growing both individually and together, with a larger

vision beyond themselves. Instilling the notion of social responsibility of married couples is important, and we are heartened
to see marrying couples who are well off refuse gifts and ask for
contributions to their chosen charities instead.

Additionally, clinicians must be open-minded, embracing
different forms and ways of being married. The question is not
what the preconceived way to be married or coupled is, but
what ways the evidence suggests works. There will be more than
one good way to be together. The proof is in the pudding, and
clinicians should be guided by what they see, not by what they
think they know.

A word about politics in our profession before we close this
final chapter: The more conservative among us sometimes
seem most concerned about stability and preserving the institution; the more liberal seem more concerned with preserving
the satisfaction and quality of relationships, regardless of their
duration or form. We position ourselves right in the middle,
concerned about both. In fact, we see the dichotomy as false
and believe that most mental health professionals would agree.
We don't know any therapists who like the idea of divorce or
who think that couples should not work hard at their marriage.
But we also don't know any therapists who think that it is anything other than unrealistic, futile, or possibly dangerous to
inordinately pressure a miserable couple into staying together.
Going forward, let us stop thinking we are divided on these
issues when we are actually on the same page.

Further, when it comes to marriages with children, most clinicians would want an unhappy couple to try harder to improve
their relationship and stay together. Ideally, we would like every
child to have happily married parents staying together out of
choice, not obligation. But at the same time we do not find
single-parent families per se to be the problem. A child starting
out with a solid single parent who has other family, friendship,
or community support will do very well indeed, as might a child

reared in a well-functioning polygamous family. We posit that it is not the form that is necessarily problematic for children, but the insecurity and loss endured when any kind of family breaks up, compounded if either the parents are rancorous, or if either parent disappears or fades from a child's life.

"Is there hope for the American marriage?" Popenoe (2007) and Flanagan (2009) ask. We agree with Karasu (2007) who concludes that although we no longer need marriage for economic security, to produce children, or to establish parental or inheritance rights, marriage will survive because we do need it for a sense of security, continuity, and belonging.

We began *Marrying Well* with the expressed hope that more clinicians, having read this book, would develop or increase their interest in working with couples in premarital counseling and education. The premarital period is possibly the most teachable time in a couple's life and a very exciting opportunity for all involved. We believe that premarital practice, which is fast becoming a new clinical subspecialty, can help all couples have marriages that while still imperfect, are more supportive, nurturing, rewarding, encouraging of growth, and enduring than in the past.

References

Ahuru, P. (1914). The Magic Book. In E. M . Tappan (Ed.), *The world's story: A history of the world in story, song and art, Vol III. Egypt, Africa And Arabia.* trans W K. Flinders Petrie.

Amato, P.R. & Booth, A. (1997). *A generation at risk: growing up in an era of family upheaval.* Cambridge, MA: Harvard University Press.

American Association for Marriage and Family Therapy. (2001). *User's guide to the AMFT Code of Ethics.* Washington, D.C: Author.

Armstrong, K. (2001). *Buddha.* New York: Penguin Books.

Assagioli, R. (1974). *The act of will.* New York: Penguin.

———. (1965).*Psychosynthesis.* New York: Viking Press

Bennett, J. (2009, July 29). Only you, and you and you. *Newsweek.*

Biale, R. (1995). *Women and Jewish law: The essential texts, their history, and their relevance for today.* New York: Schocken.

Blackstone, Sir W. (2005). *The commentaries of Sir William Blackstone on the laws and constitution of England.* London: Elibron Classics. (Original work published 1796)

Bodenmann, G. (2005). Dyadic coping and its significance for marital functioning. In T. Revenson, K. Kayser, G. Bodenmann (Eds.), *Couples coping with stress: emerging perspectives on dyadic coping.* Washington, DC: American Psychological Association.

———. (1997). Dyadic coping: systemic-transactional view of stress and coping among couples: Theory and empirical findings. *European Review of Applied Psychology. 47,* 137–140.

Boodman, S.G. (2006, February 28). Rules of engagement: before saying 'I do,' many couple are seeking help in resolving inevitable conflicts—to better their odds against divorce. *Washington Post.*

Boszormenyi-Nagy, I. & Spark, G. (1984). *Invisible loyalties: Reciprocity in intergenerational family therapy.* New York: Brunner/Mazel.

Boszormenyi-Nagy, I., & Ulrich, D. N. (1981). Contextual family therapy. In A. S. Gurman & D. P. Kniskern (Eds.), *Handbook of family therapy* (pp. 159–160). New York: Brunner/Mazel.

Bowen, M. (1978/1994). *Family therapy and clinical practice.* Lanham, Maryland: Jason Aronson.

Bramler, M.D. & Mosher, W.D. (2002). Cohabitation, marriage divorce and remarriage in the United States . *Vital Health Statistics,* 23(2). Washington, D.C.: National Center for Health Statistics.

Busby, HolmanRef, & Taiguchi, (2001). RELATE: Relationship evaluation of the individual, family, cultural and couple contexts. *Family Relations, 54,* 254–264.

Carroll, J.S., & Doherty, W.J. (2003). Evaluating the effectiveness of premarital prevention program: A meta-analytic review of outcome research. *Family Relations, 52*(2), 105–118.

Carter, B., & McGoldrick, M. (2005). *Expanded family life cycle: Individual, family and social perspectives, 3rd edition.* Boston, Massachusetts: Allyn and Bacon.

Chesler, P. (1972). *Women and madness: When is a woman mad and who is it who decides?* New York: Doubleday.

Cherlin, A.J. (2009a, May 29). Married with bankruptcy. (Op Ed.) *New York Times,* A25.

———. (2009b). *The Marriage-go-round.* New York: Alfred Knopf

Chesler, P. (1972/2005). *Women and madness.* New York: MacMillian

Christensen, A., Atkins, D. C., Berns, S., Wheeler, J., Baucom, D. H., & Simpson, L. E. (2004). Traditional versus integrative behavioral couple therapy for significantly and chronically distressed married couples. *Journal of Consulting and Clinical Psychology, 72,* 176–191.

Christensen A., Atkins, D.C., Yi, J., Baucom, D.H., & George, W.H. (2006). Couple and individual adjustment for 2 years following a randomized clinical trial comparing traditional versus integrative behavioral couple therapy. *Journal of consulting and clinical psychology, 74*(6), 1180–1191.

Cole, C.L. & Broussard J. (2006) Divorce in the U.S. *Family Therapy Magazine*

Coonz, S. (2005). *Marriage, A history.* Penguin Group: New York

———. (2000). *The way we never were.* New York: Basic Books

Cordova, J., Jacobson, N., & Christiansen, A. (1998). Acceptance versus change interventions in behavioral couple therapy: Impact on couple in session communication. *Journal of Marital and Family Therapy, 24,* 437–455.

de Shazer, S., Dolan, Y.,Korman, H., Trepper, T.S., McCollum, E.E. & Berg, I.K.(date). *More than miracles: The state of the art in solution focused brief therapy.* New York: Haworth Press.

Department of Health and Human Services (n.d.). *Healthy marriage initiative: Building real solutions for real people.* Washington, D.C.: Author.

Doherty, W.J.& Anderson, J.R. (2004). Community marriage initiatives. *Family Relations, 53*(5), 425–433.

Dunne, H. P. (1991). *One question that can save your marriage.* New York: Perigee Books, The Putman Publishing Group.

Erikson, E.H. (1980). *Identity and the Life Cycle.* New York: Norton.

Ezzeldine, M. L. (2006). *Before the wedding: Questions for Muslims to ask before getting married.* Irvine, CA: Izza Publishing.

Flanagan, C. (2009, July 2). Is there hope for the American marriage? *Time.*

Friedman, T. (2008). *Hot Flat And Crowded: Why We Need A Green Revolution And How It Can Renew America.* New York: Farrar, Straus & Giroux.

Friedan, B. (1963/2001). *The feminine mystique.* New York: Norton.

Gates, G. (2006, October). *Same-sex couples and the gay, lesbian, bisexual population: New estimates from the American Community Survey.* Los Angeles, The Williams Institute—UCLA School of Law.

Gielen, U. P., Draguns, J.G. & Fish, J.M. (2008). Principles of multicultural counseling and therapy: An Introduction. In U.P. Gielen, Draguns, J.G. & Fish, J.M. (eds). *Principles of multicultural counseling and therapy.* New York: Routledge.

Gilmore, C. P. (1892/1997. *The yellow wallpaper.* Mineola, New York: Dover Publications.

Goleman, D.P. (2005). *Emotional intelligence: Why it can matter more than IQ.* New York: Bantam Books.

Goodnough, A. (2009, April 8) Gay rights groups celebrate victories in marriage push. *New York Times.*

Gottman, J.M. (2008). On marriage. In J.Buckingham (ed). *What's next?* New York: Harper.

———. (1999). *The marriage clinic: A scientifically based marital therapy.* New York: Norton.

Gottman, J., Coan, J., Carrere, S., & Swanson, C. (1998). Predicting marital happiness and stability from newlywed interactions. *Journal of Marriage and the Family, 60*(2), 5–23.

Gottman, J.M. & Gottman J.S. (2006). *Ten lessons to transform your marriage.* New York: Three Rivers Press.

———. (1999). The marriage survival kit: A research-based marital therapy. In R. Berger & M. T. Hannah (Eds.). *Preventative approaches in couples therapy* (pp. 304–330). Philadelphia: Brunner/Mazel.

Gottman, J.M., & Levenson, R.W. (1992). Marital processes predictive of later dissolution: behavior, physiology and health. *Journal of Personality and Social Psychology, 63,* 221–233.

Gottman, J. M., & Notarius, C.I. (2002). Marital research in the 20th century and a research agenda for the 21st century. *Family Process, 41*(2), 159–197.

Gottman, J. M., & Silver, N. (2009). *The seven principles for making marriage work: A practical guide from the country's foremost relationship expert.* New York: Crown.

Gray, J. (1992). *Men are from mars, women from Venus.* New York: Harper Collins.

Guerin, P., Fay, F., Burden, S., & Kautto, J. (1987). *The evaluation and treatment of marital conflict: A four-stage approach.* New York: Basic.

Guerney, B. G. Jr, (1977). *Relationship enhancement: Skill training programs for therapy, problem prevention and enrichment.* San Francisco, CA: Jossey Bass.

Guttentag, M. & Secord, P.F. (1983). *Too many women? The sex ratio question.* California: Sage Publications, Inc.

Halford, W.K. (2004). The future of couple relationships education: Suggestions on how to make a difference. *Family Relations, 53*(5), 559–566.

Halford, W.K., Markman, H.J. Kline, G.H. & Stanley, S.M. (2003). Best practices in relationship education. *Journal of Marital and Family Therapy, 29*(3) 385–406.

Halford, W.K., Markman, H.J., & Stanley, S. (2008). Strengthening couples' relationships with education: Social policy and public health perspectives. *Journal of Family Psychology, 22*(3), 497–505.

———. (2003). Best Practice in Couple relationship education. *Journal of Marital and Family Therapy, 29*(3) 385–406.

Halford, W.K., O'Donnell, C., Lizzio, A. & Wilson, K.L. (2006). Do couples at high risk of relationship problems attend premarriage education? *Journal of Family Psychology, 20*(1), 160–163.

Halsall, P. (ed) (n.d.). Internet History Sourcebook Project. Retrieved August 2009 from *www.fordham.edu./halsall/ancineyt/ mesopitania-contracts-html.*

Hartman, M. S. (2004). *The household and the making of history.*

Hawkins,A.J., Blanchard, V.L., Baldwin, S.A., & Fawcett, E.B. (2008). Does marriage and relationship education work? A meta-analytic study. *Journal of Counseling and Clinical Psychology, 76*,723–734.

Hendrix, H. & Hunt, H.L. (2008). *Getting the love you want.* New York: Henry Holt and Company

————. (1999) Imago relationship therapy: Creating a conscious marriage or relationship. pp. 169–195. In R. Berger & M T. Hannah (eds), *Preventive approaches in couples therapy.* Philadelphia, Pennsylvania: Brunner/Mazel

Hendrix, H., Hunt, H.L., Hannah, M.T. & Luquet, W. (eds) 2005). *IMAGO relationship therapy: Perspectives on theory.* San Francisco, California: Jossey-Bass.

Holman, T.B. (2001). *Premarital prediction of marital quality or breakup: Research, theory and practice.* New York: Kluwer Academic/Plenum Publishers.

Holman, T. B., & Li, B. D. (1997). Premarital factors influencing perceived readiness for marriage. *Journal of Family Issues, 18*(2), 124–144.

Humphry, M. (1897/1993a). *Manners for men.* London, England: Pryor Publications

————, (1897/1993b). *Manners for women.* London, England: Pyror Publications

Hunt, R., Hof, L., & DeMaria, R. (1998). *Marriage enrichment: Preparation, mentoring and outreach.* Philadelphia, Pennsylvania: Brunner/ Mazel.

Imber-Black, E. (2009, May 8) Presentation at NYAMFT meeting at Ackerman Institute for the Family. New York.

————. (1999). *The secret life of families: Making decisions about secrets: When keeping secrets can harm you, when keeping secrets can heal you— And how to know the difference.* New York: Bantam.

Jacobson, N.S., & Christensen, A. (1996). *Integrative behavior couple therapy.* New York: Norton

Jacobson N.S., Follette W.C., & Pagel, M. (1986). Predicting who will benefit from behavioral marital therapy. *Journal of Consulting Clinical Psychology, 54,* 518–522.

Jacobson, N. S., & Margolin, G. (1979). *Marital therapy: Strategies based on social learning and behavior exchange principles.* New York: Brunner/Mazel.

Jakubowski, S.F., Milne, E.P., Brunner, H., & Miller, R.B. (2004). A review of empirically supported marital enrichment programs. *Family Relations, 53*(5), 528–537.

Johnson, S. (2008). *Hold me tight: Seven conversations for a lifetime of love.* New York: Little Brown & Co.

———. (2004). *The practice of emotionally focused couple therapy.* New York: Brunner-Routledge.

———. (2003). The revolution in couples therapy: a practitioner-scientist perspective. *Journal of Marital and Family Therapy,* 29 (3), 365–384

———. (2002). *Emotionally focused couple therapy with trauma survivors.* New York: Guilford Press.

Johnson, S., & Lebow, J. (2000). The "coming of age" of couple therapy. *Journal of Marital and Family Therapy, 26*(1), 23–38.

Johnson, S. M., Hunsley, J., Greenberg, L., & Shindler, D. (1999). Emotionally focused couples therapy: Status and challenges. *Clinical Psychology, 6,* 67–79.

Kantor, J. (2009, October 26) The Obamas'marriage. *New York Times Magazine.*

Karasu, S. R. (2007). The institution of marriage: Terminable or interminable? *American Journal of Psychotherapy, 61*(1), 1–16.

Katbamna, M. (2009, October 27). 'Half a good man is better than none at all.' *The Guardian.*

Kerr, E. & Bowen, (1988). *Family evaluation: An approach based on Bowen theory.* New York: Norton.

Krakauer, J. (2004). *Under the banner of heaven.* New York: Anchor Books .

Kübler-Ross, E. (1969). *On death and dying.* New York: Scribner & Co.

Lamb, M. E. (1997). *The role of the father in child development.* (3rd ed.). New York: Wiley.

Larson, J.H. & Homan, T.B. (1994). Premarital predictors of marital quality and stability. *Family Relations, 43*(2), 228–237.

Larson, J.H., Newell, K., Topham, G. & Nichols, S. (2002). A review of three comprehensive premarital assessment questionnaires. *Journal of Marital and Family Therapy, 28*(2), 233–239.

Larson, J.H., Vatter, R.S., Galbraith, R.C., Holman, T.B. & Stahman, R.F. (2007). The Relationship evaluation (RELATE) with therapist-assisted interpretation: Short-term effects on premarital relationships. *Journal of Marriage and the Family, 33*(3), 364–374.

Lawrence, D.H. (1928/2005). *Lady Chatterley's lover.* New York: Barnes and Noble.

Licata, N. (2002). Should premarital counseling be mandatory as a requisite to obtaining a marriage license? *Family Court Review, 40* (4), 518–532.

Markey, B., Micheletto, M., & Becker, A. (1985). *Facilitating open couple communication, understanding and study (FOCUS).* Omaha: Nebraska: Archdiocese of Omaha.

Markman, S., Stanley, S.M., Blumberg, S.L., Jenkins, N.H., & Whiteley, C. (2004). *12 hours to a great marriage.* San Francisco, California: Jossey-Bass.

McManus, M. (1995). *Marriage savers.* Grand Rapids, Michigan: Zondervan.

Maqsood, R. W. (2000). *The Muslim marriage guide.* Beltsville, MD: Amana Publications.

McGoldrick, M., & Gerson, R. (1985). *Genograms in family assessment.* New York: Norton.

McGoldrick, M., Gerson., & Petry, S. (2008). *Genograms: Assessment and intervention, 3rd edition.* New York: Norton.

Mitchell, J. (1986/1987). *The selected Melanie Klein.* New York: The Free Press.

Mitchell, S. (2002). *Can love last? The fate of romance over time.* New York: Norton.

Muncy, R.L. (1974). *Sex and marriage in utopian communities: Nineteenth century America.* New York: Penguin.

Murray, C.E. & Murray, T.L. (2004). Solution-focused premarital counseling: Helping couples build a vision for their marriage. *Journal of Marital and Family Therapy, 30*(3), 349–358.

National Institute of Relationship Enhancement. (n.d). *Couple enhancement weekend.* Retrieved December 2009 from http://www.nire.org

Northey, W. F. Jr. (2009). Effectiveness research: A view from the USA. *Journal of Family Therapy, 31,* 75–84.

Olson, D. H. (1996). *PREPARE/ENRICH Counselors manual: Version 2000*. Minneapolis, MN: Life Innovations

Olson, D. H., & Olson, A.K. (2002). PREPAE/ENRICH Program Version 2000. In R. Berger & M. T. Hannah (Eds). *Preventive approaches in couple therapy*. Philadelphia, PA.: Brunner Mazel.

Ooms, T. & Wilson, P. (2004). The challenge of offering relationship and marriage education to low-income populations. *Family Relations, 53*(5), 440–448.

Ooms, T. (2002). Role *of the federal government in strengthening marriage. Virginia Journal of Social Policy & the Law, 9*(1).

Phillips, A. (1988) *Winnicott*. Cambridge: Harvard University Press.

Piaget, J., & Inhelder, B. (1966/2000). *The psychology of the child*. New York: Basic Books.

Polyamorous paralegal (2009, May 18). The Polyamorous paralegal. *New York Magazine.*

Popenoe, D. (2007). *The state of our unions: The social health of marriage in America*. Piscataway, NJ: Rutgers University National Marriage Project.

Rogers, C. (1995). *On becoming a person: A therapist's view of psychotherapy*. New York: Houghton Mifflin Harcourt. (Original work published 1961)

Rogers, C. (2003). *Client-centered therapy: Its current practice, implications and theory*. London: Constable. (Original work published 1951)

Ryan, K.D. & Gottman, J. M. (n.d). Psycho-educational intervention with moderately and severely distressed married couples— One year follow-up. Available from www.gottman.com/research/about. Accessed June 2009.

Scharff, D.E. & Scharff, J.S. (1991). *Object relations couple therapy*. North Vale, NJ: Aronson.

Sexton, Gilman, & Johnson-Erickson (2005). Evidence-based practice. In T. P. Gullota & G. R. Adams (Eds.), *Handbook of adolescent behavioral problems: Evidence-based approaches to prevention and treatment*. (pp. 101–128). New York: Springer Science Media.

Snyder, D.K., Castellani, A.M., & Whisman, M.A. (2006). Current status and future directions. *Annual Review of Psychology, 57,* 317–344.

Sprenkle, D.H.,& Blow, A.J. (2004). Common factors and our scared models. *Journal of Marital and Family Therapy, 30*(2), 113–129.

Sprenkle, D.H., Davis, S.D., & Lebow, J.L. (2009). *Common factors in couple and family therapy: The overlooked foundation for effective practice.* New York: Guilford.

Stanley, S.M., Amato, P.R., Johnson, C.A., & Markman, H.J. (2006). Premarital education, marital quality, and marital stability: Findings from a large, random household survey. *Journal of Family Psychology, 20*(1), 117–126.

Stanley, Blumberg, & Markman. (1999). Helping couples fight for their marriages: The PREP approach. In R. Berger & M. T. Hannah (Eds.), *Preventive Approaches in Couples Therapy.* (pp. 279–303). New York: Bruner Mazel.

Stevenson, B. & Wolfors, J. (2007). Marriage and divorce: Changes and their driving forces. *Journal of Economic Perspectives, 21*(2), 27–52.

Sullivan, K.T., & Anderson, C. (2002). Recruitment of engaged couples for premarital counseling: An empirical examination of the importance of program characteristics and topics to potential participants. *The Family Journal: Counseling and Therapy for Couples and Families,* 10(4), 388–397.

Sullivan, K.T., Pasch, L. A., Cornelius, T., & Cirigliano, E. (2004). Predicting participation in premarital prevention programs: The health belief model and social norms. Family Process. 43(2), 175–193.

Tennov, D. (1999). *Love and limerence: The experience of being in love.* Second Edition. Chelsea, MI: Scarborough House.

Tolstoy, L. (1878/2004). *Anna Karenina.* New York: Barnes and Noble Classics

Trepper, T.S., Dolan, Y., McCollum, E.E., & Nelson, T. (2006) Steve de Shazer and the future of solution based therapy. *Journal of Marriage and the Family,* 32(2), 133–140.

Tulchin, A. (2007). Same-sex couples creating households in old regime France: The uses of the affrèrement. *Journal of Modern History, 79,* 613–647.

Vasileff, L. A. (2008). Three sure fire indicators he is about to file for divorce. *Divorce matters and money matters!* Available from http://www.divorcematters.com. Accessed July 15, 2008.

Vasileff, L. A., & Palatnik, M. (2008, February). The changing land-

scape of divorce. *Law Journal Newsletters*. Available from http://
www.divorcematters.com/library.html. Accessed July 15, 2008.

Wallerstein, J. (2001). Children after divorce: Wounds that don't
heal. In K. Scott & M. Warren (Eds.). *Perspectives on marriage: A
reader.* New York: Oxford University Press.

Wallerstein, J. Kelly, J.B. & Blakeslee, S. (1996). *Surviving the break up.*
New York: Basic Books.

Weisstein, N. (1970). Kinder, kuche, kirche as scientific law: Psychology constructs of the female. In R. Morgan (Ed), *Sisterhood is powerful: An anthology of writings from the women liberation movement.*
New York: Random House.

Whelan, C. B. (2007, July 6). Close encounters of the engaged kind.
Wall Street Journal.

Williams, A. (2008, October 3). Hopelessly devoted to you, you and
you. *The New York Times.*

Williams, L., & Jurich, J. (1995). Predicting marital success after five
years: Assessing the predictive validity of focus. *Journal of Marriage
and Family Therapy, 21*(2), 141–153.

Witte, J. (1997). *From sacrament to contract: Marriage, religion, and law
in the Western tradition.* Louisville, Kentucky: Westminister John
Knox Press.

Wolff, Z. (2005, June 16). Going to the therapist en route to the altar.
The New York Times.

Woolf, V. (1929/1989). *A room of one's own.* New York: Houghton Mifflin Harcourt.

Index